Look Smarter Than You Are with Oracle Hyperion Planning 11.1.2

Advanced Hyperion Planning

interRel Consulting
Tracy McMullen
Edward Roske

1st Edition

interRel Press, Arlington, Texas

Look Smarter Than You Are with Oracle Hyperion Planning 11.1.2: Advanced Hyperion Planning

interRel Consulting
Tracy McMullen
Edward Roske

Published by:

interRel Press
A Division of interRel Consulting Partners
1000 Ballpark Way, Suite 304
Arlington, TX 76011

Library of Congress Cataloging-in-Publication Data
Roske, Edward; McMullen, Tracy
 Look Smarter Than You Are with Oracle Hyperion Planning
11.1.2: Advanced Hyperion Planning

Edward Roske, Tracy McMullen 1st ed.
 p. 469 cm.
 Includes index.
 978-1-300-62818-7

This book is dedicated to Hyperion Pillar. Pillar was the distant ancestor of Hyperion Planning and though it is now ancient technology, without Pillar, Planning would never have been able to exist.

Hyperion Pillar, may you rest in peace.

Edward Roske, Tracy McMullen

ABOUT THE AUTHORS

Edward Roske fell in love with Hyperion at first sight. In 1995, Edward was working for the Moore Business Forms printing facility in Mundelein, Illinois. When he saw his first demonstration of Arbor Essbase (as it was known at the time), he quit his job to become a full-time Essbase consultant (becoming in the process one of those rare individuals who quit a stable job to consult on a product for which he had absolutely no experience).

Edward is a pioneer. He was one of the first Essbase Certified consultants in the world. He was also one of the first people in the world to become certified in Hyperion Planning and he has been using both Planning and HFM since their creations in the early 21st century. While at Moore, he also obtained his first patent proving that there are still new ideas waiting to be discovered and exploited for financial gain.

In May of 1997, Edward left his senior consulting position with a Chicago-based firm to co-found interRel Consulting along with Eduardo Quiroz. Proving that being humble will get you nowhere, Edward helped write interRel's original motto: "Reaching for perfection, we deliver the impossible in record time." He has been the CEO of interRel Consulting since its inception growing them to be a multi-million dollar firm with offices from coast-to-coast.

Edward still keeps his Essbase and Hyperion skills sharp. He has overseen successful Hyperion implementations at over 100 companies. His optimizations have resulted in Essbase calculation improvements of more than 99.99%.

Continuing his quest to become the world's foremost Oracle EPM-evangelist, Edward has been a regular speaker at annual Hyperion user conferences since 1995 and he is noted for his humorous slant to technically boring information; in the last ~20 years, he has spoken to over 10,000 people in 15+ countries on 5 continents. He was the first Essbase Domain Lead for the Oracle Applications Users Group (OAUG) and was two-time chair for the Oracle Developer Users Group's (ODTUG) annual Kscope conference. Recently, Oracle awarded him the title of "Oracle ACE Director" and "Fusion UX Advocate" to acknowledge that at least in a couple of minor areas, Oracle feels Edward knows more than they do. Visit Edward's blog at http://looksmarter.blogspot.com/ or follow him on Twitter at @ERoske.

Though not especially relevant, if Edward ever found a busload of nuns and orphans in need of help, he would totally save them.

ABOUT THE AUTHORS

Tracy McMullen, Oracle ACE Director, has been leading the development of Enterprise Performance Management and Data Warehousing applications for over 10 years. Roles on projects have ranged from developer, to architect and project manager on technologies from Hyperion and Business Objects to Cognos and Oracle. She's seen all of the business intelligence tools and Hyperion is her favorite.

Tracy started her career at Arthur Andersen Business Consulting on a project programming in RPG (fun stuff!). Thankfully, her next project introduced her to the world of multi-dimensional databases with a Cognos PowerPlay implementation for an oil and gas client (many years ago Tracy was certified in Cognos PowerPlay and Impromptu). Next, she helped clients from various industries revolutionize their information delivery with Hyperion and other technologies. After years of successful business intelligence implementations, a few shredded documents changed her career path from future Partner to eliminating cancer.

Tracy next joined The University of Texas M.D. Anderson Cancer Center where she lead the charge in implementing budget and planning solutions utilizing Hyperion Planning.

Fate stepped in once again with relocation to the South Texas Coast and Tracy found her new home with interRel Consulting. She has served as Architect, Trainer, Project Manager, tap dancer, and Director of Consulting Services with interRel. She is currently the Director for Product Strategy.

Tracy helped co-write the Oracle Essentials certification exams with Oracle for Hyperion Planning, Hyperion Financial Management, Essbase, and Data Relationship Management. She is a Certified Project Management Professional (PMP). Tracy has been a regular instructor at interRel, user conferences and other professional seminars since 2000 on topics including information delivery, business intelligence, data warehousing, and Hyperion implementations. Her strong technical background is complimented by comprehensive practical experience in project management, a skill important not only on the job but at home as well where she manages her kids on a daily basis (ok, she attempts to manage with moderate success).

ABOUT INTERREL CONSULTING

Integrated solutions are key to providing our clients the timely information they need to make critical business decisions. Our philosophy, experience, and methodologies are integral components of our application development, project management, optimization and training. As a result of our experience and commitment to excellence, interRel has become one of the premier providers of analytical solutions using Oracle BI and Hyperion solutions.

interRel solves business problems through utilizing Business Intelligence (BI) and Enterprise Performance Management (EPM) technologies. Our EPM Assessments are designed to identify an organization's current EPM current state relative to the corporate strategy.

interRel has been in business since 1997, and we take pride in delivering our solutions with small teams composed of members with an average of over eight years of Oracle Hyperion and BI related tools, application and consulting experience.

Exclusive EPM/BI consultancy

- 100% of our revenue is from Oracle EPM / BI products
- 100% of our Consultants specialize in Oracle EPM Systems (Hyperion)
- 100% of our Senior Consultants are Hyperion Certified
- Senior Consultants have 8+ years of experience
- "Junior" Consultants have 5+ years of experience

Oracle Hyperion Community - Training, Free Webcasts, and More

Through our various outlets, our focus is always to interact and help others in the Oracle Hyperion community.

If you like this book, join us in person for a hands-on training class. interRel Consulting offers classroom education on a full spectrum of Oracle EPM solutions, including standard course offerings such as *Essbase and Planning Accelerated Fundamentals*, tailored for new Administrators, as well as unique advanced courses like *Hyperion Calc Scripts for Mere Mortals* and *Oracle Data Integrator (ODI) for Hyperion*. All classes are taught by knowledgeable, certified trainers whose experience averages more than 8 years per instructor. This interactive environment allows attendees the opportunity to master the skill set needed to implement, develop and manage Hyperion solutions successfully. All classes are held at our headquarters in Dallas and offer CPE accreditation. interRel Consulting also provides custom training on-site to clients.

interRel Consulting proudly offers free twice-weekly webcasts. These webcasts include the full scope of Oracle BI and EPM System (Hyperion) products, including Essbase, Planning & Hyperion Financial Management. Webcasts are primarily held every non-holiday week and twice in most weeks. Topics include 'Tips, Tricks & Best Practices,' which gives you an insider's guide to optimize the usage of your solution. The 'Administration' series focuses on making your job easier and giving a snapshot of the Accelerated Fundamentals course outline while the 'Overview' webcasts discuss the highlights of a solution and how it can be used effectively. All webcasts include interactive examples and demonstrations to see how the products really work.

Awards & Recognitions

- Two-Time Oracle Titan Award winner for "EPM & BI Solution" of the year
- 2008 Oracle Excellence Award winner with Pearson Education
- interRel has also received honorable mentions in both the "Financial Management & EPM" and "Energy & Utilities Industry" categories at the Oracle Titan Awards
- Inc. magazine's 5000 fastest-growing private companies in the country (AKA: "Inc. 5000.") – 2008 through 2012
- The only Hyperion consulting partner with three Oracle ACE Directors

interRel's commitment to providing our customers with unsurpassed customer service and unmatched expertise make interRel the partner of choice for a large number of companies across the world. Learn more at www.interrel.com.

ACKNOWLEDGEMENTS

If we were to thank all of those who assisted us in the creation of this book, we would have to not only personally mention hundreds of people but also several companies and one or two federal agencies (though we will give a special shout-out to those wacky guys over at the Internal Revenue Service: keep it real, yo!). Suffice to say, if this book stands tall, it is only by balancing on the heads of giants.

Thanks to several people at interRel including Troy Seguin, Dyana Brune, Lynne McDaniels, Jeff Dietz, Margot Sylvain, Rodrigo Becerra, and Christopher "CTI" Solomon of interRel Consulting; your contributions for the book go way beyond your paychecks. Thank you to Alla Oriente, John Infantolino, and Steve Press for being long-time, strong supporters. We would like to thank some of the product folks at Oracle for their insight and advice: thanks to Matt Milella, Shubhomoy Bhattacharya, Guillaume Arnaud, Shankar Viswanathan, Al Marciante, Aneel Shenker, John O'Rourke, Nick Moscaritolo, and Balaji Yelamanchili.

Edward also wants to say "thank you" to Melissa Vorhies Roske, Vanessa Roske, and Eliot Roske for giving up their time with him on evenings and weekends, so he could make his publishing deadline. On a related note, Edward would also like to thank in advance anyone who can figure out a way to get rid of publishing deadlines. Tracy McMullen would like to thank her family for their never-ending support.

We give our sincerest gratitude to all the people above, and we hope that they feel that this book is partly theirs as well (just without the fame, glory and most importantly, the royalties).

DISCLAIMER

This book assumes you are familiar with Hyperion Planning or have read the book *Look Smarter Than You Are with Hyperion Planning: Creating Planning Applications*. This book is a "Part 2" and the basics of Planning are not covered in this book. You'll have to buy *Look Smarter Than You Are with Hyperion Planning: Creating Planning Applications* for "Part 1" the basics .

This book is designed to provide supporting information about the related subject matter. It is being sold to you and/or your company with the understanding that the author and the publisher are not engaged by you to provide legal, accounting, or any other professional services of any kind. If assistance is required (legal, expert, or otherwise), seek out the services of a competent professional such as a consultant.

It is not the purpose of this book to reprint all of the information that is already available on the subject at hand. The purpose of this book is to complement and supplement other texts already available to you. For more information (especially including technical reference information), please contact the software vendor directly or use your on-line help.

Great effort has been made to make this book as complete and accurate as possible. That said, there may be errors both typographic and in content. Therefore, use this book only as a general guide and not as the ultimate source for specific information on the software product. Further, this book contains information on the software that was generally available as of the publishing date.

The purpose of this book is to entertain while educating. The authors and interRel Press shall have neither liability nor responsibility to any person living or dead or entity currently or previously in existence with respect to any loss or damage caused or alleged to be caused directly, indirectly, or otherwise by the information contained in this book.

If you do not wish to abide by all parts of the above disclaimer, please stop reading now and return this book to the publisher for a full refund.

TABLE OF CONTENTS

Scene 1:
Oracle Hyperion Planning:
The Adventure Continues

Welcome to the greatest advanced Hyperion Planning book ever written.

Note! As of the time of this writing, this is the only advanced Hyperion Planning book ever written. This is how we're able to make the claim in the opening sentence without inviting lawsuits.

Our goal for this book is to walk you through many of the more advanced and esoteric topics of Hyperion Planning 11.1.2.2 and 11.1.2.3. If you are not on 11.1.2.2 (and you should be on at least that version, but enough with the soapboxing), the majority of the examples in this book still apply. The navigation is the same for most features though things like the Data Form Designer and Approvals changed dramatically starting in version 11.1.2.1. For those sad individuals on older versions, when we go through things only in 11.1.2.2 and 11.1.2.3, you'll just have to sit back, drool over what you can't have, and figure out how to work around it in your version. Or you could spend the same time convincing your IT department to upgrade.

This book is designed to be a companion book to *Look Smarter Than You Are with Oracle Hyperion Planning 11.1.2: Creating Planning Applications.* While it can be purchased separately for those who already understand the basics of Hyperion Planning, we won't be going back and reviewing everything in that book (or this book would quickly become twice as long).

In the first book (and if you haven't read it, we told it in the form of a musical and that will be continued in this book), we followed our main character, Penny, and her team of all-knowing consultants as they created their Hyperion Planning application and enter the plans into the system. Many of the examples in this book assumed you created the ENTPLN application in the first book. If you haven't created this application, you can, for the most part, follow along with either the Planning Sample application or one of your existing applications.

In the finale of Act 1 (the first book), Penny, Eddie and the consultants finished the plan and submitted it for approval just as Dr. Dementor (our evil antagonist with a heart of gold) surprises them with his deathray. Is Hyperion Planning doomed?

Find out in Act 2, *Look Smarter Than You Are with Hyperion Planning 11.1.2: Advanced Hyperion Planning.*

MANAGE ORACLE HYPERION PLANNING

Scene 2:
Planning Under the Covers

Dr. Dementor shoots his evil deathray of death... and it jams (as foretold by prophecy).

"Darn deathray!" he shouts angrily, shaking the weapon of destruction. "I knew I should have prototyped this thing." He quickly darts toward the door in escape. Before disappearing through the exit, he turns and says ominously in a governor-of-California-sort-of-way, "I'll be back."

Penny turns to the Translator. "There must be something we can do to prepare for the return of Dr. Dementor. How can I make sure Hyperion Planning is indestructible?"

"Maintenance is key to an unstoppable Planning application. It is time to teach you how Planning works 'under the covers.' This knowledge will definitely help you defeat Dr. Dementor."

To become an all knowing, all seeing Planning administrator, you have to understand some of the more complex aspects of Planning and Essbase.

To begin with, realize that although Essbase is the main database used to power Hyperion Planning, there is also information stored relationally. These two repositories, Essbase and relational, work together to power everything custom you see in the planning applications. The metadata is stored in a relational repository (one database per application) and the data or numbers are stored in Essbase block storage databases.

RELATIONAL REPOSITORY

Planning stores most of its metadata in an underlying relational repository. Along with a DBA, it can be helpful to understand the tables and information. The Planning utilities installed with Hyperion Planning provide supported ways to add or update data in these tables (discussed later in the book), though you can, if you want to potentially void your warranty, access the tables directly. For those of you who like hacking the underlying schemas, here are some of the tables you can access (all the table names start with "HSP_" which is short for "Hyperion Solutions Planning").

One of the main Hyperion Planning tables is the HSP_Object table, which contains the listing of all objects in Planning. HSP_OBJECT_TYPE is the reference table for items in the HSP_OBJECT table:

	Hyp_Plan_Samp		HSP_OBJECT_TYPE	

Columns | Data | Constraints | Grants | Statistics | Column Statistics

Sort... Filter: Enter Where Clause

	OBJECT_TYPE	TYPE_NAME
1	8	Attribute Dimension
2	30	Attribute Member
3	7	Form
4	38	Year
5	2	Dimension
6	31	Scenario
7	1	Folder
8	6	Group
9	32	Account
10	10	Alias
11	5	User
12	35	Version
13	37	Currency Member
14	50	User Defined Dimension Member
15	33	Entity
16	11	Cube
17	9	Currency
18	4	Calendar
19	8	FX Table
20	12	Planning Unit
21	45	Shared Member
22	34	Time Period

The HSP_Member table contains member properties for dimension members. To view dimension member names, join the MEMBER_ID to OBJECT_ID in HSP_OBJECT:

	MEMBER_ID	DIM_ID	DATA_STORAGE	TWOPASS_CALC	C...	...	...	...	...	USED_FOR_CONSOL	HAS_MBR_FX	BASE_MBRID
1	32	32	1	0	S	S	S	S	S	0	0	(null)
2	30	30	1	0	S	S	S	S	S	0	0	(null)
3	35	35	1	0	S	S	S	S	S	0	0	(null)
4	37	37	1	0	S	S	S	S	S	0	0	(null)
5	38	38	1	0	S	S	S	S	S	0	0	(null)
6	33	33	1	0	S	S	S	S	S	0	0	(null)
7	31	31	1	0	S	S	S	S	S	0	0	(null)
8	34	34	1	0	S	S	S	S	S	0	0	(null)
9	850	37	0	0	S	S	S	S	S	0	0	(null)
10	1000	37	0	0	S	S	S	S	S	0	0	(null)
11	1500	35	0	0	S	S	S	S	S	0	0	(null)
12	50002	38	0	0	S	S	S	S	S	0	0	(null)
13	50003	38	0	0	S	S	S	S	S	0	0	(null)

Note! You will be unsupported by Oracle if you change data in the tables directly although Oracle is okay with you querying the tables. Be very careful if you try this and again, check out the utilities to see if one will perform your desired task in a supported manner.

Reporting Against the Metadata

Smart Lists are controlled lists of text values for users to review and input. Users may not type in the cell of a Smart List member but can select text values from a drop down list:

Text and Date measures allow free form entry from the end user:

	Jan	Feb	Mar	Apr	May	Jun	Jul	Aug
BAS	New Customer!	Production Issu..						
HTAS								
BB								

FiscalYear: FY13

N/A | Product Note | Budget | Final

This textual information (smart lists and free form text and dates) is stored in the relational repository. So if users want to report and analyze smart list data or free form text data, they will need to use one of the following options:

- Planning data forms and ad hoc grids
- Planning connection in Smart View
- Planning ADM driver in Financial Reporting

If you use an Essbase connection for reporting and analysis, users will see the stored IDs in Essbase, not the correct text values.

ESSBASE REPOSITORY

Planning stores all of its numeric data in Essbase databases. In versions prior to 11.1.2.3, block storage option (BSO) databases are supported. The Essbase BSO database structure is determined by the dimensions defined within the Essbase outline whether they are tagged "dense" or "sparse". In version 11.1.2.3 aggregate storage option (ASO) databases are supported in addition to BSO databases.

DENSE AND SPARSE FOR BSO

Before we define dense and sparse and how these settings affect your BSO database, let's start with defining a member combination. A member combination is the intersection of members from each dimension. See the following examples of member combinations for the following sample outline:

⊟‑**Year** Time (Active Dynamic Time Series Members: H-T-D, Q-T-D) (Dynamic Calc)
   ⊞‑**Qtr1** (+) (Dynamic Calc)
   ⊞‑**Qtr2** (+) (Dynamic Calc)
   ⊞‑**Qtr3** (+) (Dynamic Calc)
   ⊞‑**Qtr4** (+) (Dynamic Calc)
⊟‑**Measures** Accounts (Label Only)
   ⊞‑**Profit** (+) (Dynamic Calc)
   ⊞‑**Inventory** (~) (Label Only)
   ⊞‑**Ratios** (~) (Label Only)
⊟‑**Product** {Caffeinated, Intro Date, Ounces, Pkg Type}
   ⊞‑**100** (+) (Alias: Colas)
   ⊞‑**200** (+) (Alias: Root Beer)
   ⊞‑**300** (+) (Alias: Cream Soda)
   ⊞‑**400** (+) (Alias: Fruit Soda)
   ⊞‑**Diet** (~) (Alias: Diet Drinks)
⊟‑**Market** {Population}
   ⊞‑**East** (+) (UDAS: Major Market)
   ⊞‑**West** (+)

Example member combinations:
- Qtr1->Profit->100->East->Actual
- Year->Profit->100->East->Actual
- Jan->Sales->100-10->New York->Budget
- Jan->Sales->100->New York->Budget

Tip! The symbol "->" is known as a cross dimensional operator in Essbase (more on this later). For now, when you see the "->", think of the word "at". We are referencing the data value for Qtr1 at Profit at 100 at East at Actual.

Dense data is data that occurs often or repeatedly across the intersection of all member combinations. For example, you will most likely have data for all periods for most member combinations. You will most likely have data for most of your accounts for member combinations. Time and accounts are naturally dense (unless you have time or accounts at very low levels such as Time by day or Accounts by a 1,000+ item long chart of accounts).

Sparse data is data that occurs in few member combinations. For example, you probably don't sell every one of your products in every one of your markets. Product, Market, and Employee dimensions are usually sparse:

Products

Time

Markets					
X				
		X		
X				
	X			
			X	

Measures					
X	X		X	
X	X	X	X	X
X	X	X		X
	X	X	X	X
X		X	X	X

Sparse   **Dense**

You as the administrator will assign a dense / sparse setting to each dimension. This will dictate how the Essbase database is structured.

To set density for Planning dimensions in a BSO plan type,

1. Open the ENTPLN Planning application in the Workspace.
2. Select *Administration >> Manage >> Dimensions*.
3. Select *Performance Settings* tab.
4. Select the plan type for Sum.
5. Set dimensions in the following order (use the up and down arrow keys to move dimensions) with dense and sparse settings:

Dimensions	Performance Settings	Evaluation Order

Select Plan Type   [Sum ▼]

Position △ ▽	Dimensions	Members	Density
1	Period	19	⦿ Dense ○ Sparse
2	Account	22	⦿ Dense ○ Sparse
3	Entity	152	○ Dense ⦿ Sparse
4	FiscalYear	6	○ Dense ⦿ Sparse
5	Scenario	5	○ Dense ⦿ Sparse
7	Version	4	○ Dense ⦿ Sparse

Why can't you see the dense / sparse setting for the Product Manager dimension or any other attribute dimensions? If you answered "attribute dimensions are always sparse and dynamic", pat yourself on the back. You're coming along, my fledgling administrator.

BLOCK STRUCTURE

The Essbase BSO database is composed of a number of blocks. A block is created for each intersection of the sparse dimensions that contain data values. In the example below, Market and Product are sparse. See a block for each sparse member combination in the example below:

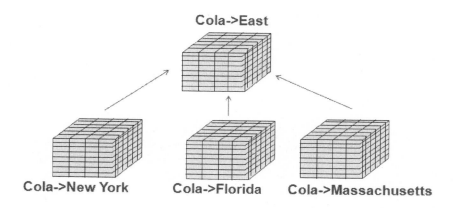

There are four types of blocks (and some blocks can be multiple types):

- Input blocks are blocks where data is loaded or input.
- Calculated blocks are blocks that are created through consolidation or calculation.
- Level zero blocks are blocks that are created from the level zero members of all sparse dimensions.
- Upper-level blocks are all blocks that contain at least one upper level member (non-level zero).

Each block is made up of cells. These cells are created for each intersection of the dense dimensions. In the example below, Time, Measures, and Scenario are dense dimensions. See the cells for each dense member combination in the example below (we've highlighted one specific cell "Profit" at "Jan" at "Actual"):

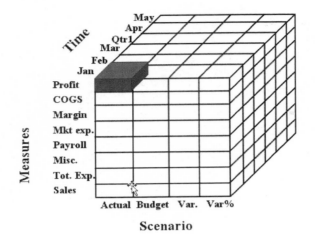

Scenario

OUTLINE CONSOLIDATION

Essbase is built to perform outline consolidations. You assigned a consolidation attribute to each member that tells Essbase how to perform the consolidation, whether it should add to the total, subtract from the total, and so forth. Unary operators include +, -, *, /, %, ^, and ~. The consolidation will use these operators and follow the path of the hierarchies for each dimension.

So what do outline consolidation and dense/sparse have to do with each other? Essbase will perform dense calculations first and then sparse calculations. The default calculation order for Essbase is the following:

1. Accounts (whether it's dense or not)
2. Time (whether it's dense or not)
3. Remaining dense dimensions (in the order they're in the outline)
4. Remaining sparse dimensions (in the order they're in the outline)
5. Two Pass calculation members

Note!

While we never advise running the default calculation (there are so many more optimal calculations to run), the default calculation is especially bad when either Accounts or Time are sparse dimensions. Because of the default order Essbase calculates dimensions, if Accounts or Time are sparse, the default calculation will pass through the database at least two times during a full aggregation. This takes a lot of time and is to be avoided at all costs.

Let's follow the path of an Essbase consolidation to help you better understand. In the example below, the highlighted cells indicate cells loaded with data.

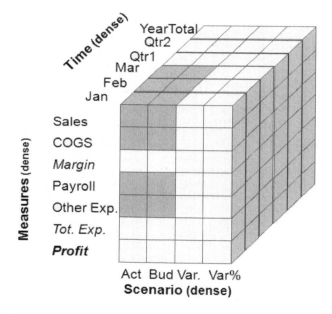

Next you see those cells populated with the Accounts dimension calculation (see Profit, Margin, Tot. Exp) assuming stored upper-level dense members (which is actually to be avoided for optimization reasons).

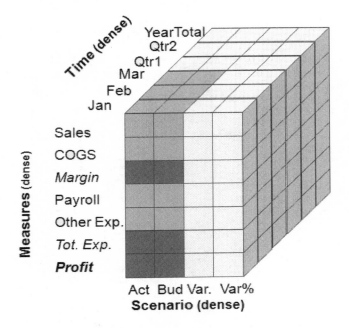

Finally the cells in the upper portion of the block represent those cells populated with the Time dimension calculation (Qtr1, Qtr2, YearTotal). Sometimes we dynamically calculate our dense, upper-level Time members to improve calc script performance.

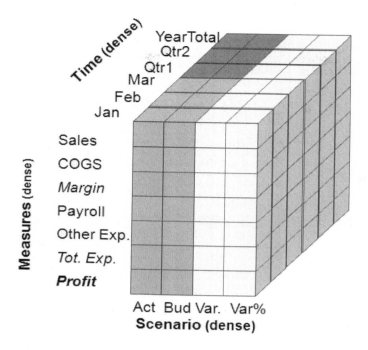

Why don't the "Var" and "Var %" (Var is short for Variance) members show calculated data values? 99% of the time you will tag these two members with the dynamic calc property so data will never be stored and in most cases, you won't need to calculate the Scenario dimension (and in most cases, this is a sparse dimension instead of a dense dimension; but we're getting a bit ahead of ourselves).

Here is another view of this dense calculation. Data is loaded to Sales and COGS members for each month. We are looking at the block for Vermont, Cola, and Actual (there's that cross dimensional symbol that means "at").

Vermont -> Cola -> Actual

Accounts	Jan	Feb	Mar	Qtr1
Sales	124.71	119.43	161.93	
COGS	42.37	38.77	47.28	
Margin				

First we consolidate the Accounts dimension, calculating the Margin member.

Vermont -> Cola -> Actual

Accounts	Jan	Feb	Mar	Qtr1
Sales	124.71	119.43	161.93	
COGS	42.37	38.77	47.28	
Margin	82.34	80.66	114.65	

Next we consolidate the Time dimension, calculating the Qtr1 member.

Vermont -> Cola -> Actual

Accounts	Jan	Feb	Mar	Qtr1
Sales	124.71	119.43	161.93	406.07
COGS	42.37	38.77	47.28	128.42
Margin	82.34	80.66	114.65	277.65

Once the Dense calculation is complete, the sparse calculation is next. The Vermont -> Cola -> Actual block and the New York -> Cola -> Actual block are added together to create the East -> Cola -> Actual block.

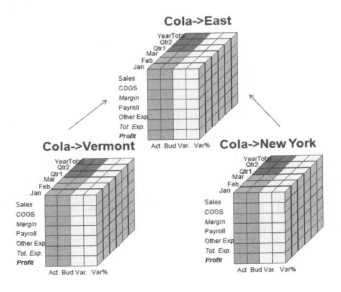

CALCULATE THE BLOCK SIZE

Now that you know the basics about the Essbase block structure, let's learn how to calculate block size for BSO plan types. Data block size is determined by the amount of data in a particular combination of dense dimensions. Data block size is $8n$ bytes, where n is the number of cells that exist for that combination of stored members of dense dimensions.

Note! There are also bytes that make up the block header for each sparse combination, but since we can't control the block header size, it's irrelevant for our purposes.

Here is an example:

Measures (Dense): 40 stored members
Time (Dense): 17 stored members
Scenario (Dense): 2 stored members

Block size = 40 * 17 * 2 * 8 = 10880 bytes or 11 Kb

Note! Use the number of stored dense members when calculating block size, not the total number of members.

Despite what the Essbase Database Administrator's Guide says, we recommend a block size of about 8 Kb in 32 bit Essbase. Larger block sizes will hurt parallel calculations (which is what most of your calculations will be these days). Too small block sizes may result in an increased index file size. This forces Essbase to write and retrieve the index from disk, slowing calculations When in doubt, err on the side of smaller. That is, 1 Kb is better than 40 Kb.

If you're using 64-bit Essbase, larger blocks actually perform better so test the sparse and dimension settings to find the right block size for your application. We often find that blocks upwards of 1 Mb can be effective if your hard drives or storage area networks are particularly speedy.

Tip!

As with anything in Essbase, these guidelines are not definitive and are just a starting point. Hence, the term "guideline". We have implemented applications that violated the block size guideline and still realized fast performance. Optimization tips are very much influenced by your hardware, data, requirements and much more. Test to find the right block size for your database!

Let's calculate the block size for our Entpln.Sum database. We have two dense dimensions right now: Account and Period. In the screenshot below, the period dimension has 14 stored members and the account dimension has 9 stored members:

Database Properties: [localhost.ENTPLN.Sum]

Database: **localhost.ENTPLN.Sum**   Status: **Loaded**

Statistics | Caches | Transactions | Storage | Currency | Modifications

General | Dimensions

Number of dimensions **6**

Dimension	Type	Members in Dimension	Members Stored
Period	Dense	21	14
Account	Dense	22	9
Entity	Sparse	152	119
FiscalYear	Sparse	6	6
Scenario	Sparse	5	4
Version	Sparse	4	4

So the block size for the Sum plan type is 14*9*8 = 1008 bytes or 1 Kb.

Try It!

Calculate the block size for the Entpln.Rev plan type.

Essbase also calculates the block size for you (of course we waited to tell you that until you understood how to calculate it manually first). Select the database and right-click. Select *Edit >> Properties*. Select the Statistics tab:

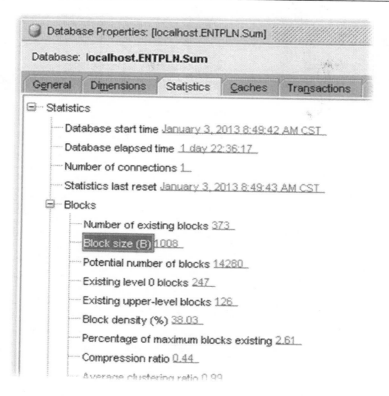

So why did we teach you how to calculate block size? One, it is important to understand the concept of what members make up a block. Getting the block size to a reasonable level is important in tuning. You can reduce block size by making more members dynamic and changing a dense dimension to sparse. Two, you may want to use this calculation when you are performing an initial design to figure out your starting point for dense and sparse dimensions.

Note!

How you configure what is dense and sparse can have significant impact on your cube performance, size and memory requirements.

CALCULATE THE NUMBER OF BLOCKS

Now we know the size of the data blocks. But how many blocks could we possibly have? A block is created for each unique intersection of stored sparse members. To calculate the total possible blocks, multiply the number for stored members for each sparse dimension. The sparse dimension member counts for Entpln.Sum are:

Database Properties: [localhost.ENTPLN.Sum]				
Database: localhost.ENTPLN.Sum		Status: **Loaded**		
Statistics	Caches	Transactions	Storage	Currency	Modifications
General			Dimensions		

Number of dimensions 6

Dimension	Type	Members in Dimension	Members Stored
Period	Dense	21	14
Account	Dense	22	9
Entity	Sparse	152	119
FiscalYear	Sparse	6	6
Scenario	Sparse	5	4
Version	Sparse	4	4

Number of Possible Blocks = 119*4*4*6 = 11424

This time we will mention up front that Essbase also calculates the total possible blocks for you. Select the database and right-click. Select *Edit >> Properties*. You can view the *Potential number of* blocks on the Statistics tab.

When you see this number for a production database, you may get really scared. This number will probably be really big, sometimes into the quadrillions. But remember, we've tagged these dimensions sparse for a reason. The likelihood that data exists for every single combination is very, very rare. So we recommend you understand this concept but don't worry about it any further (don't you just love it when the teacher teaches you something that you won't ever really use?). In certain cases, really large potential block counts (in excess of 100 trillion) can cause inefficient calcs, so watch out if you see this occurring.

The more helpful statistic is the *Number of existing blocks*. Make sure you have loaded and calculated the database before you check this statistic. Under Database Properties, go back to the *Statistics* tab and view the *Potential number of blocks, Existing level-0 blocks* and *Existing upper-level blocks*:

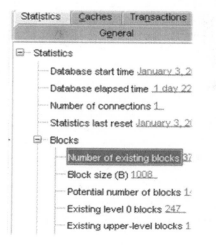

Essbase also tracks the number of existing level-zero blocks and upper level blocks.

INDEX AND PAGE FILES

The index file is a file that contains pointers to all of the different blocks in the BSO database. The index file is named ess*n*.ind and is stored in your database directory (n starts with 00001 and increments by 1 every time the file size reaches 2 GB). Essbase uses this file to locate the blocks that are requested during Essbase operations.

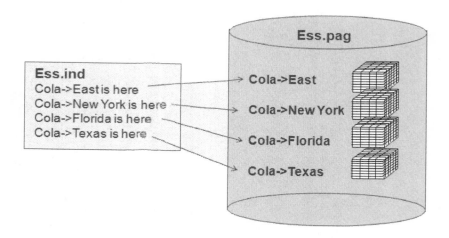

Data is stored in page files for BSO databases, named ess*n*.pag and stored in the database directory (also starting with 00001 and incrementing every 2 GB). These files are stored in the database directory. Essbase uses both the index and page files when performing operations on data blocks.

Try It!

Find the index and page files for the Entpln Sum plan type. Let's open the page files and take a look at the data. Kidding: do not open the page or index files. Ever. Always leave these files alone (unless you are backing them up). You cannot view data via the page files or a list of sparse blocks in the index file. If you open these files, not only will you see quite a bit of random hexadecimal characters, you will probably corrupt your application and database if you then save them. Don't say we didn't warn you.

Memory (index and data caches) can be set aside to help performance during operations. The index cache stores a portion or all of the index in memory for quicker access. The data cache stores a portion of the data blocks in memory for quicker access. We'll show you how to tune these memory caches in the tuning chapters later in the book.

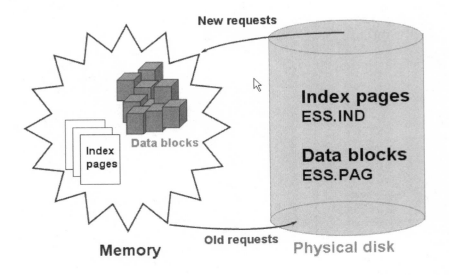

Did you know that interRel Consulting provides free concierge service for every paying client? Just kidding. We wanted to make sure you were still awake and paying attention through this valuable but dry and slightly boring section (OK, really boring section).

INTRODUCTION TO ASO

We've learned that Essbase allows two database types: aggregate storage databases (ASO) and block storage databases (BSO). ASO databases are designed to handle more dimensions and members, smaller batch windows for loads and aggregations of sparse data, and smaller database footprints. In versions prior to 11.1.2.3, only BSO plan types (databases) were supported.

Hyperion Planning supports aggregate storage option (ASO) plan types in Hyperion Planning version 11.1.2.3. ASO plan types can be created during application creation or added in the new Plan Type Editor (11.1.2.3 new interface to build both ASO and BSO plan types). Users can use ASO plan types to provide write back to databases with larger number of dimensions and members.

Benefits of an ASO plan type include unified dimension maintenance and security for BSO and ASO planning and reporting. There is no longer a need to create a separate Essbase only cube in Essbase Administration Services. ASO plan types provide a higher level of granularity for requirements that dictate detailed planning. No aggregation is required for ASO databases so results at upper levels are available immediately. You can build composite forms that present data from both ASO and BSO plan types together.

A single ASO plan type maybe created during application creation. An ASO plan type can also be added later in the application via the Plan Type Editor. Planning applications can still have up to 3 BSO plan types. The number of ASO plan types allowed in an application equals the number of BSO cubes created plus one.

ASO Basics

Remember how you learned Essbase block storage option concepts for Hyperion Planning (e.g. dense, sparse, outline order)? You will need to learn ASO concepts to successfully build ASO plan types in Planning. If you have built an ASO cube in Essbase, then you just need to apply this knowledge within Planning to create the ASO application and database. If you are new to ASO, we recommend you read *Look Smarter Than You Are with Hyperion Essbase: Administrator's Guide.* Here are a few highlights that you will apply when creating ASO plan types.

Essbase requires a separate application for each ASO database so the ASO plan types will not be part of the Essbase application containing the BSO plan types. If you are creating an ASO plan type, you must specify an application name. All ASO application names must be unique across the enterprise.

The dimension types supported in ASO (like BSO) are Accounts, Time, Time Date, and Attribute. You can also have "None" or no dimension type assigned. Planning and Essbase provide built in functionality associated with each one of these dimension types. However dynamic time series (DTS) members are not supported for ASO plan types.

Hierarchy Types. In ASO databases, there are three types of hierarchies: stored, dynamic, or multiple hierarchies ("Hierarchies Enabled"). Stored hierarchies will aggregate according to the structure of the outline. In our example, months will roll up to quarters up to a year total in the Period member. This aggregation is really fast (the nature of ASO databases); however, stored hierarchies may only have the + for any member and ~ consolidation tags for members under a label only parent (other assigned consolidation tags are ignored). Also stored hierarchies cannot have member formulas and there are a few other restrictions on label only assignments.

Dynamic hierarchies are calculated by Essbase (vs. aggregated like in stored hierarchies) so all consolidation tags and member formulas are processed. The evaluation order for the calculation of members is dictated by the solve order. Dynamic hierarchies as expected do not calculate as quickly as stored hierarchies.

You can also have multiple hierarchies within a single dimension. The hierarchies within a dimension can be stored, all dynamic or have one hierarchy stored and the other hierarchies dynamic. Multiple hierarchies can contain alternate hierarchies with Shared Members or completely different hierarchies.

A new property in Hyperion Planning, Hierarchy Type, is available for dimensions in an ASO plan type. ASO dimensions are automatically enabled to support multiple hierarchies. The first hierarchy in a multiple hierarchy dimension must be stored.

For members with a stored hierarchy type, the only valid plan type aggregation options are Addition or Ignore. In a stored hierarchy, the first member must be set to Addition. For members with a dynamic hierarchy type, all plan type aggregation options are valid. Stored hierarchy members that are not children of Label Only members must have Addition set as the consolidation operator. Children of Label Only members can be set to Ignore.

Most of the member properties are the same across ASO and BSO plan types.

Consolidation. Consolidation operators tell the outline how to rollup the members in a hierarchy. Should Jan, Feb, and March be added together to reach a total for Q1? Should units sold be multiplied by price to calculate revenue? Consolidation operators tell Essbase how to aggregate members in a dimension. Valid ASO consolidation operators include: Addition (+) – This is the default consolidation property, Subtraction (-), Multiplication (*), Division (/), Percent (%), and No consolidate (~) (in the same dimension). Never Consolidate (^) is not supported for ASO plan types.

In most cases you will use the default Addition consolidation tag. The second most common consolidation tag is *No consolidate* (~). Use this in places where it doesn't make sense to add up members.

Data Storage. The Data Storage property tells Essbase how the member should be stored. Valid ASO data storage options include:

- Store: Store the data value with the member (default for ASO databases).
- Never share: Do not allow members to be shared implicitly.
- Label Only: Create members for navigation and grouping.
- Shared Member: Share data between two or more members.

Data Type. A member in the dimension tagged Accounts may be one of four types: numeric, smart list, text or date.

Member Formulas. Member Formulas allow you to define specific logic for calculating a member in both BSO and ASO plan types. However ASO databases use MDX syntax. This logic can range from very simple to highly complex. For example, you will probably create member formulas to calculate variances, averages, ratios and more. **The formula syntax for ASO is different than the syntax for BSO.** You must add member formulas in EAS for ASO plan types and assign the HSP_UDF user defined attribute to the member (so the formula will remain after Refresh). Member formulas in the Planning web are not supported in 11.1.2.3.0. Planning does not generate XREF member formulas on ASO databases.

Time Balance. Time balance attributes are only available in the dimension tagged as Accounts, and are used to tell Essbase how a given member should be aggregated up the Time dimension. Depending on your requirements, you can assign Time Balance

Last, Time Balance First or Time Balance Average along with specifications on how to handle periods with missing data.

Solve Order. The solve order member property is specific to ASO and it tells Essbase "here is the order to complete calculations" for ASO databases. Why is this important? You want to calculate the correct numbers in the correct order. Think order of operations for basic math. 4+5*2 does not equal (4+5)*2. Solve order is way you control the order of calculations in ASO databases. However solve order is not supported in the first release of 11.1.2.3 but will be patched soon. This property does not apply to BSO.

Now that version 11.1.2.3 supports ASO databases, we'll begin our less than exciting topic of "ASO Under the Covers" where we will introduce tablespaces instead of index and page files. Snort some caffeine because while this isn't quite as exciting as building your Planning application and retrieving data, it is important to understand some of the underlying structures for aggregate storage databases.

If you ask some of the greatest minds in the business how ASO works, you'll hear the same resounding answer: "It's a black box" or "it is top secret and hard to understand". Under the covers, our handy Essbase developers designed a database to handle more dimensions and members, smaller batch windows for loads and aggregations of sparse data, and smaller database footprint. If you're familiar with blocks and dense / sparse, those concepts don't apply. Aggregate storage databases stores data in highly optimized aggregation nodes.

Let's jump into some more details about ASO "under the covers".

ASO TABLESPACES

Aggregate storage databases utilize tablespaces for data file and work file storage and retrieval. Each ASO application has 4 tablespaces: Default, Temp, Log, and Metadata. These tablespaces will show up as folders under the application folder. The Default tablespace stores the data structure and database values. The Temp tablespace is a temporary work space for the application and is used during data loads, aggregations and retrievals. The Log tablespace houses a binary transaction log file of default tablespace updates and the Metadata tablespace stores information about the file locations, files, and objects contained in the database.

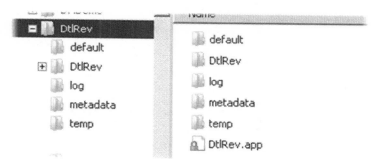

For the default and temp tablespaces, you can define multiple locations and sizes. A file location specifies a physical disk space for storing database files. Each tablespace may contain one or more file locations and can span multiple physical drives and/or logical volumes. You can also define tablespace "location" properties like the directory path locations, maximum disk space to be used for each location, and maximum file size allowed for each location. For example, you set the Max File Size to 16 MB, a .dat file will be created and loaded until it reaches the 16 MB limit. When the limit is met, another .dat file is created.

```
Ess00001.dat (16MB)
Ess00002.dat (8 MB)
```

You cannot change the location or size of the metadata and log table spaces.

To control and manage the tablespaces for your aggregate storage database, use the Tablespace Manager.

1. In the Administration Services Console, right click on the desired ASO application (in our example below we choose an ASO application called "DtlRev".

2. Select *Edit Properties:*

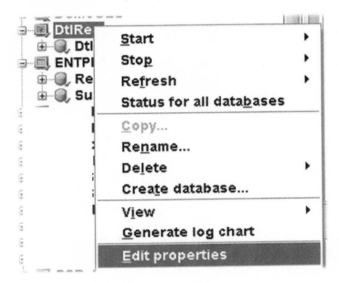

3. Choose the *Tablespaces* tab:

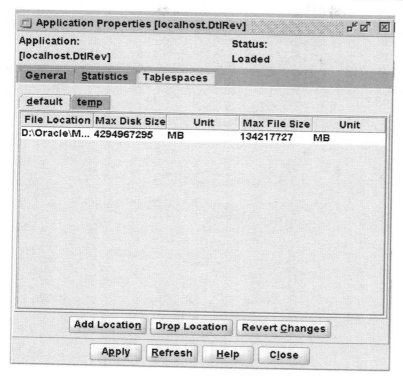

From this window you can edit the file locations for the default and temp tablespaces (by selecting either the default or temp tabs). Once you have chosen the desired tablespace, simply click in the existing file location and make the desired changes:

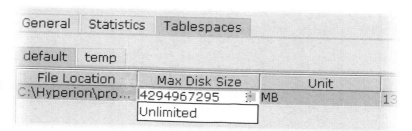

Click the *Add Location* or *Drop Location* to add and remove locations.

4.   Close the application properties window.

Sizing Tablespaces

During the data load and aggregation process, data is stored in both the Temp and Default directories. ASO will always build the full .dat file in the temp tablespace while the default tablespace still has the production .dat open. Hence, for your maximum database size you have to plan on *at least* **3 times your maximum bloated .dat size**. We recommend you play it safe since there is no guarantee that the operating system is not "paging the buffer" (which sounds naughty, by the way). Basically, make sure you have plenty of disk space for your ASO databases.

ASO FILES

Let's also review some of the other files that you will see in your application and database directory folders:

Directory or File	*Location*	*Description*
appname.app	*ARBORPATH*\app\ *appname*\	Application file containing application settings
appname.LOG	*ARBORPATH*\app\ *appname*\	Application log file
dbname.db	*ARBORPATH*\app\ *appname*\dbname\	Database file containing database settings
dbname.dbb	*ARBORPATH*\app\ *appname*\dbname\	Backup of database file
dbname.ddb	*ARBORPATH*\app\ *appname*\dbname\	Partition definition file
dbname.otl	*ARBORPATH*\app\ *appname*\dbname\	Outline file
dbname.otl.keep	*ARBORPATH*\app\ *appname*\dbname\	Temporary backup of *dbname*.otl (created by operations that modify the outline and write it to a new file.)
trigger.trg	*ARBORPATH*\app\ *appname*\dbname\	Trigger file
essn.dat	*ARBORPATH*\app\ *appname*\default\ *ARBORPATH*\app\	Aggregate storage data file

	appname\log\	
	ARBORPATH\app\ *appname*\metadata\	

Can you open and edit any of these files directly? No! And don't try it: doing so may cause database corruption.

ESSBASE DIRECTORY STRUCTURE

Now that you understand the Essbase database structure, let's take a look at the file directory structure on the server for Essbase. The Essbase directory structure contains folders and files created when you install the program. In the 11x version, Essbase uses a system variable called ESSBASEPATH for this directory structure. Older versions of Essbase used a system variable called ARBORPATH (we love you Arbor Software, may you rest in pieces).which you might see hanging around in 11x. These environment variables are %ESSBASEPATH% and %ARBORPATH% in Windows and $ESSBASEPATH and $ARBORPATH in UNIX:

- Essbasepath\bin stores Essbase executables, the Essbase.CFG configuration file, the Essbase.sec security definition file, and the Essbase.bak backup security file.
- Essbasepath\app stores server-based applications (more on this shortly).
- Essbasepath\client stores any client based files and applications.
- Essbasepath\docs stores online documentation.
- Essbasepath\locale contains the character-set files necessary for multi-language use.

Need To Know – Essbase Executables

Helpful
Info

Stored in *arborpath*\bin
- Essbase.exe – Essbase server agent process
- Esssvr.exe – application process
- Essmsh.exe – MaxL shell
- Esscmd.exe – Esscmd command line interface

Stored in *eas*\Server\bin
- Starteas.exe – start the Administration Server executable
- Admincon.exe – Administration Services Console application

The *Essbasepath*\app directory contains all of the application files. An application will contain databases. For a single Hyperion Planning application in versions prior to 11.1.2.2, you may have up to three BSO databases or plan types (more if you are using the Project Financial Planning, Public Sector Budgeting, Workforce Planning or Capital Asset Planning modules). In 11.1.2.3 Planning supports an ASO application/database for every BSO database plus one.

Each database will contain one outline file. Other objects like calc scripts in databases and rules files can be stored at the application or database level.

Let's take a look at the snapshot of the Essbase ASO directory structure:

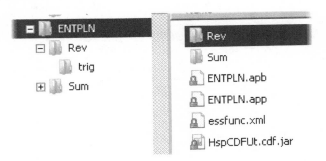

Let's take a look at the snapshot of the Essbase BSO directory structure:

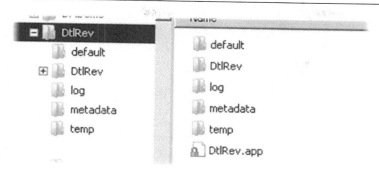

Tip!
You can store rules files, calc scripts, and report scripts at the application OR database level. If you have a calc script that will be run against one or more databases, store this script at the application level once instead of stored multiple times at the database level.

RESTRUCTURING FOR ESSBASE

Restructuring of your Planning databases takes place after the outline changes, like when you add new, edit, and delete members and dimensions. Any and every change forces Essbase to restructure the database, so think of it as "re-saving" the database. This can be a time consuming process depending on the type of restructure and database size.

For BSO, a full restructure, the most time consuming type of restructure, will take place when an outline is updated with the movement, deletion, or addition of a member from a dense dimension. This will reorganize every data block in the page file and regenerate the index. A re-calculation will also be required.

For BSO, a sparse restructure is a much faster type of restructure and takes place when you move, delete, or add a member from a sparse dimension. This type of restructure regenerates the index file but does not restructure the data blocks.

If you delete or move a member in an ASO database, a full outline restructure will take place which could take some time. Make sure to have up to three times the size of the database available so this restructure can complete without error.

A full restructure will take place and aggregation views will be cleared for a hierarchy that is moved, deleted or added. Changing the top member of a stored hierarchy from label only to stored (and vice versa) and changing dynamic hierarchies to stored hierarchies (and vice versa) will have the same end result.

If you add, delete or move a standard dimension, data will be cleared from the database and you'll have to reload data, and for ASO plan types you will have to recreate aggregation views and run the materialization process.

For ASO, a "light" restructure with low performance impact will take place when you make the following types of changes: renaming a member, changing a formula, and changing an alias. A slightly more intensive restructure takes place when you make those same changes to an alternate hierarchy or attribute dimension. If any aggregate views have been created using the updated attribute dimension or alternate hierarchy, they will be cleared, requiring the user to rerun any aggregations.

An outline restructure is the last type of restructure and will take place when you make a change that impacts the outline only, like changing an alias or member formula. This restructure will not regenerate the index file or restructure the data blocks, so is very quick indeed for both BSO and ASO.

Note!   Each action you perform on Planning dimensions will cause some type of restructure. For a full list of the actions and what type of restructure will occur, see the Essbase Database Administrator's Guide and search for a table called "How Actions Affect Databases and Restructuring".

If your BSO restructuring times are too long and impacting your users, consider the following tuning tips:

- If you change a dimension frequently, make it sparse.
- Use incremental restructuring to control when Essbase performs a required database restructuring.
- Push dense dimension changes to a nightly process where a longer batch window is acceptable.

Tip!   Full restructures of ASO databases will require 3x the database size.

While Penny is moving and grooving in the more technical aspects of Planning (this can be fun stuff for the IT oriented), you may be ready to jump ship. Don't put on your swimsuit just yet, the Translator is about to break out in song for Planning Administration.

Scene 3:
Planning Administration

APPLICATION SETTINGS

Planning provides a number of settings that can be defined by application: *Current application defaults, Display settings,* and *Advanced settings.* For each application, you can enable certain application defaults like:

- *Enable email notification* (users receive an email when they become the new owner of a planning unit)
- *Copy the owner* (application owner receives a copy of all email notifications),
- Default alias table
- Whether to show alias and/or description for member selection
- Whether to show Planning unit aliases in Approvals and show Planning units that have not been started
- *Display full user names*

Display settings can also be defined under application settings. Options include *Specify number formatting, Retain page and POV selections, Enable warnings for large forms* and more. Follow along with us as we set application settings for our Entpln.

In the *Advanced system settings,* you specify the email server and administrator email address, task list date format, and Shared Services registration information. You can choose to show the full user name instead of id for Approvals. An important setting that you will definitely use is *Application Maintenance mode.* You define when users or other administrators can access the application. For example, if you want to take the system down for maintenance, you can turn off access for end users:

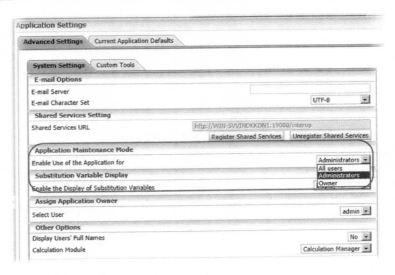

Advanced System Settings is also where you can change the application owner.

Under *Advanced Settings >> Custom Tools*, you can add customized links to your Planning application by user type (Basic, Interactive, or Administrator). Users access the links by selecting *Tools >> Links*.

To hit home some of the application settings, let's set the application settings for Entpln or Planning Sample application.

1. Select *Administration >> Application>> Settings*.
2. Select the *Current Application Defaults* tab.
3. Review all of the available Current Application Defaults - Application Settings.
4. On the Application Settings tab, change the following options:
   a. *Show Planning Units as Aliases – Yes*:

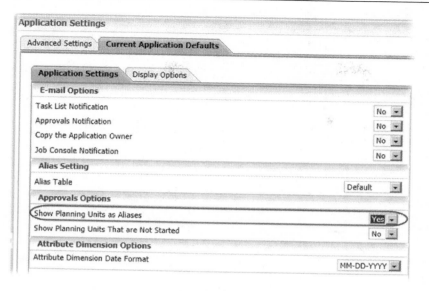

5. On the *Display options tab,* change the following options:

a. Allow *Search When Number of Pages Exceeds:* "5"

b. *Indentation of Members on Page:* Indent based on Hierarchy.

c. *Set Warn if data form larger than cells specified:* "7500"

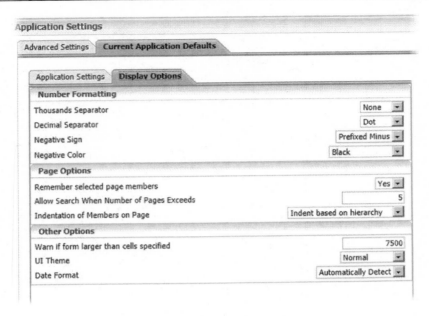

6. Click *Save*.
7. Select the *Advanced Settings* tab.
8. Review all of the available options.
9. On the System Settings tab, set *Enable Use for Application* for *Administrator* (helpful when you want to keep users out of Planning):

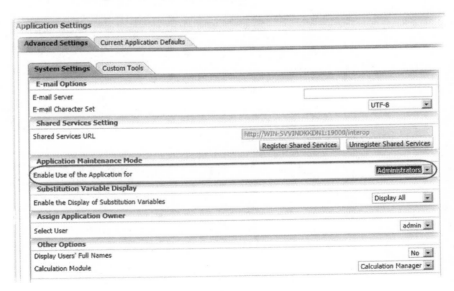

10. Select the *Custom Tools* tab.
11. Add a link to interRel's website – www.interrel.com – for interactive users to view:

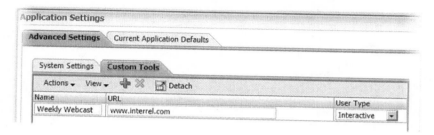

Now make sure to communicate to users that they can choose to accept application defaults or set their own preferences.

1. Select *File >> Preferences.*
2. Select *Planning* preferences (scroll down to see the icon for Planning).
3. For *Application Settings*, check all of the boxes to use Application Defaults (users can choose to use the application defaults or set their own preferences):

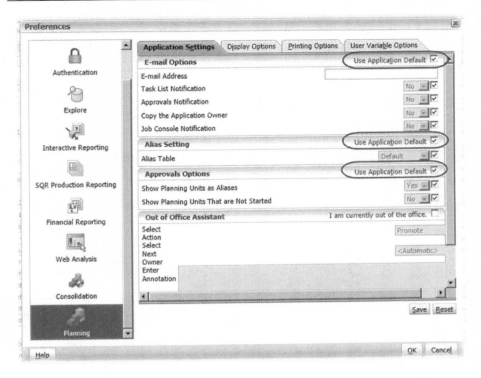

4. For *Display Options* tab, check all of the boxes to *Use Application Defaults*.

5. Open the a data form and note the changes.

Note!

Version 11.1.2.3 provides new preference settings for aliases and grid fetch settings.

APPLICATION PROPERTIES

A number of Planning application properties exist. Select *Administration >> Application>> Properties* to define settings for the Planning application. The properties are saved in the HSPSYS_PROPERTIES system database table. In earlier versions, you updated this information in a file on the server manually.

You can update the properties listed and also add new properties.

Manage Properties

Application Properties	System Properties		

Actions ▾   View ▾   ✚ ✖   ⬚ Detach

Property Name	Property Value
ADD_HSP_RATES_DTURL_PATTERN	/*HyperionFDM*/
EDIT_DIM_ENABLED	true
ENABLE_FOR_OFFLINE	true
JDBC_MAX_CONNECTIONS	10
JDBC_MIN_CONNECTIONS	1
OLAP_MAX_CONNECTIONS	10
OLAP_MIN_CONNECTIONS	1
SUBS_VAR_DISPLAY_OPT	1
SUPPORTING_DETAIL_CACHE_SIZE	20
SYNC_USER_ON_LOGON	true

One helpful property is to allow users to open more than one form at one time using the DATA_GRID_CACHE_SIZE property. This property specifies the number of data grids cached per user for an application. This property is set to "1" by default, allowing only one form to be opened for each user at a time. You can increase this setting to "2" or "3" but more memory is required to support the cached data grids. If you have a large number of users or large data forms, performance test this setting before using in production.

In 11.1.2.2, you can also change application skin of the end user interface. The application skin can either be a a BLAF (Browser Look and Feel) or a "Fusion" skin. The Fusion skin is the default style for the 11.1.2.2 Planning web interface (developed in Application Development Framework (ADF)).

To set the skin setting,
1. Select *Administration >> Application>> Properties*
2. Click the + icon.
3. Create an application property called "SKIN_FAMILY".
4. Set the value to "blafplus-rich" or "fusion".
5. Click *Save.*
6. Log out of the application and workspace.
7. Clear the cache.
8. Log back in and the new skin setting will display.

Note!   Values for the application properties may be case sensitive.

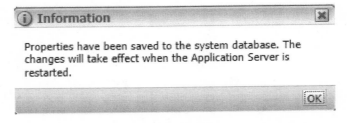

Another property that can be added or changed is the HOME_PAGE property. By default, users will see the Task List view in the Planning application navigation. You can change the starting point to start at the form folder navigation by setting HOME_PAGE to "Forms". You can also set the property to "Approvals" to default to the Approvals process management screen.

You must restart the Planning application server for properties to take effect:

> ⓘ **Information**   ☒
>
> Properties have been saved to the system database. The changes will take effect when the Application Server is restarted.
>
> OK

PLAN TYPE EDITOR IN 11.1.2.3

New Plan Type Editor

You can add or delete plan types to an existing Planning application via the Plan Type Editor in 11.1.2.3. Select *Administration >> Manage >> Plan Types* to access the Plan Type Editor:

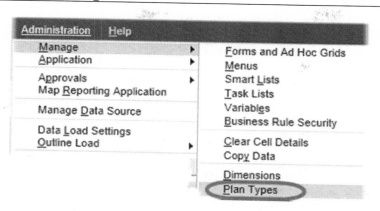

The Plan Type Editor displays:

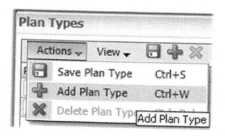

You can *Add* or *Delete* plan types from an application:

When adding a new plan type, you can choose *ASO* or *BSO*:

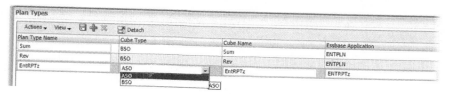

You may create up to 3 BSO plan types within a single application (just like before) and X ASO plan types where X equals the number of BSO plan types +1.

Plan Type Name	Cube Type	Cube Name	Essbase Application
Sum	BSO	Sum	ENTPLN
Rev	BSO	Rev	ENTPLN
EntRPTz	ASO	EntRPTz	ENTRPTz
DtlRev	ASO	DtlRev	DtlRev

VIEW STATISTICS

As an administrator, you can view the names of users logged on to the Planning application as well as the last time a user has accessed the Planning application. You can also tell how much available supporting detail cache exists (if this is 100%, then you may want to increase this cache setting).

To view statistics,

1. Select *Administration >> Application>> Statistics*:

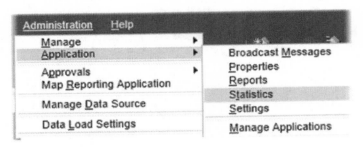

The stats will display:

View Statistics

Application ENTPLN
Users 1
Supporting Detail Detection Cache Usage 0%

User Name	Time since last access (hh:mm:ss)
Administrator	00:00:00
Administrator	00:00:00
Administrator	00:00:00
Administrator	00:00:00
Administrator	00:00:00

COPY DATA

Another handy admin feature is the copy data feature. Planning administrators can copy the entire plan from one year to another or from a specific intersection to another. For example, the Planning Administrator may be ready to copy revenue data to the final version while expenses are still in draft versions. The Copy Data feature copies all relational data, including supporting detail, account annotations, comments and documents, from one dimensional intersection to another dimensional intersection. The settings that you select in the *Copy Data* page are preserved for the current session only. Members and dimensions that you copy must be present in the selected plan types and data must be copied into cells that can accept data.

Note!   You cannot copy planning unit annotations.

Note!   Calculations must be run after using the Copy Data feature.

To copy data,
1. Select *Administration >> Manage >>Copy Data.*

In the following example, you need to copy all expense data for North America for all periods for next year's Budget from Sandbox to Final.

2. Set the following options to do so including *Comments* and *Supporting detail*:

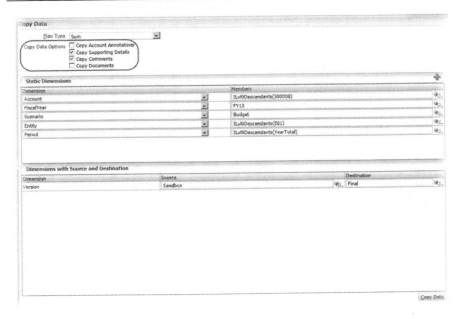

3. Click *Copy Data*.

Just as you've done in the other member selection windows, you can use functions and variables to identify members. You can type directly into the text box if you know the exact member name or use the member selection icon.

CLEAR CELL DETAILS

You may at times want to clear cell details for a dimensional intersection like supporting detail or cell text. In version 9.3.1, you have to go to the backend tables to do this. Beginning in version 11, you have the *Clear Cell Details* feature in the Planning web client.

Note!

CAREFULLY use this feature! You don't want to accidentally clear unintended plan data. We recommend you back up data (both relational and Essbase) before running the *Clear Cell Details* task).

To clear cell details,

1. Select *Administration >> Manage >>Clear Cell Details:*

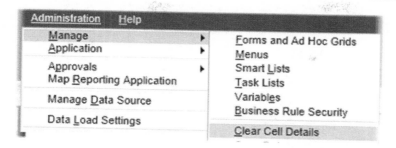

2. Select the plan type, dimensions, members and clear options:

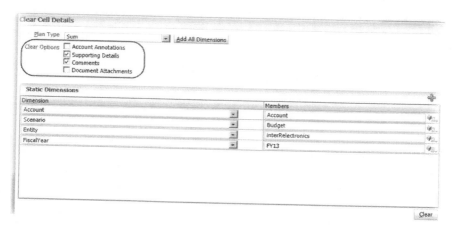

3. Click *Clear*.

REPORTING

Reports on Data Forms and Planning Annotations

Planning provides standard administration reports available for data forms and planning unit annotations. They also included audit tracking features under Reporting (for some strange reason) even though no audit reports are actually available.

To run Planning reports,

1. Click *Administration >> Application >> Reports*.
2. Create a Form Definition report by selecting one or more data forms on the Data Forms tab.
3. Move the selected data forms into the Selected Data Forms section.

4. Optionally check *Include Member Selection List* and *Business Rules*:

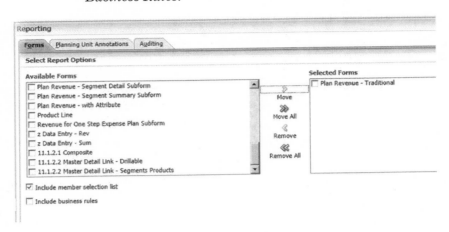

5. Click *Create Report*.

This is a helpful documentation tool for form definitions.

Select *Administration* >> *Application* >> *Reports* and choose the Planning Unit Annotations tab to run Planning unit annotations reports. Choose the desired Scenario, Version and Entity members and then select options to apply filters based on Approvals status:

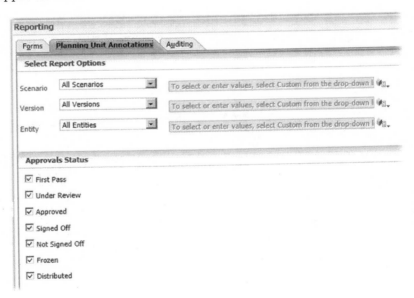

AUDITING

Next lets discuss auditing, a Planning feature that tracks the who, when, and what of Planning actions.

Audit details capture the following information:

- Data Form: Expenses 04
- Group: Marketing
- User: SBakey
- Time Posted: 12/12/2013 9:17
- Action: Add
- Property: Currency
- Old value: Default
- New value: USD

Beginning in 11.1.2.2, users can view the audit details from the data forms. This includes all actions except impact from business rules executed on the cell:

Smart list and free form text changes are also captured:

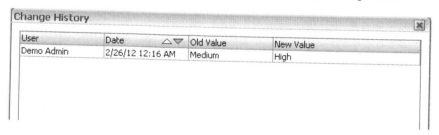

There is a performance consideration so only track those items you need. For example, if you only have 1 or 2 administrators that manage Planning, don't worry about tracking the administrative tasks. We recommend focusing on tracking those actions of end users like data changes, business rules and copy version.

To turn on auditing,

1. Click *Administration >> Application >> Reports.*
2. Select the Auditing tab.

3. Choose the actions to track:

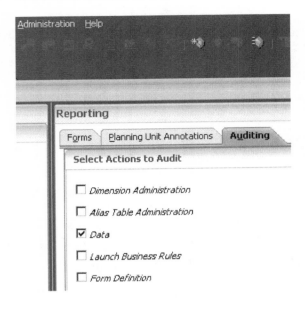

4. Click *Save*.
5. Restart the Planning web server.

You must restart the Planning services for auditing selections to take effect.

Note!

You need to set up a back end process against the Planning relational database archive this data periodically. You must use SQL to access backend table. To clear the audit tables you will run a SQL delete statement similar to the following:

```
DELETE FROM HSP_AUDIT_RECORDS
```

Note!

Once you clear the HSP_AUDIT_RECORDS table, end users will no longer be able to view the data history through the Planning user interface.

To view audit records, sorted by the time they were posted will as expected require SQL:

```
SELECT * FROM HSP_AUDIT_RECORDS ORDER BY TIME_POSTED
```

The next Planning administration topic is an important one: the Planning utilities. These utilities can save you hours in development and administration so definitely read this scene.

Scene 4:
Planning Utilities

With your installation of Hyperion Planning, many utilities are available to make the Planning administrator's job a bit easier. The utilities provide a supported way to update Planning components and the underlying relational tables. You can also schedule tasks to run in off hours using the utilities.

The Hyperion Planning utilities can be found in the HYPERION_HOME\products\Planning\bin folder. The picture below shows the Planning\bin folder and all the utilities available in version 11.1.2.2 (note a few of these are not available in 9.3.1). In this section we will review and show you examples of each utility.

Oracle ▾ Middleware ▾ user_projects ▾ epmsystem1 ▾ Planning ▾ planning1

New folder

Name	Date modified	Type	Size
BroadCastMessage.cmd	6/3/2012 6:06 AM	Windows Command ...	1 KB
BuildEntity.bat	1/24/2013 11:19 AM	Windows Batch File	1 KB
CalcMgrCmdLineLauncher.cmd	6/3/2012 6:06 AM	Windows Command ...	1 KB
CubeRefresh.cmd	6/3/2012 6:06 AM	Windows Command ...	1 KB
DeleteSharedDescendants.cmd	6/3/2012 6:06 AM	Windows Command ...	1 KB
ExportPFPSampleApp.cmd	6/3/2012 6:06 AM	Windows Command ...	1 KB
ExportPFPTemplates.cmd	6/3/2012 6:06 AM	Windows Command ...	1 KB
ExportSecurity.cmd	6/3/2012 6:06 AM	Windows Command ...	1 KB
FormDefUtil.cmd	6/3/2012 6:06 AM	Windows Command ...	1 KB
HBRExport.cmd	6/3/2012 6:06 AM	Windows Command ...	1 KB
HBRMigrateSecurity.cmd	6/3/2012 6:06 AM	Windows Command ...	1 KB
HspUnlockApp.cmd	6/3/2012 6:06 AM	Windows Command ...	1 KB
ImportFormDefinition.bat	6/3/2012 6:06 AM	Windows Batch File	1 KB
ImportSecurity.cmd	6/3/2012 6:06 AM	Windows Command ...	1 KB
ImportUsers.cmd	6/3/2012 6:06 AM	Windows Command ...	1 KB
MaintenanceMode.cmd	6/3/2012 6:06 AM	Windows Command ...	1 KB
MemberFormula.cmd	6/3/2012 6:06 AM	Windows Command ...	1 KB
MemberFormulaSync.cmd	6/3/2012 6:06 AM	Windows Command ...	1 KB
MenuDefUtil.cmd	6/3/2012 6:06 AM	Windows Command ...	1 KB
OutlineLoad.cmd	6/3/2012 6:06 AM	Windows Command ...	1 KB
PasswordEncryption.cmd	6/3/2012 6:06 AM	Windows Command ...	1 KB
PFPImportUtility.bat	6/3/2012 6:06 AM	Windows Batch File	9 KB
PropFileMig.cmd	6/3/2012 6:06 AM	Windows Command ...	1 KB
ProvisionUsers.cmd	6/3/2012 6:06 AM	Windows Command ...	1 KB
PushData.cmd	6/3/2012 6:06 AM	Windows Command ...	1 KB
setHPenv.bat	6/3/2012 6:06 AM	Windows Batch File	3 KB
SortMember.cmd	6/3/2012 6:06 AM	Windows Command ...	1 KB
TaskListDefUtil.cmd	6/3/2012 6:06 AM	Windows Command ...	1 KB
UpdateUsers.cmd	6/3/2012 6:06 AM	Windows Command ...	1 KB

Note! Some utilities require the planning application owner to run.

Note! The utilities must be run on the Planning server. If you don't have access to the Planning server, start to make friends with IT and make your case on why you need access. Good news though – Oracle is continuing development into web based user interfaces to perform Planning utility tasks. Version 11.1.2.3 provides a web user interface to run the Outline Load utility.

We will start with PasswordEncryption.cmd as the output password file can be used by the other utilities. PasswordEncryption.cmd and OutlineLoad.cmd were introduced in version 11.1.1. Planning utilities need to be run on the server where Planning is installed, they can be executed from the command line or from batch files that can be scheduled using third party scheduling tools.

PASSWORD ENCRYPTION

PasswordEncryption.cmd

The Password Encryption utility, introduced in version 11.1.1, creates files that store an encrypted password for use by other Planning utilities. Each file may contain only one password. You choose the location and the name of each file when running the utility. Once you create a password file, you can run other utilities from the command line or from batch files with the option "[-f:passwordFile]" as a parameter instead of typing the password.

This utility is normally located in the HYPERION_HOME\Products\Planning\bin folder with the other Planning utilities.

In order to create a password encryption file with the Password Encryption utility in a Windows environment, use: PasswordEncryption.cmd with the name and path of the password File; In a UNIX environment use: PasswordEncryption.sh with the name and path of the password File, you will be prompted to enter the password to encrypt.

Open the command line, go to the Planning bin folder, enter PasswordEncryption.cmd with the name and path of the password File, and enter the password to encrypt.

```
PasswordEncryption.cmd
H:\A_RB\PlanningUtilityScripts\EncryptionFile1.
txt
```

Try
It!

You will see a notification that your password has been encrypted and stored in the location you indicated:

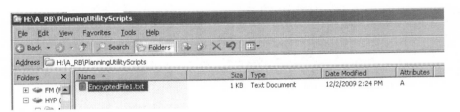

Go to the specified folder location and you will see the file:

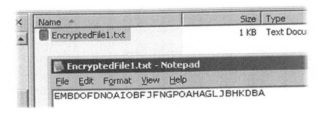

Open the file:

You will see the password is stored in the file in encrypted form:

This password file can be used as a first parameter in the utilities that are explained in the remainder of the utilities section.

SECURITY UTILITIES

ExportSecurity.cmd

With the Export Security utility you can export access permissions to a Planning security file SecFile.txt. It can export security for selected groups or selected users or all groups and users in the planning application. It can export security for members, data forms, data form folders, task lists, Calculation Manager business rules, Calculation Manager business rules folders. By exporting a security file you can then import access permissions into other applications using the Import Security utility that is explained in the following section of this scene. The syntax and parameters are:

```
ExportSecurity.cmd [-f:passwordFile]
/A=appname,/U=username,
[/S=searchCriteria|/S_USER=user|/S_GROUP=group],
[/S_MEMBER=memberName|/S_MEMBER_ID=memberName
|/S_MEMBER_D=memberName|/S_MEMBER_IC=memberName|/S_M
EMBER_C=memberName],[/DELIM=delim] ,
[/DEBUG=true|false],[/TO_FILE=fileName],[/HELP=Y]
The mandatory parameters are:
/A=appname,/U=username. If a password file is setup
it can be used as an option. Just as with the other
utilities, if a password file is set up, it can be
used as the first parameter,
```

If you specify only the mandatory parameters, the utility will export access to all artifacts for all users and groups in the application. You can't export access permissions to task lists for administrators but you can manually add those records into the file for future importing.

Optional parameters are:

/S	Search criteria (search for a user or group)
/S_USER	user (specify a user)
/S_GROUP	group (specify a group)
/S_MEMBER	member name (specify a member)
/S_MEMBER_ID	member name (specify a member and its descendants)

/S_MEMBER_D	member name (specify a member's descendants)
/S_MEMBER_IC	member name (specify a member and its children)
/S_MEMBER_C	member name (specify a member's descendants)
/DELIM	delimit (specify a delimiter)
/DEBUG	true/false
/TO_FILE	(specify the path to the SecFile.txt (
/HELP	Y

In this example we are going to export all security from a Planning application. Open the command prompt, go to the Planning\Bin directory, and execute the ExportSecurity.cmd utility with the mandatory parameters as shown below.

Try
It!

\H:\HYSL\products\Planning\bin\ExportSecurity.c md -f: H:\A_RB\PlanningUtilityScripts\passwordfile.txt /A=totplan, /U=Planningadmin

The Output SecFile.txt looks like:

```
secFile.txt - Notepad
File  Edit  Format  View  Help
Planner,Depreciation Summary,READ,MEMBER,SL_FORM
Planner,11 Balance Sheet,READWRITE,MEMBER,SL_FORM
Henry,E01_101_1110,READWRITE,MEMBER
Henry,Sales Manager,READ,MEMBER,SL_TASKLIST
Frank,TotalGeography,READ,@IDESCENDANTS
Frank,Var %,READ,MEMBER
Planner,Plan,READWRITE,MEMBER
Planner,Target,READ,MEMBER
Planner,Final,READWRITE,@ICHILDREN
Planner,working,READWRITE,MEMBER
Planner,Forecast,READWRITE,MEMBER
Planner,Actual,READ,MEMBER
Planner,CashFlow,READ,@IDESCENDANTS
Planner,BalanceSheet,READ,@IDESCENDANTS
Planner,IncomeStatement,READWRITE,@DESCENDANTS
Planner,515000,READ,@IDESCENDANTS
Planner,511000,READ,@IDESCENDANTS
Planner,511100,READWRITE,MEMBER
Planner,506560,NONE,MEMBER
Planner,506321,READ,MEMBER
Planner,506311,READ,MEMBER
Planner,400000,READ,@IDESCENDANTS
Planner,Statistics,READWRITE,@DESCENDANTS
Planner,COSRate,READ,MEMBER
Planner,01 Facilities Allocation,READWRITE,MEMBER,SL_FORM
Planner,02 IT Allocation,READWRITE,MEMBER,SL_FORM
Planner,03 Marketing Allocation,READWRITE,MEMBER,SL_FORM
Planner,02 Product Revenue,READWRITE,MEMBER,SL_FORM
```

The exported SecFile.txt includes fields for: user or group,member name in the application, access permissions, relationship funtion. Artifacts are include SL_FORM, SL_COMPOSITE, SL_TASKLIST, SL_CALCRULE, SL_FORMFOLDER and SL_CALCFOLDER

ImportSecurity.cmd

The Import Security utility loads access permissions for users and groups from a text file. The utility imports security for these items: members, data forms, data form folders, task lists, Calculation Manager Business Rules, Calculation Manager Business Rules folders. Permissions are overwritten for existing members while all other existing permissions are not. You can clear existing access permissions with SL_CLEARALL parameter. All users, groups and objects must be defined in the application before running the Import utility.

The text file must be named "SecFile.txt" and must be placed in the HYPERION_HOME\Planning\Bin folder. You can use the SecFile.txt extracted with the Export Security utility to update security across applications or you can manually create the SecFile.txt file. Available delimiters for the secfile.txt include comma, tab, semi-colon, pipe, colon, and space. Comma is default delimiter.

After running the utility, verify results in importsecurity.log. You can improve import security performance by disabling the display of full names of users; this change is made in the Planning Web client under advanced system settings.

The syntax and parameters are:

```
ImportSecurity.cmd [-f:passwordFile] appname,
username, [delimiter], [RUN_SILENT], [SL_CLEARALL]
```

An example would be:

```
ImportSecurity.cmd "entbud,admin,SL_TAB,1"
```

Try
It!

Create a simple security file (the name must be SecFile.txt) and import it using the utility.

Open the command line, go to the Planing\Bin folder and enter this:

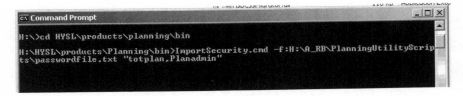

You should receive a success notification:

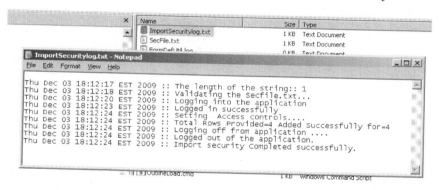

Look at the ImportSecuritylog.txt located in the Planning\bin folder. All rows should have loaded successfully.

ProvisionUsers.cmd

The Provision Users utility synchronizes Planning users, groups and roles in Shared Services with a Planning application and with Essbase. It is an alternative to refreshing security filters from the Planning Web client.

The syntax and parameters are:

```
ProvisionUsers [-f:passwordFile] /ADMIN:adminName
/A:appName [/U:user1[;user2;user3]]
```

Mandatory parameters:	
/ADMIN	adminName
/A	appName
Optional parameters:	
[-f:passwordFile]	If the password file is set up, use as first parameter
/U:	Specifies the users to sync

/R:n	Specifies the interval in minutes for the sync to run (no argument runs the sync once)

Try
It!

Open the command line and enter the mandatory parameters as shown below.

If you don't get a success message, you can look at the log in the Planning\Bin folder the log is called UserProvisionSync.Log. If you execute the utility from a batch file, the log will go to the same folder as the batch file:

Other examples:

ProvisionUsers /ADMIN:admin /A:Entpln syncs all users for Entpln application.

ProvisionUsers /ADMIN:admin /A:entpln /U:eddie /R:60 syncs user eddie in entpln every 60 minutes.

UpdateUsers.cmd

The Update Users utility is used with the UpdateNativeDir Shared Services utility to synchronize identities between Planning and Shared services. Update Users must be run after running the UpdateNativeDir Shared Services utility. Users and groups can lose their assigned access when their identities (SIDs) change, and the only way to prevent this is to synchronize identities between Planning and Shared services. Synchronization is required when the authentication provider is changed, users and groups are moved in an external provider, or when migrating an application from one environment to another with different Shared Services instances.

The two utilities need to run in a specific order. First, run the UpdateNativeDir utility to update user and group identities in Shared Services. This utility and its documentation are in the HYPERION_HOME/Common/Utilities/SyncOpenLDAPUtility directory. Second, run the UpdateUsers.cmd to update SIDs in Planning with the changes in Shared Services. The server needs to be local host. Check results in UpdateUsers.log in the bin directory.

The syntax and parameters are:

```
updateusers.cmd [-f:passwordFile] serverName
adminName applicationName
```

Open the command line and enter the mandatory parameters as shown below:

Try It!

```
UpdateUsers.cmd –
f:H:\A_RB\PlanningUtilityScripts\passwordfile.txt
server planadmin TotPlan
```

You should receive a completion message:

To view details, look at the UpdateUsers.log in the bin directory.

UserMigrUtil.cmd

This utility was used to delete the underscore users when you were migrating from Planning 3.5 or 4x .

Export/Import Utility

The last utility we will cover is not actually a Planning utility but you can use it to help maintain security for the users and groups used by Planning.

The CSS Import/Export Utility is a command-line utility that enables you to export, import, and validate user provisioning data in the native Open LDAP directory. This utility is part of Shared Services (not Planning). You can use the utility to create, modify, and delete users, groups, and roles that originate from the native user directory bundled with Shared Services, and you can modify relationship data for users/groups stored externally. You can export data from ALL directories, but you can import data to the NATIVE directory only, the utility lets you validate the import file for errors prior to import.

You can find the utility and its documentation in the Shared Services　　　　　　Server　　　　　　under Hyperion_Home\common\utilities\CSSImportExportUtility.　　All the components of the utility, including the documentation, are contained in a zip file called cssimportexport.zip. Install the utility by extracting the content of the zip file into folder where the user running the utility has read, write and execute access. The zip file extraction creates the importexport directory that contains all required files the documentation file is called impexp.pdf. In the extracted directory you will find the properties file, sample.CSV and .XML export files, and three batch scripts: CSSExport, CSSImport and CSSValidate. Before starting the import export operations, back up the Shared Services relational repository, ensure Shared Services is running, and prepare the importexport.properties file.

ADMINISTRATIVE TASKS

BroadCastMessage.cmd

You can use the Broadcast Message utility to send text messages to all Planning users who are logged into the application at the time the message is sent. With broadcast messaging you can ask folks to log out of the system or communicate upcoming maintenance; the text message only appears in Planning and can be up to 127 characters. The utility is an alternative to sending broadcast messages using the Planning Web Client. Using the web client, messages go to users of the application from which you are sending; using the utility you can specify the application and schedule messages using a third party scheduler.

The syntax and parameters are:

```
Broadcastmessage.cmd -f:passwordfile  server_name,
application_name, username, message
```

Try It!

Open the command line, go to the Planning\Bin folder, and enter: **BroadcastMessage.cmd -f: the name and path of the password File [space]** *server name*, **Entpln**, *youruserid,* **"Eddie - Dr. Dementor is right behind you".**   Or in real life, you might actually type "This is a test message – Please ignore". Do not use a comma between the password file and the server name and the server name for this utility needs to be "localhost".

All planning users connected to the specified application receive the following message:

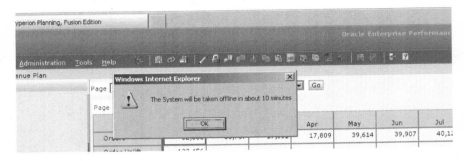

Tip!

You can execute the Planning utilities from a batch file. For example, you can create a batch file to send a broadcast message to your Planning users and schedule it using a third party tool to execute 10 minutes before the application is taken offline for maintenance.

Try It!

Create a new text document, change the file extension from "txt" to "bat", edit the file and add: the path to the utility: **HYPERION_HOME\Planning\Bin folder\ BroadcastMessage.cmd -f: the name and path of the password File [space] server name, application name, user, "I'm about to kick you out of the system for the midday process."**
You can now execute the batch file with a double click or schedule it using a third party tool.

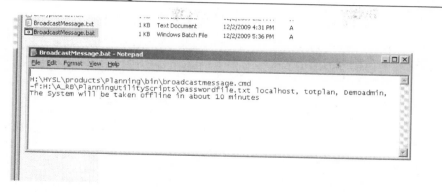

HspUnlockApp.cmd

Use this utility when a Planning application becomes locked. This utility clears the HSP_Lock table. It must be run from the Planning server.

The syntax and parameters are:

```
HspUnlockApp.cmd[-f:passwordFile] servername
username appname
```

Open the command line and unlock the app.

Try It!

You should get a confirmation message:

```
taskSequence =

task =

*******H:\HYSL\common\config\9.5.0.0\registry.properties
using Java property for Hyperion Home H:\HYSL
Setting Arbor path to: H:\HYSL\common\EssbaseRTC\9.5.0.0
d{ISO8601> INFO main com.hyperion.audit.client.runtime.AuditRuntime - Entering A
udit Client http://demodrive.oracle.com:28080/interop/Audit
d{ISO8601> INFO main com.hyperion.audit.client.runtime.AuditRuntime - Initializi
ng Manager for the serverhttp://demodrive.oracle.com:28080/interop/Audit
d{ISO8601> INFO main com.hyperion.audit.client.manager.AuditContext - Creating N
ew Audit Client Instance .... http://demodrive.oracle.com:28080/interop/Audit
d{ISO8601> INFO main com.hyperion.audit.client.runtime.AuditRuntime - Audit Clie
nt has been created for the server http://demodrive.oracle.com:28080/interop/Aud
it
The application has been successfully unlocked
d{ISO8601> INFO Thread-15 com.hyperion.audit.client.runtime.AuditRuntime - Writi
ng Audit Records for migrated Artifacts ...
d{ISO8601> INFO Thread-15 com.hyperion.audit.client.runtime.AuditRuntime - Store
d Audited Data Successfully !!!
Usage:    HspUnlockApp.cmd
          HspUnlockApp.cmd  [-f:passwordFile] servername username appname
Example:  HspUnlockApp.cmd  localhost xyz app1
H:\HYSL\products\Planning\bin>
```

CubeRefresh.cmd

Use the Cube Refresh utility to refresh the Planning Application via the command line or from a batch file that can be scheduled using a third party tool. It refreshes Planning metadata and security filters to Essbase application via command line, pushing all Planning web client changes to the Essbase databases. Take the same cautions when refreshing the application using this utility as you do when refreshing through the web client (e.g., you don't delete members that have data and the Essbase outlines are not locked). Like other utilities, this one needs to run on the Planning server.

The syntax and parameters are:

```
CubeRefresh.cmd [-f:passwordFile]
/A:application_name /U:user_name [/C|/R] /D
[/F[S|V]][/RMIPORT:rmi_port] [/L] [/DEBUG]
```

[-f:passwordFile]	If the password file is set up, use as first parameter
/C	Creates the database outline
/R	Refreshes the database outline
/D	Specify the database during create or refresh
/F	Refreshes all security filters
/FS	Generate shared member security filters
/FV	Validate security filters but don't save
/FSV	Validate the shared member security filters
/RMIPORT	Specify an RMI port number if is different

	than default
/-L	Default option (connecting to an app server locally or remote)
/L	Create or refresh without connecting to the application server
/DEBUG	Specify detailed error messages

For example if you want to refresh the outline and security filters, type the following:

```
CubeRefresh.cmd -f:passwordFile /A:entbud /U:eddie
/R /D /FS
```

Try
It!

Open the command line and refresh the cube, outline and security changes will be refreshed with the options below:

Look for the following confirmation message:

Note!

Be very careful with the **/C** command. You only want to create the application once!

DIMENSIONS & DATA

Introduction to the Outline Load Utility

The Outline Load utility was introduced to Planning in version 11.1.1 and you can use it to load metadata and data. You load .CSV metadata files in parent-child format directly into

Planning. The Outline Load Utility can update and build the following dimensions and outline components: Account, Period, Year, Scenario, Version, Currency, Entity, user-defined dimensions, attributes, UDAs, exchange rates, Smart Lists, Dates and Text measures. In 11.1.2.2, you can export metadata as well. In 11.1.2.3 the Outline Load Utility supports relational databases as import sources and export targets.

The syntax and parameters are as follows:

```
OutlineLoad [-f:passwordFile][/S:server]
/A:application /U:userName [/M]
[/I:inputFileName/D[U]:loadDimensionName|/
DA:attributeDimensionName:baseDimensionName] [/TR]
[/N] [[/R] [/U]] [/C] [/F] [/K]
[/X:exceptionFileName] [L:logFileName] [/?]
```

Available parameters for the Outline Load Utility in 11.1.2.2 include:

-f:*passwordfile*	Pass in encrypted password file
/S:*server*	Server
/A:*application*	Application
/U:*username*	User to log into the application
/M	Generate fully qualified header records for loadable dimensions
/I:*inputfilename*	Name of the flat file containing header record and data records in CSV format
/E:*outputfilename*	Name of output file for exported dimension
/D:*loaddimensionname*	Dimension to be updated with flat file
/DU:*userdefinedload dimensionname*	User defined dimension to be loaded; New dimension will be created if it doesn't exist
/DA[T]:*attributeload dimensionname: basedimensionname*	Text attribute dimension to be loaded:base dimension; New attribute is created if it doesn't exist
/DAN:*attributeload dimensionname: basedimensionname*	Numeric attribute dimension to be loaded:base dimension; New attribute is created if it doesn't exist
/DAB:attributeloaddim ensionname:basedime nsionname	Boolean attribute dimension to be loaded:base dimension; New attribute is created if it doesn't exist
/DAD:attributeloaddim ensionname:basedime nsionname	Date attribute dimension to be loaded:base dimension; New attribute is created if it doesn't exist
/TR	Used when loading data via the Outline Load utility

/N	"Dry run"; doesn't actually load data from flat file
/O	Maintain order of members in load file
/H	Order input records in the parent child order; /-H loads members in the order within the flat file (faster)
/R	Delete all members before performing the load
/U	Delete all planning units with the /R option
/T	Inherit unspecified plan type settings from parent when adding new members
/C	Perform a cube refresh after metadata load
/F	Create security filters when performing cube refresh
/K	Lock the dimension (recommended)
/X:*exceptionfilename*	Exception file name
/L:*logfilename*	Log file name
/DX:*Hsp_Rates*	Load Hsp Rates dimension and create exchange tables
/DS:*Hsp_SMARTLISTS*	Load Smart List dimension and the values
/?	Display usage text

New parameters for the 11.1.2.3 Outline Load Utility to support relational database source and targets include:

- /ER[:RDBConnectionPropertiesFileName]
- /ED CSV file to which to write exported data is written
- /EDD The row, column, and POV members being exported
- /ERA
- /REQ:exportQueryOrKey
- /REC:catalog
- /RED:driver
- /RER:url
- /REU:userName
- /REP:password

To follow along with Penny and run a build process for the Entity and Account dimension, please email info@interrel.com for the sample flat files.

Update the Entity Dimension from Flat File

Here is the Entity.CSV metadata file for the Entity dimension. If you ever loaded metadata into Planning using HAL, you will find this file very similar to a file you uploaded with HAL. Fields can be in any order, but headers are case sensitive and must match exactly:

	A	B	C	D	E	F	G	H	I
1	Parent	Entity	Alias: Default	Data Stor	Plan Type Aggregati		Plan Type Aggregation (Rev
2	Entity	interRelectronics	interRelectronics, Inc.	Store	1 +		1 +
3	interRelectronics	E01	North America	Store	1 +		1 +
4	E01	E01_0	North America Corporate	Store	1 +		1 +
5	E01	E01_101	USA	Store	1 +		1 +
6	E01_0	E01_101_1000	USA Sales	Store	1 +		1 +
7	E01_101_1000	E01_101_1100	East Sales	Store	1 +		1 +
8	E01_101_1100	E01_101_1110	MA	Store	1 +		1 +
9	E01_101_1100	E01_101_1120	NY	Store	1 +		1 +
10	E01_101_1100	E01_101_1130	PA	Store	1 +		1 +
11	E01_101_1000	E01_101_1200	West Sales	Store	1 +		1 +
12	E01_101_1200	E01_101_1210	CA	Store	1 +		1 +
13	E01_101_1200	E01_101_1220	CO	Store	1 +		1 +
14	E01_101_1200	E01_101_1230	WA	Store	1 +		1 +
15	E01_101_1000	E01_101_1300	North Sales	Store	1 +		1 +
16	E01_101_1300	E01_101_1310	IL	Store	1 +		1 +
17	E01_101_1300	E01_101_1320	MN	Store	1 +		1 +
18	E01_101_1000	E01_101_1400	South Sales	Store	1 +		1 +
19	E01_101_1400	E01_101_1410	FL	Store	1 +		1 +
20	E01_101_1400	E01_101_1420	TX	Store	1 +		1 +
21	E01_101	E01_101_2000	USA Admin	Store	1 +		1 +
22	E01_101_2000	E01_101_2100	Admin Serv	Store	1 +		1 +
23	E01_101_2100	E01_101_2110	Info Technology	Store	1 +		1 +
24	E01_101_2100	E01_101_2120	Human Resources	Store	1 +		1 +
25	E01_101_2100	E01_101_2130	Facilities	Store	1 +		1 +
26	E01_101_2000	E01_101_2200	Finance	Store	1 +		1 +
27	E01_101_2200	E01_101_2210	Accounting	Store	1 +		1 +
28	E01_101_2200	E01_101_2220	Payroll	Store	1 +		1 +
29	E01_101_2200	E01_101_2230	Corp Finance	Store	1 +		1 +
30	E01_101_2000	E01_101_2300	Marketing	Store	1 +		1 +

1. Create an Entity.CSV file with the same rows and columns as the sample file above. Place this file on the C drive of the Planning server (in real life you will place this folder in a more secure, clearly defined location).

Valid headers for the Entity dimension (and other dimensions) include:

Required Header Name	Required Values (if any)
Entity	
Parent	
Alias: Default	
Data Storage	Store, Dynamic Calc, Never Share, Shared, Label Only
Description	
Formula	

Required Header Name	Required Values (if any)
Two Pass Calculation	True, False (or 1, 0)
Base Currency	
UDA	
Smart List	
Data Type	Unspecified, Currency, Non-Currency, Percentage, Smart List, Date, Text
Operation	Update (default), delete level 0, delete idescendants, delete descendants
Plan Type (*Plan1*)	True, False (or 1, 0)
Aggregation (*Plan1*)	+-*/%~ Never
Plan Type (*Plan2*)	True, False (or 1, 0)
Aggregation (*Plan2*)	+-*/%~ Never
Plan Type (*Plan3*)	True, False (or 1, 0)
Aggregation (*Plan3*)	+-*/%~ Never

The only required column is the Entity name.

2. Create a batch file and place it in the C:\Hyperion\products\Planning\bin directory (or whichever directory contains your Planning utilities if you've installed it differently). The .BAT file should contain the following syntax :

```
OutlineLoad /A:Entpln /U:admin /M /I:c:\entity.csv
/D:Entity /L:c:\outlineLoad.log
/X:c:\outlineLoad.exc
```

```
BuildEntity.bat - Notepad
File  Edit  Format  View  Help
OutlineLoad /A:Entpln /U:admin /M /I:c:\Entity.csv /D:Entity /L:c:/outlineLoad.log /X:c:/outlineLoad.exc
```

Depending on the folder structure on your Planning server you may need to update the file paths to match your specific directory structure.

3. Double click on the batch file to execute the utility from within the batch. (To create a batch file for each dimension, you simply "Save As" each file and change the parameters as needed.)

Notice the syntax above doesn't include anything about a password. You will be prompted to enter the password for the user defined in the syntax. Beginning in version 11, you can use a password encrypted file to supply the password.

4. Execute the batch file with the OutlineLoad.cmd script to update the Entity dimension. You may be prompted to enter the password if you did not include in the script.

You can also run the script / syntax live from the command line. Now let's take a look at the log:

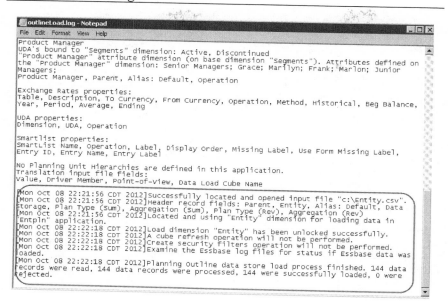

According to the log, the Entity dimension was updated successfully. Let's take a look at the Entity dimension in the Planning web client:

Update the Account Dimension from a Flat File

While we won't do this as part of the book workshops, we want to review the Account build process via the Outline Load Utility. Here is a sample Account.csv metadata file for the Account dimension. Remember, fields can be in any order, but headers are case sensitive:

You follow the same process to load the Account dimension. Create an account.csv file with the same rows and columns as the sample file above. Place this file on the C drive of the Planning server (in real life you will place this folder in a more secure, clearly defined location).

Valid headers for the Account dimension are similar to the Entity headers with a few more properties for accounts (only the Account name is required):

Required Header Name	Required Values (if any)
Account	
Parent	
Alias: Default	
Data Storage	Store, Dynamic Calc, Never Share, Shared, Label Only
Description	
Formula	
Two Pass Calculation	True, False (or 1, 0)
Base Currency	
UDA	
Smart List	
Data Type	Unspecified, Currency, Non-Currency, Percentage, Smart List, Date, Text
Operation	Update (default), delete level 0, delete idescendants, delete descendants
Plan Type (*Plan1*)	True, False (or 1, 0)
Aggregation (*Plan1*)	+-*/%~ Never
Plan Type (*Plan2*)	True, False (or 1, 0)
Aggregation (*Plan2*)	+-*/%~ Never
Plan Type (*Plan3*)	True, False (or 1, 0)
Aggregation (*Plan3*)	+-*/%~ Never
Source Plan type	Plan type name
Account Type	Expense, Revenue, Asset, Liability, Equity, Saved Assumption
Time Balance	Flow, First, Balance, Average, avg_actual, avg_365_fill
Use 445 / Use 544 / Use454	True, False (or 1, 0)
Skip Value	None, Missing, Zeros, Missing and Zeros

Required Header Name	Required Values (if any)
Exchange Rate Type	Non, Average, Ending, Historical
Variance Reporting	Non-Expense, Expense

Create a batch file that contains the following syntax:

```
OutlineLoad /A:Entpln /U:admin /M /I:c:\Account.csv
/D:Account /L:c:\outlineLoad.log
/X:c:\outlineLoad.exc
```

Depending on the folder structure on your Planning server you may need to update the file paths to match your specific directory structure. Double click on the batch file to execute the utility from within the batch. Enter the password when prompted.

Once the script is complete, review the OutlineLoad.log and verify a successful load.

What if the outline load utility ran into errors? You will find some helpful messages to help determine which records errored out and why. See the sample exception file below:

```
[Fri Jan 01 13:55:34 CST 2010] Error occurred loading data record 6:
312000,312100,Interest
Income,Update,Store,,Revenue,Flow,,Currency,Average,Non-Expense,1,+,1,+,Rev
[Fri Jan 01 13:55:34 CST 2010] java.lang.RuntimeException: Unable to set source plan
type of member 312100 to Rev. The parent does not exist in this plan type.
[Fri Jan 01 13:55:34 CST 2010] Error occurred loading data record 8:
312000,312300,Dividends from LT Inv in
Subs,Update,Store,,Revenue,Flow,,Currency,Average,Non-Expense,1,+,1,+,Rev
[Fri Jan 01 13:55:34 CST 2010] java.lang.RuntimeException: Unable to set source plan
type of member 312300 to Rev. The parent does not exist in this plan type.
[Fri Jan 01 13:55:34 CST 2010] Error occurred loading data record 9:
312000,312400,Gain (Loss) on
Disposal,Update,Store,,Revenue,Flow,,Currency,Average,Non-Expense,1,+,1,+,Rev
[Fri Jan 01 13:55:34 CST 2010] java.lang.RuntimeException: Unable to set source plan
type of member 312400 to Rev. The parent does not exist in this plan type.
[Fri Jan 01 13:55:34 CST 2010] Error occurred loading data record 10:
312000,312500,Exchange Rate Gain
(Loss),Update,Store,,Revenue,Flow,,Currency,Average,Non-Expense,1,+,1,+,Rev
[Fri Jan 01 13:55:34 CST 2010] java.lang.RuntimeException: Unable to set source plan
type of member 312500 to Rev. The parent does not exist in this plan type.
[Fri Jan 01 13:55:45 CST 2010]Planning outline data store load process finished with
exceptions: exceptions occured, examine the exception file for more information. 125
data records were read, 125 data records were processed, 121 were successfully loaded,
4 were rejected.
```

According to the log, the Account dimension was updated successfully, although 4 records were rejected. We see that one member "312000" is missing. Since it does not exist in the file or in the outline, no children can be added to this member.

To view flat file format and header definitions for other dimensions and Planning components, see the Planning Administrator Guide (search "Outline Load utility").

Load Data via the Outline Load Utility

Before we leave the Outline Load utility, let's review an example of using the Outline Load Utility to load data. Log on to the

Hyperion Planning Web client, go to Administration, go to Manage properties, and select the System Variables tab:

> Properties have been saved to the system database. The changes will take effect when the Application Server is restarted. ⊠

Application Properties | System Properties

Add

Property Name	Property Value
DATA_LOAD_FILE_PATH	C:\HyperionWorkFiles\OutlineLoad\PlanSamp.txt
DIRECT_DATA_LOAD	False
SECURITY_PROVIDER	CSS
SMART_VIEW_DISPLAY_WARNING	yes
SMART_VIEW_FORCE_INSTALL	no
SMART_VIEW_INSTALL_FILES_DIR	C:\Hyperion\products\Planning\bin\SmartView
SMARTVIEW_COMPRESSION_THRESHOLD	-1

When DIRECT_DATA_LOAD is set to True or empty, the utility loads data directly into Essbase. For this option to work the Planning and Essbase outlines must be in synch. When DIRECT_DATA_LOAD is set to false, the utility generates a .TXT data file and a .RUL file that can be used on demand.

Example: load data into the salary account for all employees. "Salary" account is the driver account. "Employee" is the load dimension:

```
Employee,Salary,Point-of-View,Data Load Cube Name
Emp1,50000,"Local,entity1,Current,Ver1,FY08,BegBalance",Plan1
Emp2,30000,"Local,entity1,Current,Ver1,FY08,BegBalance",Plan1
Emp3,55000,"Local,entity1,Current,Ver1,FY08,BegBalance",Plan1
Emp4,73000,"Local,entity1,Current,Ver1,FY08,BegBalance",Plan1
```

Tip!

Sample files for Project Financial Planning applications are provided and use the Outline Load utility.

Outline Load Utility over the Web

Planning administrators can run the Outline Load utility from the web in version 11.1.2.3 (instead of command line on the Planning server). Planning admins can import and export data and metadata from Planning web client by choosing *Administration >> Outline Load*:

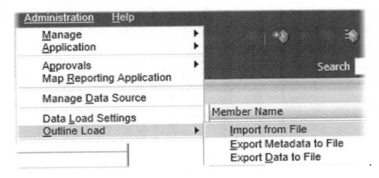

Check out the What's New appendix for more information.

SortMember.cmd

You can use the Sort Member utility for sorting dimension members that are children or descendants of a specified member in Planning, similar to the sort order functionality of the Planning Web client. Period, Year and currency dimension members cannot be sorted with this utility.

Syntax:

```
SortMember [-f:passwordFile] servername username
application member children|descendants
ascend|descend
```

Let's sort the children of Ratios in ascending order.

Try It!

This is the order of the children of "Ratios" before running the utility:

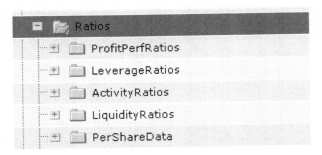

Open the command line and sort the children of "Ratios" in ascending order:

You should receive a completion message "Sorting Member Completed":

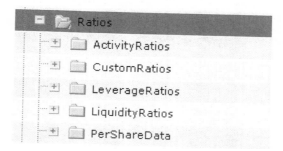

The result shows new sorted children of Ratios:

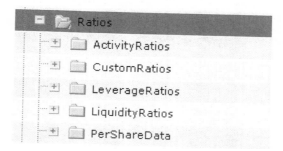

DeleteSharedDescendants.cmd

Use this utility to delete shared members that are descendants of a given member. When running this utility you might see "java.rmi" or "port already in use" errors but they do not affect the functionality of the utility. To view results, check out the following logs in the bin directory: DeleteSharedDescendants.log for status, and DeleteSharedDescendantsExceptions.log for errors.

The syntax and parameters are:

```
DeleteSharedDescendants [-f:passwordFile] servername
username application "member name"
```

For example, if you wanted to delete the descendants under member Southwest region, you would type:

```
DeleteSharedDescendants -f:passwordFile epm111server
eddie entbud "Southwest Region"
```

Try It!

Let's open the command line and delete shared members under a specific member.

Look for a a confirmation message. If there were no shared members under the specified member, the utility lets you know:

```
C:\ Command Prompt                                                      _□×
H:\HYSL\products\Planning\bin>DeleteSharedDescendants.cmd -f:H:\A_RB\PlanningUti
lityScripts\passwordfile.txt localhost Planadmin TotPlan "Ratios"
[INFO] RegistryLogger - REGISTRY LOG INITIALIZED
[INFO] RegistryLogger - REGISTRY LOG INITIALIZED
H:\HYSL\common\config\9.5.0.0\product\planning\9.5.0.0\planning_1.xml
displayName = Planning
componentTypes =

priority = 50
version = 9.5.0.0
build = 1
location = H:\HYSL\products\Planning
taskSequence =

task =

using Java property for Hyperion Home H:\HYSL
Setting Arbor path to: H:\HYSL\common\EssbaseRTC\9.5.0.0
d{ISO8601} INFO main com.hyperion.audit.client.runtime.AuditRuntime - Entering A
udit Client http://demodrive.oracle.com:28080/interop/Audit
d{ISO8601} INFO main com.hyperion.audit.client.runtime.AuditRuntime - Initializi
ng Manager for the serverhttp://demodrive.oracle.com:28080/interop/Audit
d{ISO8601} INFO main com.hyperion.audit.client.manager.AuditContext - Creating N
ew Audit Client Instance .... http://demodrive.oracle.com:28080/interop/Audit
d{ISO8601} INFO main com.hyperion.audit.client.runtime.AuditRuntime - Audit Clie
nt has been created for the server http://demodrive.oracle.com:28080/interop/Aud
it
No shared descendants of Ratios were found.
d{ISO8601} INFO Thread-15 com.hyperion.audit.client.runtime.AuditRuntime - Writi
ng Audit Records for migrated Artifacts ...
d{ISO8601} INFO Thread-15 com.hyperion.audit.client.runtime.AuditRuntime - Store
d Audited Data Successfully !!!

H:\HYSL\products\Planning\bin>
```

MemberFormulaSync.cmd

You can use this utility to push the member formulas in the Planning application to Essbase.

The syntax is:

```
MemberFormulaSync /A:appname
```

Let's open the command line and push the member formulas in the Planning app to Essbase.

Try It!

You don't get any message when it completes the refresh:

So look at the log file:

TASK LISTS & DATA FORMS

TaskListDefUtil.cmd

You can use the Task List definition utility to move task lists between applications. You can export or import task list definitions to or from XML files, and like to the form definition utility discussed next, it allows you to export/import task lists one by one or all at the same time by using the –all parameter.

The syntax and parameters are:

```
TaskListDefUtil [-f:passwordFile]
import|exportFILE_NAME|TASK_LIST_NAME|-all
SERVER_NAME USER_NAME APPLICATION
```

Try It!

In this example we are going to export all task lists from a Planning application using the –all function. You could create a batch file with the parameters below to execute the utility. The folder where we save and execute the batch file will be the destination of the exported .XML files.

You will receive a completion line for each exported task list:

By default the XML files go to the Planning\Bin folder:

	Name	Size	Type	Dat
	TaskListDefExportAl.bat	1 KB	Windows Batch File	12/
	TaskListDefUtil.log	0 KB	Text Document	12/
	HYSL Banking.xml	6 KB	XML Document	12/
	HYSL Credit Cards.xml	5 KB	XML Document	12/
	HYSL Insurance Premiums.xml	7 KB	XML Document	12/
	HYSL Treasury Transactions.xml	5 KB	XML Document	12/

ningUtilityScripts\TaskListExportFolder

Look at the TaskListDefUtil.log file for errors. An empty log file means all task lists were imported/exported successfully.

FormDefUtil.cmd

You can use the Form Definition utility to move data forms between Planning applications. It exports or imports form definitions to and from XML files. You can import or export one by one or you can use the –all parameter that allows you to import or export all the forms. When you export forms, the xml files go to the directory from which you execute the utility, by default the bin directory. You can copy the utility to another directory, if you want to export the files to that directory. You can execute the export from a batch file and the xml will go to the same folder as the batch file. Exporting/importing forms does not export/import assigned access.

The syntax and parameters are:

```
formdefutil [-
f:passwordFile]import|exportfilename|formname|-all
server name user name application
```

Try It!

In this example we are going to export all forms from a Planning application. Let's create a batch file with the parameters below to execute the utility. The folder where we save and execute the batch file will be the destination of the exported .XML files.

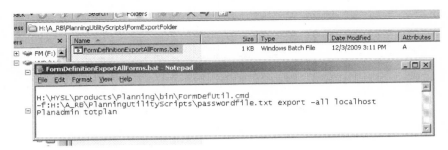

If the file executes successfully, you will see all the expected .XML files in the same folder and an empty log file. Take a look at the log, if not all the expected forms are exported:

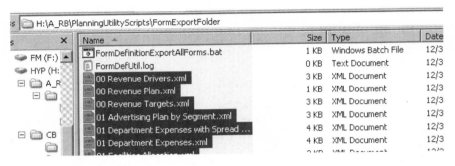

To import all forms, you can use the same batch file changing the parameter from "export" to "import":

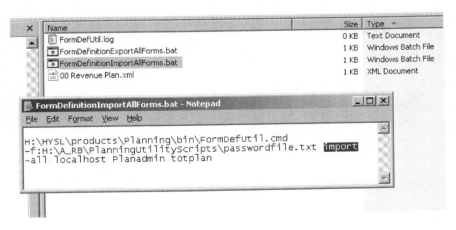

Tip!

If you want to import or export a selected form or a selected list of forms, you can leave only those forms (delete or move the rest) in the folder from which you run the utility, and use the –all parameter in the script. This is a lot easier than typing the name and the location for each form you want to import or export.

If you are exporting or importing a form that already in the target, the process will stop at that point and prompt you if you want to overwrite it:

```
C:\windows\system32\cmd.exe                                    _ □ ×
Form exported complete.
Form exported complete.
Form exported complete.
Form exported complete.
Form exported complete.
Form exported complete.
Form exported complete.
Found form file with same name, do you want to overwrite the existing file - 00
Revenue Targets.xml? (y/n)
```

```
Start importing form definition file - 00 Revenue Plan.xml
Found form with same name.Importing the form will delete the existing security a
ssignments and need to be recreated. Do you want to update it using form definit
ion xml file? (y/n)
```

Respond "Y" for yes and hit enter to continue and replace the existing form, or respond "no" and hit enter to stop the process.

To import a form definition from a specific location,

```
FormDefUtil.cmd import
c:\Hyperion\products\Planning\bin\form1.xml
localhost admin entbud
```

To export a form definition:

```
FormDefUtil.cmd export Form1 localhost admin entbud
```

Check out results in FormDefUtil.log.

RUN BUSINESS RULES

CalcMgrCmdLineLauncher.cmd

With the Calc Manager Command Launcher utility you can launch business rules or rules sets created with the Calculation Manager. It can run for a business rule or ruleset but not both. The errors are displayed on console or written to the Calc Manager log file. A runtime prompts file is required when the business rule or rule set contains one or more run time prompts (RTPs). The Validate option checks the command syntax for the utility, not the business rule or rule set syntax.

The syntax and parameters are:

```
CalcMgrCmdLineLauncher.cmd [-f:passwordFile]
/A:appname /U:username /D:database [/R:business rule
name | /S:business ruleset name] /F:runtime prompts
file [/validate]
```

If the business rule contains runtime prompts, you must create a file containing the runtime prompt values. There are two ways: specify the name of the runtime prompt values file that you generated on the RunTimesPrompt page, or create a runtime prompt ASCII file. In the runtime prompt file, list each runtime prompt and its value in separate lines. Separate name and value with "::". For example: MarketRTP:: East. You can save the file in the Planning\bin directory or specify full path when running the utility.

Try It!

In this example we are going to execute a Business Rule using the utility.

Create a run-time-prompt file. You can put it in the Planning\Bin folder or specify the location as a parameter in the utility:

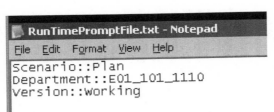

Open the command line and specify all the parameters, the business rule will take the prompts from the file:

You should receive a completion message:

Just when Penny thought she was through with administration topics after learning all about the Planning utilities, SuperManager jumps in with the next topic near and dear to all Planning administrators' hearts: Essbase Administration.

Scene 5:
Essbase Administration

Because Planning sits on top of Essbase, you are not just a Planning administrator. You are an Essbase administrator. So let's jump into some Essbase specific items (for lots of Essbase detail, check out the sister guide to this book, Look Smarter Than You Are with Essbase: An Administrator's Guide).

ESSBASE ADMINISTRATION SERVICES

You should be familiar with Administration Services by now (also known as *Essbase* Administration Services – EAS – or *Analytic* Administration Services – AAS – depending on your version). Administration Services is a central administration tool for managing and maintaining all of Essbase.

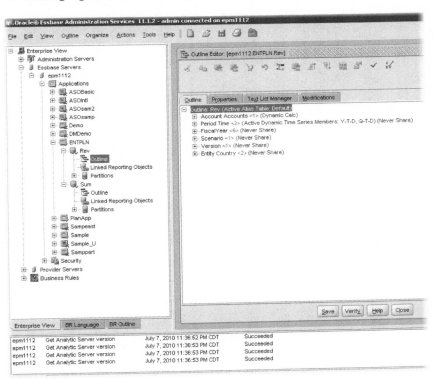

In the case of Planning you won't be making any changes to the outline in EAS. You should only make changes in the Planning web client (or EPMA if using EPMA).

The Administrative Services Console (EAS) is a provides a graphical interface that Essbase administrators and designers use to build and manage Essbase applications. The Administration Services Console talks to a middle-tier application server (the "Administration Server").

The Administration Server serves as a centralized management point as it communicates directly with multiple Essbase servers and allows multiple administrators to focus their work in a single shared environment.

The Administration Server communicates directly with Essbase servers. One Administration Server can talk to multiple Essbase servers. All Administration Services components are J2EE-compliant. J2EE stands for Java 2 Enterprise Edition, which in English-speak means that they're java-based. For those who believe a picture is worth a thousand words, here's a diagram to illustrate all those tiers:

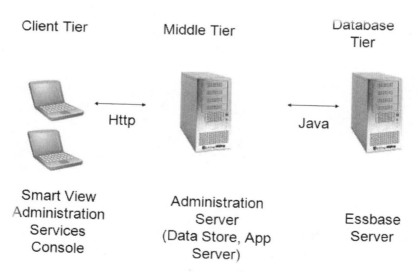

Client Tier	Middle Tier	Database Tier
Http		Java
Smart View Administration Services Console	Administration Server (Data Store, App Server)	Essbase Server

In the console, you can view and manage all Administration servers installed in your environment. In most cases, you have one Administration Server that manages all of your Essbase servers including development and production:

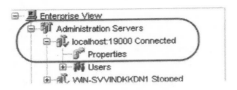

To view and manage all of the Essbase servers installed in your environment, expand the *Essbase Servers* section of the Enterprise View:

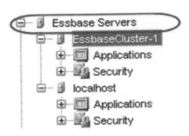

One of the big benefits of Administration Services is that you can manage development, QA, test, and production environments in one window. Copying objects across Essbase servers (even if they are different platforms like Unix and Windows) becomes child's play in Administration Services. Use the appropriate user provisioning to meet SOX, audit and security requirements across environments.

An Essbase administrator once deleted a production application, thinking he was connected to the development Essbase server. This same administrator also copied an unfinished development application from the development Essbase server to the production server, mixing up the 'to' and 'from' server during the copy. If you don't want to get fired, make sure you know which server you are connected to before you start performing potentially serious actions.

Navigate in Administration Services

There are three main ways to perform actions in the Administration Services console:

1. Menu items:

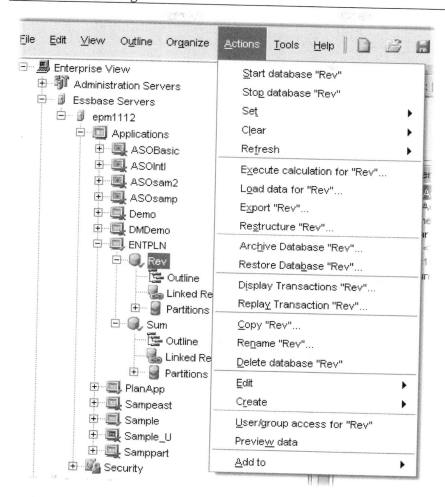

2. Icons:

3. Right-click:

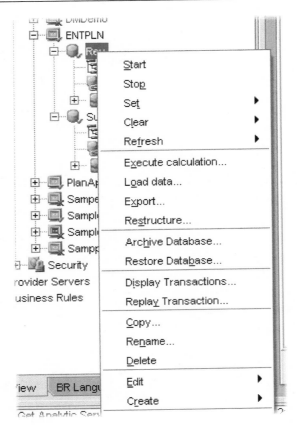

We personally prefer right-clicking since it's an easy way not to have to remember which actions are available for a specific item. Right-click on an object in the Enterprise View (the pane on the left) and you'll see all the relevant actions available to you.

Generally, when you open an item on the left (in the View pane), it will open in the pane to the right. There is another important pane in Administration Services: Messages. This section is found (unless you went to the *View* menu and turned it off) in the lower part of your window. Messages about whether actions are successful or not will be posted here:

Administration Services may not send up a big, flashy error message so be mindful of the information communicated in this section. Although messages will almost always be displayed here, the messages displayed here will almost always be highly summarized, and in computer-speak.

Stare at the messages a while and at least you'll be able to tell if the message is informational or it's a major error. For example, if a message was displayed saying "It's currently sunny with a chance of rain late in the day," this would be informational. If the message "Fatal error occurred: self-destruct sequence initiated" appears, stare at it for a nanosecond and then run.

Note!

You are very unlikely to see a "self-destruct" message.

What Can You Do in Administration Services for Planning applications?

Helpful
Info

- View the database outline
- Create data load rules
- Create calculation scripts
- Partition databases
- Review log reports and database / server information
- Manage Essbase servers
- Set Caches and configuration
- Review filter creation
- Run command and scripts

ESSBASE.CFG

The Essbase.CFG file is the main configuration file for Essbase, and it is simply a text file stored in the arborpath\bin directory. Administrators may add or change parameter values in this file to customize Essbase functionality. Many of these settings apply to the entire Essbase Server. Essbase reads the configuration file at startup of the Essbase Agent and every time an Application is loaded. Be aware of the potential requirement to restart the system or an application when you are making changes to this file.

In this file you can define settings that control TCP/IP ports and connections, define how detailed you would like your log files, specify cache settings for performance improvements, define query governors for the server or specific application, and much more highly technical gobbledygook. Here is a sample Essbase.CFG file:

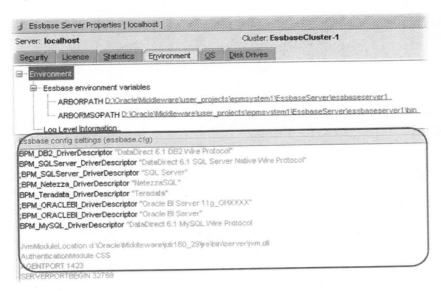

For a full listing of the Essbase.CFG settings, see the Technical Reference provided by Hyperion. We cover more of the Essbase configuration settings later in the book under optimization.

To update the Essbase.CFG,

1. In the Administration Services console, right-click on the Essbase server and select *Edit >> Properties*.
2. Choose the *Environment* tab.
3. Update the parameters by typing directly in the Essbase.CFG.
4. Restart the Essbase server for settings to take effect.

The "old school" way to update the Essbase.CFG settings is as follows:

1. Edit the file in text format with any text editor, such as Windows Notepad.
2. Enter each setting on a separate line in the file. You do not need to end each line with a semicolon.
3. Make sure the file is named Essbase.CFG,
4. Save the file in the arborpath \ bin directory.
5. Restart the Essbase Server or the Essbase Application after changing the configuration file.

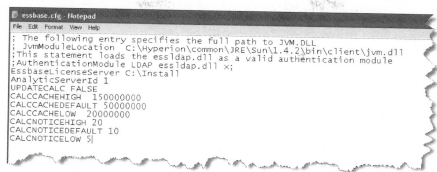

```
essbase.cfg - Notepad
File  Edit  Format  View  Help
;  The following entry specifies the full path to JVM.DLL
;  JvmModuleLocation  C:\Hyperion\common\JRE\Sun\1.4.2\bin\client\jvm.dll
;This statement loads the essldap.dll as a valid authentication module
;AuthenticationModule LDAP essldap.dll x;
EssbaseLicenseServer C:\Install
AnalyticServerId 1
UPDATECALC FALSE
CALCCACHEHIGH  150000000
CALCCACHEDEFAULT 50000000
CALCCACHELOW  20000000
CALCNOTICEHIGH 20
CALCNOTICEDEFAULT 10
CALCNOTICELOW 5|
```

Try It!

View the settings defined in your Essbase.CFG file.

ESSBASE.SEC

In earlier versions of Essbase, the Essbase.sec file stored information about users, groups, passwords for native security, and privileges on applications and databases. It also stored many application and database properties. A "syncing" process was required between Shared Services and the Essbase security file for Essbase users.

In 11.1.2.1, a relational database replaced OPENLDAP as the central storage for native Shared Services user accounts.

- CSS_DELEGATED_LIST
- CSS_DELEGATED_MEMBERS
- CSS_GROUP_CACHE_DELTA
- CSS_GROUP_MEMBERS
- CSS_GROUPS
- CSS_IDENTITY
- CSS_MEMBER_TYPE
- CSS_PROVISIONING_INFO
- CSS_ROLE_LOCALES
- CSS_ROLE_MEMBERS
- CSS_ROLES
- CSS_USER_PREFERENCES
- CSS_USERS

Now no "sync" is required for Essbase users because all of the user and groups security for Essbase is managed in Shared Services. So the Essbase.sec is slightly less critical than in previous versions but it does still store information on application and database properties. And if it is corrupted, it can kill your Essbase database.

This isn't a file you can open and read but it is critical to your Essbase server. It lives next door to Essbase.exe in the arborpath\bin neighborhood.

Each time that you successfully start the Essbase Server, a backup copy of the security file is created (named Essbase.bak). You can restore from the last successful backup by copying Essbase.bak to Essbase.sec. If you have a corrupt application, you often times will need to recover from the security file backup as well as recreate the application from scratch.

Try It!

Find the Essbase.sec file on your server and take a look at the security settings assigned. WAIT! This was a trick "Try It!" *Do not* open the Essbase.sec. You don't ever open up this file and read it. To view security, go to the *Security* section in Administration Services or run reports in Shared Services.

Since Essbase 9.3, you can export the Essbase.sec into a readable file. In Administration Services, right-click on *Security* and select *Export security file*:

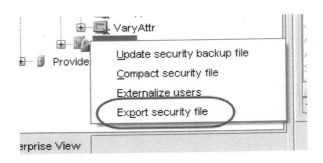

You can also use MaxL statement export security. The MaxL syntax is as follows:

```
EXPORT SECURITY_FILE to DATA_FILE file_name;
```

The resulting file will be available:

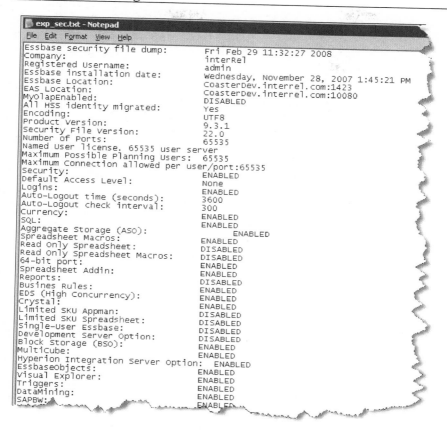

VIEW THE SERVER LOG FILE

You are going to have to troubleshoot at some point. Really? Errors? Issues with Planning? Yes, yes, and yes. The Essbase Server log file is one of your first starting points when investigating an issue (because Planning stores all of its data in Essbase, Essbase could likely be the problem). The server log file is stored in the main Essbase folder as ESSBASE.log. This log file captures all server activity, including user logins, application level activities, and database activities. We can see that Eddie, the end user, logged in at 7am on Tuesday. We can see that Trixie renamed an application at 10am (glad we're paying the big bucks for those hardworking users).

You can view this log file through Administration Services. Select the *Essbase server* from the Enterprise View panel in Administration Services. Right-click and select *View >> Log*:

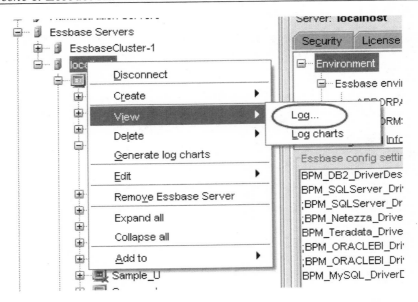

Choose *Starting Date* and enter the desired start date in most cases. Your log files will get really big and if you open the entire log file, be prepared to wait.

Have you ever tried to read text in a foreign language? Just a little confusing, right? Well, prepare yourself for a similar experience with the Essbase server log files:

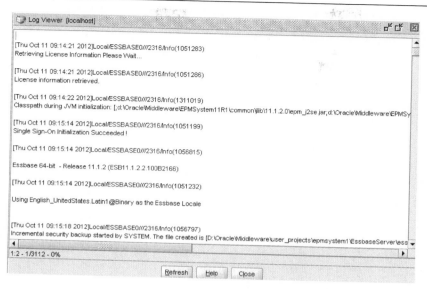

Actually, interpreting the log files isn't that bad. We'll give you a brief translation course on some of the common messages. Here are some example Startup Messages that you will see in the Essbase.log. We see the Sample application is loaded and started, and then the database Basic is loaded.

```
[Tue Nov 12 07:54:16
    2012]Local/ESSBASE0///Info(1051061)
    Application Sample loaded - connection
    established
[Tue Nov 12 07:54:16
    2012]Local/ESSBASE0///Info(1054027)
    Application [Sample] started with process id
    [1300]
[Tue Nov 12 07:54:18
    2012]Local/ESSBASE0///Info(1054014) Database
    Basic loaded
```

Here is an error message captured in the log file when user admin tried to rename an application. He received an error message stating that an application already existed with the name 'Testing'.

```
[Tue Nov 12 08:00:04
    2012]Local/ESSBASE0///Info(1051001) Received
```

```
client request: Rename Application (from user
admin)
[Tue Nov 12 08:00:04
    2012]Local/ESSBASE0///Error(1051031)
    Application Testing already exists
[Tue Nov 12 08:00:04
    2012]Local/ESSBASE0///Warning(1051003) Error
    1051031 processing request [Rename
    Application] - disconnecting
```

Here is an example of the messages you will see when you stop the Sample application and shutdown the Essbase server.

```
[Tue Nov 12 08:00:46
    2012]Local/ESSBASE0///Info(1054005) Shutting
    down application Sample
[Tue Nov 12 08:00:52
    2012]Local/ESSBASE0///Info(1051052) Hyperion
    Essbase Analytic Server - finished
```

Congratulations! You now speak Essbase-log-ish (like Elvish except that you might actually put this on your resume).

Periodically archive off the Essbase.log file. Smaller log files can help with performance.

Tip!   In 11.1.2. the Essbase log file moved to \Oracle\Middleware\user_projects\epmsystemX\diagnostics\logs\essbase\essbase\app.

Take a look at your Essbase.log file. Look for instances where applications are started and users have logged into the server. Find them?

Try It!

VIEW ESSBASE SERVER PROPERTIES

Within Administration Services you can view Essbase server level properties like username and password management settings, version information, server statistics, and OS/CPU and Memory information.

Within Administration Services, right-click on the *Essbase server*. Select *Edit >> Properties*. Select the *Security* tab:

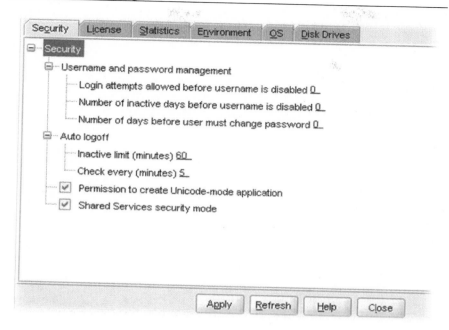

Let's say we decide to set *Login attempts allowed before username disabled* to "3" and set *Number of inactive days before username disabled"to* "365". If a user enters an invalid password, after three tries, the username is disabled. If a user hasn't logged into the server in a year, their username is disabled (don't waste those precious, costly Essbase licenses).

Select the *License* tab. This used to provide pretty important information back when Hyperion was still an independent company. Want to see what version you've installed, what additional components are installed, and when the license expires? Beginning in Essbase 9.3.1, all of the additional components are installed with Essbase (no additional licensing required):

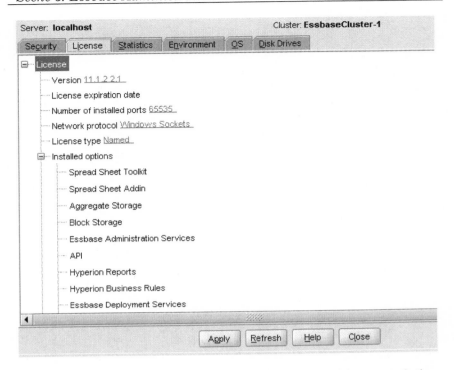

On the remaining tabs, you can view server statistics, environment information, and other hardware related information.

What is the inactive limit on your server? What version of Essbase are you running? Check out these settings and more for the Essbase server.

Try It!

VIEW SERVER SESSIONS

You can view current activity for the server: Who's connected? For how long? And more importantly, what are they doing? It is fun to be Big Brother. For example, you receive a call from a user complaining that performance has slowed significantly on the Essbase server. You check out the current sessions and see that Trixie kicked off an application copy that has brought the system to its knees.

To view Sessions, right-click on the Essbase server and select *Edit >> Sessions* in the Enterprise View panel:

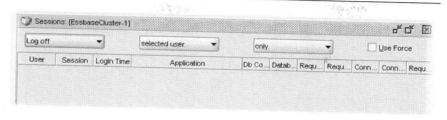

From the Sessions window, you can log off and kill users from their sessions. Why would you want to kill someone? No matter how much of a pacifist you may be, you will want to kill someone in your Essbase world.

You will definitely receive this call at some point. "I just accidentally drilled down to Dimbottom on the Product dimension which has 10,000 products. Now my computer is frozen." What is the resolution to this problem? View sessions and log off or kill this particular user. Killing may be a bit drastic but sometimes it's required. Don't worry – killing a user in Essbase is quite legal.

To log off or kill, select the desired option from the dropdown at the top of the Sessions window. Choose *Select User, All Users* or *All Instances of User*:

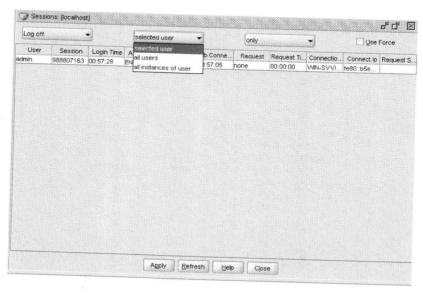

Select *On Server, On selected Application,* or *On selected Database* (the available options here depend on your two previous selections). Select *Use Force* (if necessary).

So we have some flexibility with logging off or killing. In our request above, we may only have to kill the user for a specific database. You may need to log all users off of a particular application just before the monthly load and calc takes place. You may need to log all users off of a server before nightly backups run.

As an almighty Essbase administrator, see what the minions in your domain are doing right now. View the current sessions for your Essbase server.

Try It!

SERVER DATA LOCKS

Essbase will lock cells when they are being updated whether it is through Essbase Add-In lock and send, data load, or calculation. Once the update is complete, the lock is released. Occasionally data locks are not released.

To view data locks, right-click on the Essbase server and select *Edit >> Locks*:

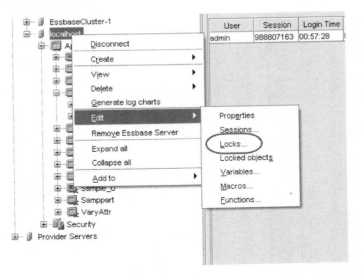

From the Locks window, you can view locks by application, database, and user. You can unlock locks by selecting *Unlock* (very tricky, we know).

LOCKED OBJECTS

Similar to data locks, you can also have locks on Essbase objects. Remember how you are prompted with the following message each time you edit an object:

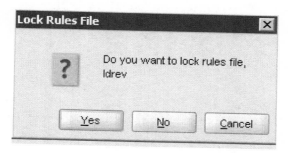

Most of the time we say *Yes* because we don't want anyone else to change the object while we are viewing or editing it. Once we save our changes and close the object, the object lock is released. But what happens if your computer freezes and causes you to reboot while you had the act.rul data load rule open? You weren't able to successfully close the rules file within Administration Services so the lock remains on the rules file.

You can unlock the rules file in the Locked Objects window. To view locked objects, right-click on the *Essbase server* and select *Edit >> Locked Objects:*

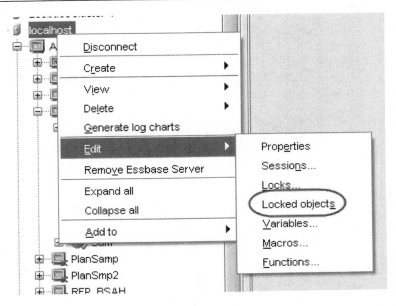

From the Locked Objects window, you can view locked objects by application, database, and user. You can unlock locked objects by selecting *Unlock*:

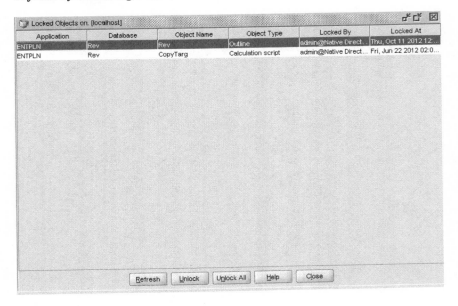

See if you have any data locks or locked objects on your Essbase server.

Try It!

VIEW AND EDIT APPLICATION PROPERTIES

The application properties and statistics tabs provide some helpful options to administrators. Remember, this is where we set the default minimum security for an application. You may want to enable *Allow Users to Start Application* for rarely used applications. This way the application and database won't take up precious memory if it is not being used. When the application is needed, it will start when the user tries to connect via Smart View or other reporting tool. This will, however, add a bit more initial response time for the user. Alternatively, if you have a highly used application, you can check *Start application when Essbase Server starts* because you know this application will need to be started and you can save some time for the first user to connect.

To view and edit application properties,

1. Select the application.
2. Right-click and select *Edit Properties.*

The Application properties window will display:

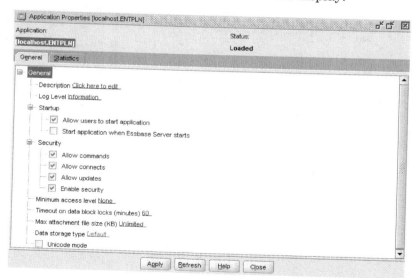

3. Click *Apply* after making any changes.

VIEW APPLICATION LOG FILE

The Application log file displays all activity for an application and its databases. There is a different application log file for each application. The log file name is the *application_name.log* and is stored in the application App file. This file tracks activity for the specific application, including the "who" and "when" of an operation and any errors of operations. For example, we can see Trixie ran a calc script on Monday at 12 p.m. We can see that Eddie performed a series of retrievals on Tuesday at 1 p.m. (more Big Brother capabilities).

You can view this log file through Administration Services. Right-click on the *application* and select *View >> Log*:

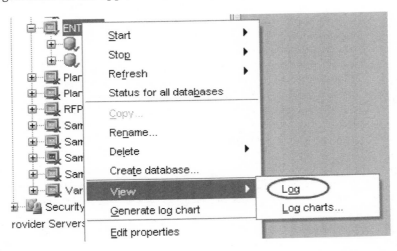

When prompted, choose the *Starting Date* option and enter the desired date (your log files will get really big and if you open the entire log file, be prepared to wait).

The application log file will display:

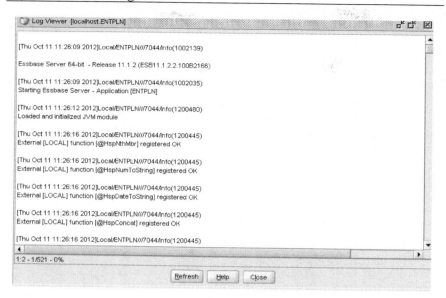

Let's learn more Essbase-log-ish. Here are some example Startup Messages that you will see in the application log file. Essbase writes information about the dimensions and members in the outline, such as the dimension sizes and dynamic calculation information, to the application log.

```
[Tue Nov 12 08:47:14
     2012]Local/Sample///Info(1002035) Starting
     Essbase Server - Application [Sample]
[Tue Nov 12 08:47:15
     2012]Local/Sample///Info(1200480) Loaded and
     initialized JVM module
[Tue Nov 12 08:47:15
     2012]Local/Sample///Info(1019008) Reading
     Application Definition For [Sample]
[Tue Nov 12 08:47:15
     2012]Local/Sample///Info(1019009) Reading
     Database Definition For [Basic]
[Tue Nov 12 08:47:15
     2012]Local/Sample///Info(1019021) Reading
     Database Mapping For [Sample]
[Tue Nov 12 08:47:15
     2012]Local/Sample///Info(1019010) Writing
     Application Definition For [Sample]
[Tue Nov 12 08:47:15
     2012]Local/Sample///Info(1019011) Writing
     Database Definition For [Basic]
[Tue Nov 12 08:47:15
     2012]Local/Sample///Info(1019022) Writing
     Database Mapping For [Sample]
[Tue Nov 12 08:47:15
     2012]Local/Sample///Info(1013202) Waiting for
     Login Requests
[Tue Nov 12 08:47:15
     2012]Local/Sample///Info(1013205) Received
     Command [Load Database]
[Tue Nov 12 08:47:15
     2012]Local/Sample///Info(1019018) Writing
     Parameters For Database [Basic]
[Tue Nov 12 08:47:15
     2012]Local/Sample///Info(1019017) Reading
     Parameters For Database [Basic
```

Essbase also writes information about the outlines for each
database to the application log.

```
[Tue Nov 12 08:47:15
     2012]Local/Sample///Info(1019012) Reading
     Outline For Database [Basic]
[Tue Nov 12 08:47:15
     2012]Local/Sample///Info(1007043) Declared
```

```
            Dimension Sizes = [20 17 23 25 5 3 5 3 15 8 6
            ]
[Tue Nov 12 08:47:15
       2012]Local/Sample///Info(1007042) Actual
       Dimension Sizes = [20 14 20 25 4 3 5 3 15 8 5
       ]
[Tue Nov 12 08:47:15
       2012]Local/Sample///Info(1007125) The number
       of Dynamic Calc Non-Store Members = [8 6 0 0 2
       ]
[Tue Nov 12 08:47:15
       2012]Local/Sample///Info(1007126) The number
       of Dynamic Calc Store Members = [0 0 0 0 ]
```

Here is an example of an error message in an application log file. The user Admin tried to load data to the Sample.Basic but the data file contained the member '500-10' which does not exist in the outline. We are told that zero records were loaded (the rules file was most likely set to abort on error).

```
[Tue Nov 12 08:49:52
       2001]Local/Sample///Info(1013210) User [admin]
       set active on database [Basic]
[Tue Nov 12 08:49:52 2001]
       Local/Sample/Basic/admin/Info(1013091)
       Received Command [DataLoad] from user [admin]
[Tue Nov 12 08:49:52 2001]
       Local/Sample/Basic/admin/Info(1003040)
       Parallel dataload enabled: [1] block prepare
       threads, [1] block write threads.
[Tue Nov 12 08:49:52 2001]
       Local/Sample/Basic/admin/Error(1003000)
       Unknown Item [500-10] in Data Load, [0]
       Records Completed
[Tue Nov 12 08:49:52 2001]
       Local/Sample/Basic/admin/Warning(1003035) No
       data values modified by load of this data file
[Tue Nov 12 08:49:52 2001]
       Local/Sample/Basic/admin/Info(1003024) Data
       Load Elapsed Time : [0.11] seconds
[Tue Nov 12 08:49:52 2001]
       Local/Sample/Basic/admin/Info(1019018) Writing
       Parameters For Database [Basic]
```

Take a look at the Entpln.Sum application log file. What date and time did we load data most recently? How long did the default calculation take place?

Try It!

Managing Log Files

We recommend you archive log files on a periodic basis (depending on the level of activity on an application). These files can become quite large and could slow performance. Application log files should be stored in Logs in your Oracle EPM / Hyperion install folder   (Oracle\Middleware\user_projects\epmsystemX\ diagnostics\logs\essbase\essbase\app). After you've made a backup of the file through the file system, you can clear the file within Administration Services.

You can change Essbase log levels at both the server and application level in the EAS Console.

Note!

View Log Charts

You can view the logs in graphical form using the log charts feature. Log charts help you review and understand Essbase activity much better than those easy-to-read log files (by "easy-to-read," we mean "easier to read than Edward's handwriting"). With log charts, Essbase-log-ish is no longer required.

To view the log file in chart format, select the application in Administration Services. Right-click and select *View >> Log Chart:*

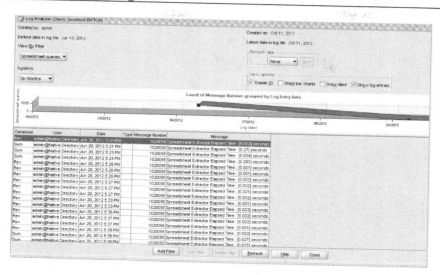

You can filter Log charts by predefined filters: errors, warnings, calculations, data loads, and spreadsheet queries:

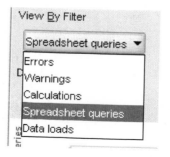

OTHER APPLICATION TASKS

Via Administration Services, several other actions for applications are available. Select an application in the Enterprise View panel and right-click. These are the other actions you can perform on applications. While you can copy, rename, and delete Essbase applications from Administration Services, you will NEVER do this for your Planning applications (unless for some reason you wanted an Essbase only copy of one the cubes for testing purposes):

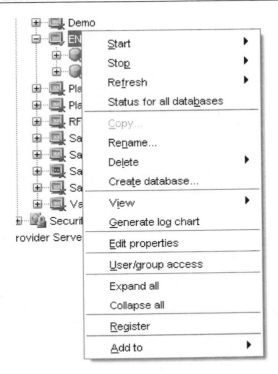

When you copy an Essbase application on the same server, all objects will be copied within Essbase including the outline, rules files, report scripts, calc scripts, and data. During the copy process, users are prohibited from accessing both the 'from' and the 'to' applications. You can copy applications across servers if desired but when you copy across servers, the data is not copied. You'll perform export and load tasks to move the data across servers. Life Cycle Management is another alternative to copying applications and data.

VIEW AND EDIT DATABASE PROPERTIES

Get to know your database properties! You can define startup options and default access privileges for databases just as you can applications. Database properties will vary depending on the database type (ASO versus BSO) and remember Planning databases are BSO, so we'll focus there.

To view and edit database properties,

1. Select the database.

2. Right-click and select *Edit >> Properties.*

BSO Database Properties

Important information is displayed for BSO databases including dimension dense / sparse settings, member counts, and other helpful ratios and statistics. You can manage commit settings, cache settings, data storage volumes, and much more via database properties. These settings are covered more detail in the optimization chapters later in the book.

Database level settings like startup options and data retrieval buffers are defined on the *General* tab:

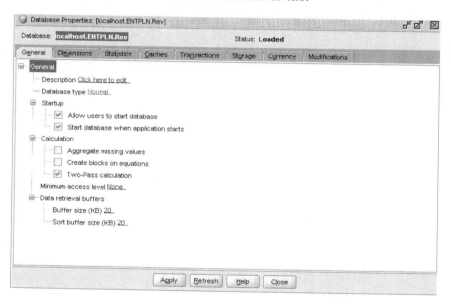

The *Dimensions* tab presents the dimensions in a helpful table, labeling dense and sparse settings and giving you a count of all members and stored members:

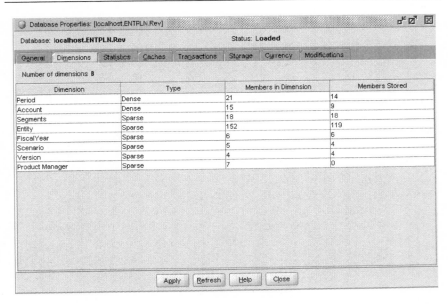

BSO statistics like cache hit ratios and block size are available on the *Statistics* tab:

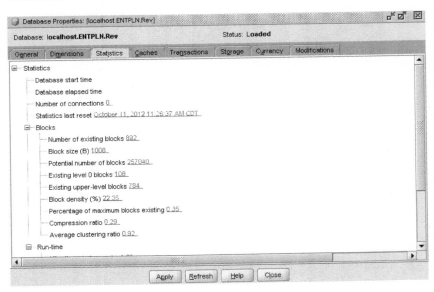

Cache settings are defined on the *Caches* tab (more on this later in the book):

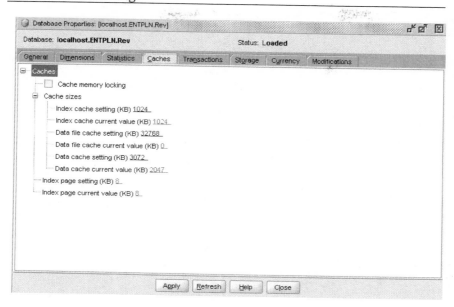

Commit settings are defined on the *Transactions* tab:

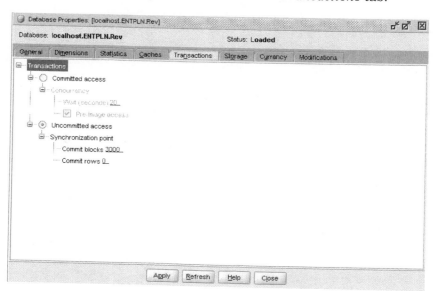

BSO compression and index and data file volumes are specified on the *Storage* tab:

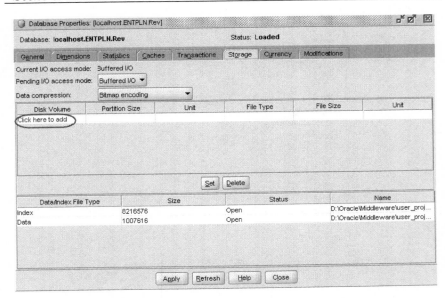

The *Modifications* tab lists any recent updates to the database:

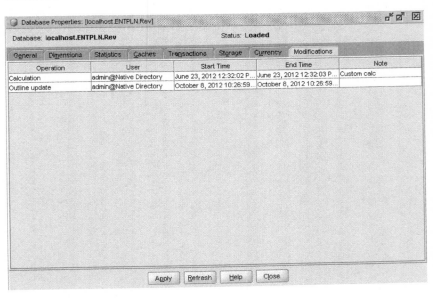

ASO Database Properties

Important information is displayed for ASO databases including dimension settings, member counts, and other helpful ratios and statistics. You can manage compression settings and much more via database properties.

General tab:

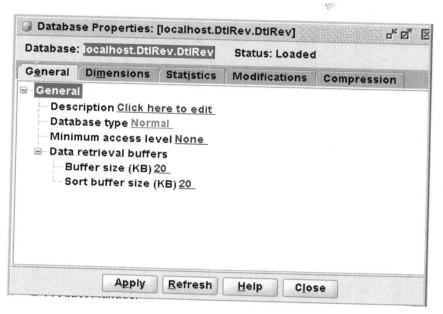

The Dimensions tab lists the dimensions and their member counts:

Dimension	Members in Dimension	Members Stored
Account	9	6
Period	19	18
FiscalYear	6	5
Scenario	5	4
Entity	5	3
Segments	5	4
Customer	4	3
Product Manager	7	7

The Statistics tab lists aggregate storage statistics:

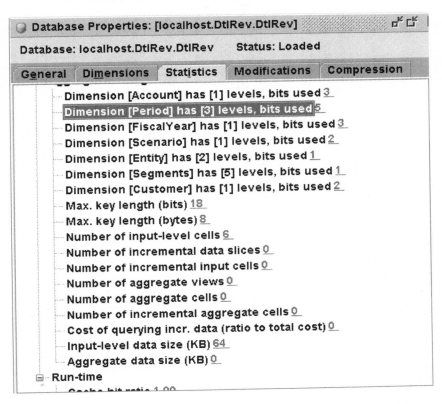

The Compression Tab is discussed in the *Look Smarter Than You Are with Essbase: An Administrator's Guide* book in the "Tune and Optimize for ASO" chapter.

Thankfully you now have the tools to manage the day to day administration tasks for Planning and Essbase. But we can't forget one of the most important action items for you as an administrator – backups!

Scene 6:
Backups and Recovery

This will probably never happen to you. Well, maybe. Actually, this will probably happen more than once in your Essbase career. An Essbase database will crash (or maybe Dr. Dementor finally gets his deathray working) just before close and you need to get the data back. Fast. Because the CFO is standing over your shoulder saying "Where are my reports?" At first you think, "Can I book my Southwest flight without him seeing"? (Wanna getaway? Eddie who?) But then you remember that you have a proven, tested backup and recovery plan and process. You are not like the girl or guy who spills beer over all of the fans at the basketball game. We can't stress how important it is to back up your applications. Listen to us – this is *really* important.

BACKUP / RESTORE FOR DATA IN ESSBASE

Essbase version 11.1.1 introduced a backup and restore functionality for block storage option databases. This backup and restore feature collects all the necessary files for backup and recovery of a BSO database (previously you had to manually perform this process). IT then backs up those files.

During the backup process, the database is placed in read-only mode and files are archived to the specified location. When a restore is launched, the database is locked while the files are restored from the archive folder. The backup and restore feature is available in the Administration Services Console and MaxL.

 Note! Because Planning creates block storage option databases, you can use the backup and restore feature on Planning databases.

In the example below, we will archive a database called "11x".

To back up a BSO database,

1. In the Administration Services Console, right-click on the *database* and select *Archive Database*:

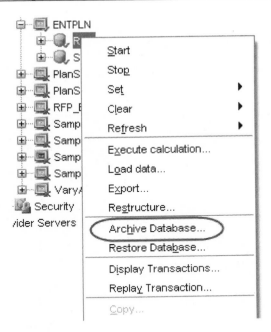

2. Provide a name for the archive:

3. Optionally, select *Force archive* and/or *Archive in the background*. Force archive will replace any archives that exist with the same name.
4. Click *OK*.

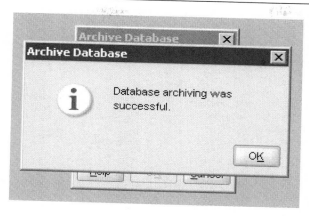

5. A file will be created in the Essbasepath\app directory:

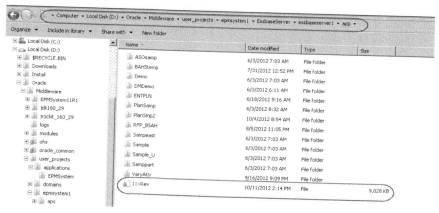

Then use your third party back up tools to backup the archive files created by Essbase.

So now when the Essbase server goes down or a database crashes and the CFO is breathing down your neck, rest assured you have a good backup file. So how do you get it back up? Fast.

To restore a database,

1. If necessary, place the archive files in the Essbase\app folder.
2. Right-click on the *database* and select *Stop* to stop the database.
3. Right-click on the *database* and select *Restore Database*.

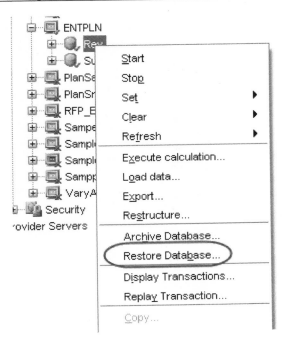

4. Choose the restore file from the drop down box:

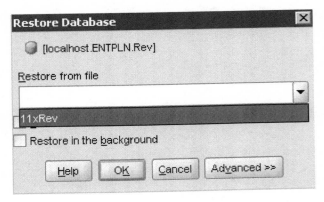

5. Optionally choose to *Force Restore* and/or to *Restore in the background.*
6. Click *OK.*

Ta-da! Like magic, the database is restored (along with some of the CFO's facial color).

Archive the Entpln application.

Try It!

TRANSACTION LOGGING / REPLAY

Another new feature that goes along with backup and restore is the transaction logging and replay capability. Essbase can now track operations in the database like data loads, calculations, and data submissions from Smart View or the Excel Add-in. This feature is similar but different to Planning's Auditing feature.

Because the events are tracked, the administrator can display and replay those transactions. The administrator can choose to replay all transactions from a certain point or she can pick and choose the transactions to replay.

The real power comes with using backup and restore along with transaction logging / play back to restore a database to a previous state. This will probably never happen... wait, actually this could definitely happen. Your budgeting and planning database crashes just after lunch and plans are due at the end of the day. You backup on a nightly basis so you could restore from last night's backup. However, your chances of getting the plan data changes from the morning were pretty slim. Now in Essbase 11, you can use transaction replay to get those data changes back, restoring the BSO database fully with minimal data loss (picture Essbase as a superhero with a big "S" emblazoned across its chest).

The replay for data loads uses a reference or pointer to the data source file (not the actual file). If the underlying data file changes, the new data will be loaded to the database.

Tip!

First you have to enable transaction logging for the desired database (by default, transaction logging is not enabled). To turn on transaction logging, update the Essbase.CFG with the following setting.

```
TransactionLogLocation AppName DbName LogLocation
Native Enable
```

For example:

```
TransactionLogLocation Sample Basic
c:\hyperion\trlog native enable
```

In this example, we'll enable transaction logging for our 11x database.

1. In the Administration Services console, right-click on the Essbase server and select *Edit >> Properties*.
2. Choose the *Environment* tab.
3. Update the TransactionLogLocation parameter in the Essbase.CFG by typing:

```
TransactionLogLocation Sample Basic D:\Oracle\TRLog
NATIVE ENABLE
```

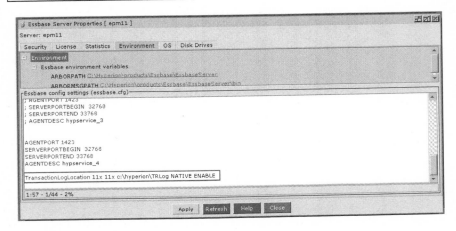

4. Click *Apply*.
5. Restart the Essbase server.
6. Create the directory and folder if necessary (we created a TRLog folder in the Hyperion directory to store the transaction log files). The name must match exactly or the application won't start.
7. Right-click on the application and select *Start*.
8. Right-click on the database and select *Start*.
9. Right-click on the database and select *Display Transactions*:

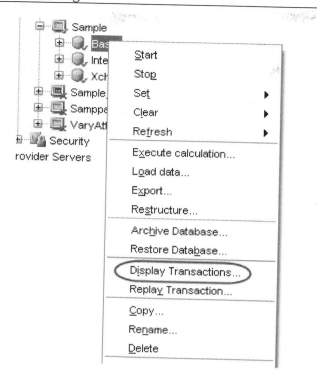

10. Display transactions based on one of the following options:
    - *Last replay time* or
    - *Since a specific date and time*

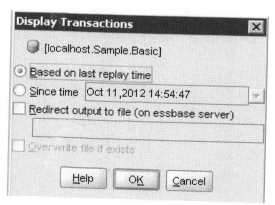

11. Check the *Redirect output to a file* if desired (and optionally overwrite the file if it exists).
12. The Transaction List displays:

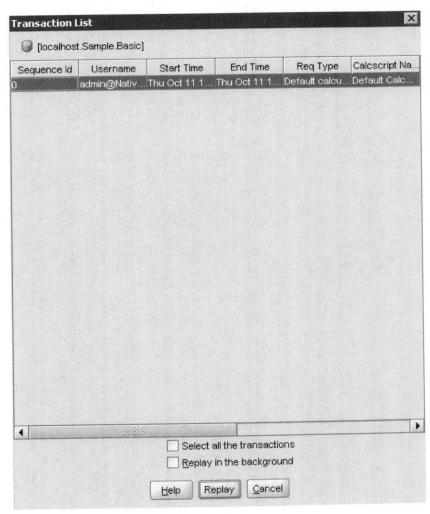

The following columns are shown: Sequence, username, start time, end time, action (or req type), Calcscript name, dataload file, dataload file type, rules file, rules file location, and sql or ftp file user name. (For you existing admins, admit it – you are saying "Wow, this is really cool. What took so long?")

So what would the recorded transactions look like? For example, if we adjusted the columns you would see that first

(Sequence 0) all data was cleared by the user *admin* Wednesday, August 1, 2012, beginning at 8:01 am and ending at 8:02 am. Next (Sequence 1) we see that user *admin* loaded data using the calcdat.txt Wednesday, August 1, 2012, beginning at 8:05 am and ending at 8:06 am. And finally (Sequence 2), we see the default calc script was run by admin on Wednesday, August 1, 2012, beginning at 8:07 am and ending at 8:08 am.

To replay a single transaction, select the desired transaction and click *Replay*.

13. Select the desired transaction and select the *Replay* button (to clear all of the data).

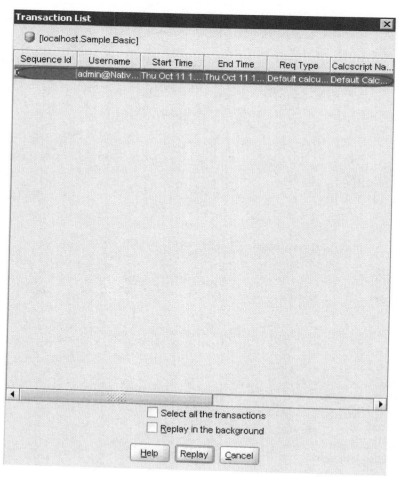

A successful message should display:

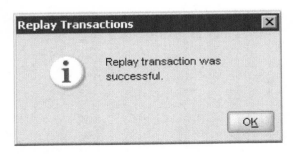

Optionally, you can choose to select all transactions and have them replay in the background.

So back to our midday budget crisis... because you turned on transaction logging for the budget database, you can easily recover last night's archive file, restoring the database. You can replay all transactions that have taken place since the backup, returning the plan data to its original state just before the crash. We think we see a budget increase for a certain Planning Administrator salary because of the quick recovery.

Enable transaction logging for the Entpln Sum database. Enter some expense data via the data forms and run a calc script for Sum. Test viewing and replaying transactions.

Try It!

Planning Auditing vs. Transaction Replay

So which feature should you use to track data changes? Or is it both? You decide but keep in mind there can be performance impacts (test to make sure you aren't slowing things down too much).

	Planning Auditing	**Transaction Replay**
Tracks data changes	Y	Y
Tracks calc scripts launch	Y	Y
Tracks business rules launch	Y	N
Tracks Essbase data load rules launch	N	Y

	Planning Auditing	Transaction Replay
Tracks data form changes	Y	N
Tracks Copy Version, Copy Data and Clear Cell Details	Y	N
Tracks changes in security	Y	N
Tracks changes in task lists	Y	N
Supported for ASO Plan types	Y	N
Visible to End Users	Y	N
Can "Replay" changes in the event of a crash	N	Y

EXPORTING THE DATA

The second method for backups is data exports. Exporting will copy data to a text file that you specify. You can export all data, level zero data, or input-level data for BSO databases and level zero data for ASO databases. The thing with exports is that they only export data. Essbase objects like outline files, rules files, etc. are not included so you will need to use file system backups for those items.

So if we have to do a file system backup anyway, why export? Use exports when you want to transfer data across platforms, when you want to back up only a certain portion of the data (level 0 blocks), or when you want to create an exported file in text format, rather than binary format. If you have a copy of the outline and data export, this can be a quick way to recover a corrupted database.

To perform a data export,
1. Select the database.
2. Right-click and select *Export* or Select *Actions >> Export "dbname"*:

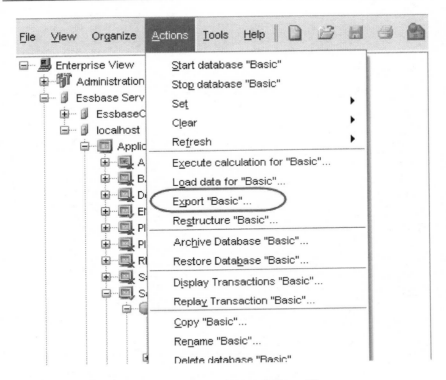

3. Specify the name for the exported data file.
4. Choose the export option:
    *   BSO - All data, Level 0 blocks, or Input blocks
    *   ASO – Level 0 blocks
5. Choose either *column* or *non-column* format.

Column format often facilitates loads to relational databases or other systems. Non-column format is faster for loading or reloading to the Essbase database. Column format exports are not available for ASO.

6. Select *Execute in the background* in most cases:

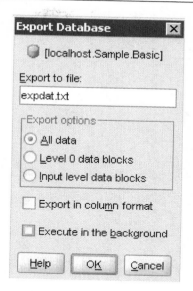

The export file is by default placed in the \arborpath\Essbase\app directory.

To reload an exported file, you will follow the same steps to load any data file though you won't need a rules file. No rules file is necessary since the data was exported in native Essbase format.

1. Right-click on the database and select *Load Data*.
2. Select *Find Data File* and navigate to the exported data file.
3. Specify the error file location and name.
4. Click *OK* to load the data.

If you are reloading a level zero export or input level export file for a BSO database, the database must be recalculated.

Tip!

Don't forget about the binary data export commands (see Oracle's Essbase Tech Ref Guide for more details); these are other good options for exporting data sets for backup purposes.

OLD SCHOOL ESSBASE BACKUPS

In the olden days of backups, before we had the 11x backup and restore feature, we had to walk to school every day in the snow with no shoes and prepare the Essbase server and applications for file system backup ourselves . To do this,

1. Place database in read-only ("archive") mode. Using MaxL, type "**alter database begin archive**".
2. Perform backup using third-party backup utility, backing up the entire Essbase directory or specific files.
3. Return database to read-write mode. Using MaxL, type "**alter database end archive**".

BEGINARCHIVE commits any modified data to disk, switches the database to read-only mode, reopens the database files in shared, read-only mode and creates a file containing a list of files that need to be backed up. By default, the file is called archive.lst and is stored in the *ARBORPATH*\app\appname\dbname directory. ENDARCHIVE switches the database back to read-write mode.

It is important to back up all .ind and .pag files related to a database because a single database can have multiple .ind and .pag files. These files could be placed on different volumes so make sure you are backing up everything.

These are the key BSO files to back up (these are captured automatically for us in the Backup and Restore feature):

ess*n*.ind	*ARBORPATH*\app*appname**dbname*
ess*n*.pag	*ARBORPATH*\app*appname**dbname*
dbname.esm	*ARBORPATH*\app*appname**dbname*
dbname.tct	*ARBORPATH*\app*appname**dbname*
dbname.ind	*ARBORPATH*\app*appname**dbname*
dbname.app	*ARBORPATH*\app
dbname.db	*ARBORPATH*\app*appname**dbname*
x.lro	*ARBORPATH*\app*appname**dbname*
dbname.otl	*ARBORPATH*\app*appname**dbname*
Database object files (.otl, .csc, .rul)	*ARBORPATH*\app*appname**dbname*

To restore files from a backup,

1. Stop the application and databases.
2. Replace the files on disk with the corresponding files from the backup.

Do not move, copy, modify, or delete any of the following files: essn.ind, essn.pag, dbname.ind, dbname.esm, and dbname.tct. Doing so may result in database corruption and/or clearing of the database.

BACKUPS FOR ASO

File system backups are the best method for aggregate storage databases.

To backup an ASO database,
1. Stop the application.
2. Using the File system to back up the *arborpath \ app \ appname* folder.

The following ASO files must be copied:

Appname.app	\ARBORPATH\app\appname
Appname.log	\ARBORPATH\app\appname
Dbname.db	\ARBORPATH\app\appname
Dbname.db	\ARBORPATH\app\appname\dbname
Dbname.dbb	\ARBORPATH\app\appname\dbname
Dbname.ddb	\ARBORPATH\app\appname\dbname
Dbname.otl	\ARBORPATH\app\appname\dbname
Dbname.otl.keep	\ARBORPATH\app\appname\dbname
Trigger.trg	\ARBORPATH\app\appname\dbname
Default	\ARBORPATH\app\appname\default
Temp	\ARBORPATH\app\appname\temp
Log	\ARBORPATH\app\appname\log
Metadata	\ARBORPATH\app\appname\metadata
Essn.dat	\ARBORPATH\app\appname\default

To restore files from a backup,
1. Stop the application and databases.
2. Replace the files on disk with the corresponding files from the backup.

OTHER ESSBASE PIECES TO BACKUP

Don't forget to backup the following files along with your Essbase application and database files:

Essbase.sec	*ARBORPATH*\bin
Essbase.bak	*ARBORPATH*\bin
Essbase.CFG	*ARBORPATH*\bin

BACKUP THE RELATIONAL REPOSITORIES

Don't forget to back up the underlying relational repository for Planning on a frequent basis. You will also want to back up the Shared Services underlying relational repository and all Shared Services files on the Shared Services server. Your DBA should be able to help with the relational databases.

Life Cycle Management (LCM) is another alternative to create application backups; we'll cover LCM in the next chapter.

Finally a last piece of advice: Regularly test your backup and recovery process. We know some of the smartest Essbase administrators who thought their backup process was working correctly but found out otherwise at the most critical time. Trust us. When you get that 2 a.m. I-need-my-data-where-is-it-and-how-could-you-be-asleep-when-the-sky-is-falling call from your panicked boss, you can calmly say "I'll have the database up shortly Mr. CFO." No need for panic and mayhem.

Scene 7:
Life Cycle Management

Life Cycle Management (LCM) provides a set of tools to consistently migrate Oracle EPM applications and/or individual artifacts within and across environments and operating systems. LCM is part of the Foundation Services component of an Oracle EPM implementation and is available in the Shared Services console.

The LCM tools are designed to facilitate the movement of objects in connected and disconnected environments for development, test & production. You might consider using LCM over some of the Planning utilities or backup and recovery options discussed in the prior chapters.

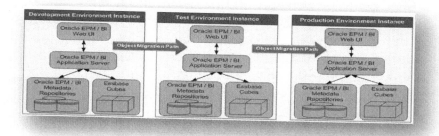

A connected environment is where development, test, and production environments are managed by a single Shared Services instance. A disconnected environment is one where each logical environment (development, test, production) has its own Shared Services instance. Most user configurations will have disconnected environments.

Let's now review some of the features of the Oracle EPM Life Cycle Management

APPLICATION & FILE SYSTEM GROUPS

An application group in Shared Services essentially maps to a product like Essbase or Planning. Previously known as "projects", application groups allow for more simplified management of the applications registered with Shared Services. The screenshot below highlights application groups:

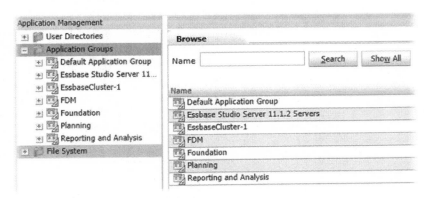

Another application group called *File System* is used in disconnected migrations (when applications need to be moved across different Shared Services instances). The File System Group references the artifacts that have been selected for migration to the file system as opposed to a target application in the same Shared Services environment. This is what allows for the support of disconnected Shared Services environments and will be used in most situations. Users can export an application and/or artifacts to a file system folder:

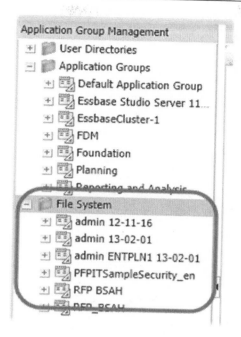

Users can then connect to the different Shared Services instance and import from the File System Folder.

Each migration that is defined to have a file system destination will get a folder created on the Shared Services server that will contain the objects in scope for the migration. Additionally each user gets a named folder to help organize the migrations. The default location on the file system is <HYPERION_HOME>/common/import_export/<USER_NAME>.

Information on LCM migrations are tracked for reporting:

User	Source	Destination	Start Time	Completed Time	Duration	Status
admin	Sample	admin 12-11-16\ESB-Sample	November 16, 2012 11:21:00	November 16, 2012 11:31:13	00:30:13	Completed
admin	PFPITSampleSecurity_en\HSS-Sh...	Shared Services	October 16, 2012 10:42:25	October 16, 2012 10:42:27	00:00:02	Completed
admin	PFPITSampleSecurity_en\HSS-Sh...	Shared Services	October 16, 2012 06:51:31	October 16, 2012 06:51:33	00:00:02	Completed
admin	RFP BSAH\HP-RFP_BSAH	RFP_BSAH	August 5, 2012 23:05:21	August 5, 2012 23:05:49	00:00:29	Completed
admin	RFP_BSAH	RFP BSAH\HP-RFP_BSAH	August 5, 2012 11:40:11	August 5, 2012 11:40:17	00:00:04	Completed
admin	RFP_BSAH\HP-BAHSdemo	RFP_BSAH	August 2, 2011 12:11:35	August 2, 2012 12:12:03	00:00:28	Completed
admin	BAHSdemo	RFP_BSAH\HP-BAHSdemo	August 2, 2012 12:09:03	August 2, 2012 12:10:08	00:00:15	Completed

APPLICATION ARTIFACTS

The Life Cycle Management tools can be used to manage a variety of artifacts from the different Oracle EPM applications. The supported applications & artifacts for Planning are:

Planning
- Configuration
- Global Artifacts
- Plan Types
- Relational Data
- Security
- Support for standalone Calculation Manager (11.1.2.1)
- Migrate Business Rules and other objects from Calc Manager to Classic FM and Planning apps (11.1.2.1)
- Support for PSB (11.1.2.1)
- Planning report scripts (11.1.2.2)

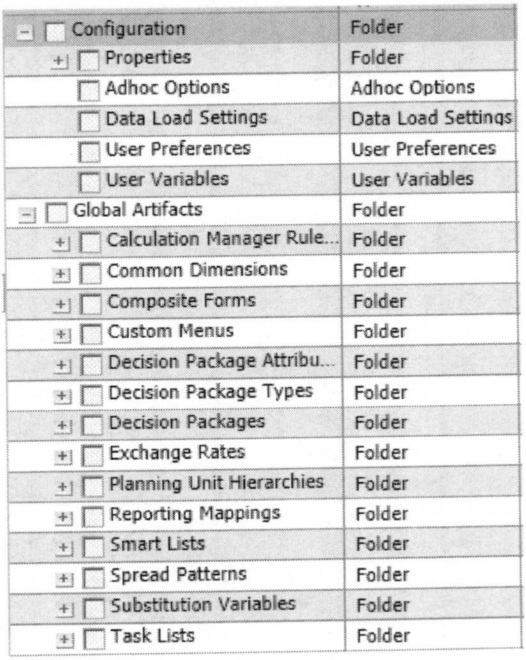

− ☐ Configuration	Folder
+ ☐ Properties	Folder
☐ Adhoc Options	Adhoc Options
☐ Data Load Settings	Data Load Settings
☐ User Preferences	User Preferences
☐ User Variables	User Variables
− ☐ Global Artifacts	Folder
+ ☐ Calculation Manager Rule...	Folder
+ ☐ Common Dimensions	Folder
+ ☐ Composite Forms	Folder
+ ☐ Custom Menus	Folder
+ ☐ Decision Package Attribu...	Folder
+ ☐ Decision Package Types	Folder
+ ☐ Decision Packages	Folder
+ ☐ Exchange Rates	Folder
+ ☐ Planning Unit Hierarchies	Folder
+ ☐ Reporting Mappings	Folder
+ ☐ Smart Lists	Folder
+ ☐ Spread Patterns	Folder
+ ☐ Substitution Variables	Folder
+ ☐ Task Lists	Folder

Plan Type	Folder
DtlRev	Folder
Attribute Dimensions	Folder
Calculation Manager...	Folder
Data Forms	Folder
Report scripts	Folder
Rule files	Folder
Standard Dimensions	Folder
Substitution Variables	Folder
Rev	Folder
Attribute Dimensions	Folder
Calc scripts	Folder
Calculation Manager...	Folder
Data Forms	Folder
Report scripts	Folder
Rule files	Folder
Standard Dimensions	Folder
Substitution Variables	Folder
Sum	Folder
Travel	Folder

Relational Data	Folder
Account Annotations	Account Annotati...
Cell Texts	Cell Texts
Planning Units	Planning Units
Supporting Detail	Supporting Detail
Text Values	Text Values
Security	Folder
Access Permissions	Folder
Groups	Folder
Users	Access

EPMA supported artifacts include Application Metadata, Data Synchronizations, Dimension Access, and Shared Library Dimensions. Shared Services (users & task flows) artifacts include Native Directory (Security) and Task flows.

APPLICATION MIGRATION

Application Migration is accomplished by exporting and importing the application artifacts. 11.1.2.2 LCM provides a more simplified migration definition file and Migration status report. Beginning in this version, application shell creation for Classic applications are supported (meaning you don't have to create a "shell" before migrating a Planning application to a brand new application / environment).

Version 11.1.2.3 further improves the application migration process through cross version LCM support (you can use LCM to migrate applications from 11.1.1.4 to 11.1.2.3) and new features to move application artifacts from one environment to another by downloading from the File System Node (saved as zip file). For faster deployment, you can import application metadata on an incremental basis using a date and time stamp.

To run migrations you must have the LCM Designer role provisioned in Shared Services.

Let's migrate an application!

1. Navigate to the *Application Groups Directory* in the Application Management window.
2. Expand *Planning*.
3. Select the Application you wish to export, the Artifact List will load in the browser window on the right. We selected Planning/ENTPLN.
4. Select the Artifacts you wish to export, there are multiple choices to accomplish this task:
   a. Select *All* button (lower right) or
   b. Check each artifact separately:

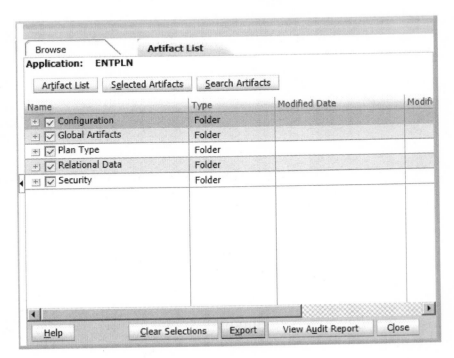

The *Search Artifacts* button (top center) gives you the ability to search for artifacts by *Artifact Name* (enter the name with or without the wildcard *), *Date Modified* (select from the drop-down, note if you select Date Range, you will also enter the Start Date and End Date, or *Modified By* (helps finding the Artifact(s) created/modified by a specific user when you may not know the artifact name).

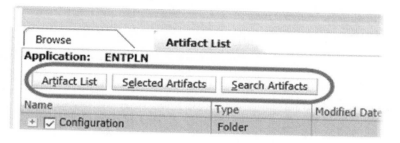

5. Once you have the artifacts selected, click the *Export* button, lower right of Artifact List window:

6. The Export to Filesystem window will open with the default File System Folder populated with: "admin yy-mm-dd'. Modify the name as desired:

7. Click the *Export* button.
The Migration Status Report will appear. Find the line for the job run, the Status column shows the progress. If the Status

column is In Progress, click the Refresh button in the lower right corner until the export shows Completed.

User	Source	Destination	Start Time	Completed Time	Duration	Status
admin	ENTPLN - ENTPLN1 admin 13-05-15\HP-ENT... 60 out of 93 artifact(s) processed		May 15, 2013 22:20:52			In Progress
admin	admin ENTPLN1 13-02-01\HP-ENT... - ENTPLN1		February 2, 2013 09:33:21	February 2, 2013 09:35:33	00:02:12	Completed
admin	ENTPLN - admin ENTPLN 13-02-01\HP-ENTPLN		February 1, 2013 14:15:22	February 1, 2013 14:15:34	00:00:12	Completed
admin	PLNEPMA - admin 13-02-01\HP-PLNEPMA		February 1, 2013 11:38:04	February 1, 2013 11:38:08	00:00:04	Completed
admin	Sample - admin 12-11-16\ESB-Sample		November 16,	November 16,	00:00:13	Completed

8. Navigate to the File System directory, below the Application Groups, find the directory you just created with the artifacts exported, select the Application artifact, in this case, HP-ENTPLN.

By selecting it, the Artifacts List in the group will load in the browser window.

9. If you are migrating this export to a new environment, check that the prerequisites are satisfied before continuing (see below).

Prerequisites:

If the Import is new to the destination Planning environment:

- Ensure Shared Services Native Directory artifacts (users, groups, and provisioning) exist. If not, migrate the directory.

- Ensure the Metadata database exists in Oracle, SQL Server, or IBM DB2. If it does not exist, create the database.
- Ensure the Datasource exists in Planning (example) by logging into the Planning UI, *Administer >> Manage Datasource*. If the datasource does not exist, *Add a New Datasource*, fill in the relevant information for the destination Database and Essbase.

Once the Pre-requisites have been verified,
10. Log into the Shared Services for the destination environment.
11. Navigate to the *File System*.
12. Locate the exported application.
13. Load the Artifact List, the window has the same options as the export window did, except the *Export* button is the *Import* button.
14. Repeat Step 3 to select the artifacts you wish to import:

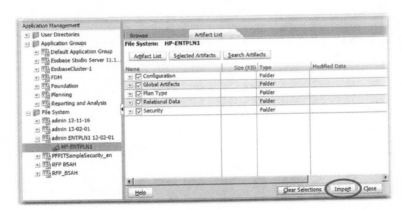

15. Click the *Import* button.
The Import to Application window appears. Ensure the information for Applications, in this case, Planning: ENTPLN1, is correct. Note the window message that "The application will be created if it doesn't exist."
16. Click the *Import* button:

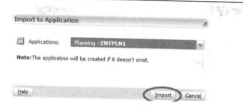

The Report will appear with the Status column showing the progress of the import.

17. Click the *Refresh* button until the Status is Completed (or just be patient):

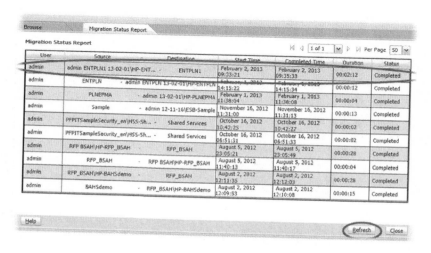

To verify that the Planning Application has been imported, open the Planning Application Group. View the list and your new Planning application should appear (in our case "ENTPLN1"). If it does not, you may have to click the *Refresh* for it to appear. The Refresh is at the top of the window, or you may go to *View >> Refresh* on the Menu.

LIFE CYCLE MANAGEMENT REPORTS

The Life Cycle Management tools have reporting capabilities to assist in the management of LCM activities. The Migration Status Report provides migration status and migration date and time. While processing, the report shows the number of artifacts it has processed. The Audit Report displays user LCM activities and must be configured prior to use.

To view the Migration Status report, log into Shared Services and select *Administration >> Migration Status Report*:

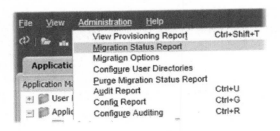

The Migration Status Report will open in the Browse window:

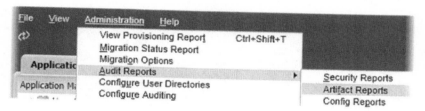

User	Source	Destination	Start Time	Completed Time	Duration	Status
admin	admin ENTPLN1 13-02-01\HP-ENT...	ENTPLN1	February 2, 2013 09:33:21	February 2, 2013 09:35:33	00:02:12	Completed
admin	ENTPLN	admin ENTPLN 13-02-01\HP-ENTPLN	February 1, 2013 14:15:22	February 1, 2013 14:15:34	00:00:12	Completed
admin	PLNEPMA	admin 13-02-01\HP-PLNEPMA	February 1, 2013 11:38:04	February 1, 2013 11:38:08	00:00:04	Completed
admin	Sample	admin 12-11-16\ESB-Sample	November 16, 2012 11:31:00	November 16, 2012 11:31:13	00:00:13	Completed
admin	PFPITSampleSecurity_en\HSS-Sh...	Shared Services	October 16, 2012 10:42:25	October 16, 2012 10:42:27	00:00:02	Completed
admin	PFPITSampleSecurity_en\HSS-Sh...	Shared Services	October 16, 2012 06:51:31	October 16, 2012 06:51:33	00:00:02	Completed
admin	RFP BSAH\HP-RFP_BSAH	RFP_BSAH	August 5, 2012 23:05:21	August 5, 2012 23:05:49	00:00:28	Completed
admin	RFP_BSAH	RFP BSAH\HP-RFP_BSAH	August 5, 2012 11:40:13	August 5, 2012 11:40:17	00:00:04	Completed
admin	RFP_BSAH\HP-BAHSdemo	RFP_BSAH	August 2, 2012 12:11:35	August 2, 2012 12:12:03	00:00:28	Completed
admin	BAHSdemo	RFP_BSAH\HP-BAHSdemo	August 2, 2012 12:09:53	August 2, 2012 12:10:08	00:00:15	Completed

To run the Audit Report, you must have the configuration set to *Enabled*). If enabled, there are two ways to access the report: selecting *Administration >> Audit Reports >>Artifact Reports*:

You can also open the Artifact List for an application and view the audit information select artifacts or all artifacts by choosing the desired option and clicking the *View Audit Report* button:

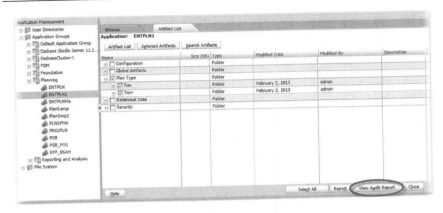

LCM COMMAND LINE UTILITY

The Life Cycle Management Utility is a command-line utility that provides an alternate way to migrate artifacts from source to destination. Lifecycle Management Utility can be used with a third-party scheduling service such as Windows Task Scheduler or Oracle Enterprise Manager.

In summary, Life Cycle Management provides a powerful set of tools that can be used to facilitate many administrative tasks within an Oracle EPM Environment:

- Application migrations with cross-product artifact dependencies
- Security migrations
- Web user interface (instead of commend line utilities)
- Configuration of Oracle EPM System products in a mixed-release environment

- Perform other manual configuration changes
- Backup & Recovery
- Import and export artifacts for editing purposes
- Edit a single artifact
- Version control
- In 11.1.2.3, migrate applications from earlier versions to 11.1.2.3

Scene 8:
MaxL Automation

You can automate Planning tasks using the Planning utilities but what about the Essbase tasks? You've learned most all of the tasks to build and maintain Essbase databases through the Administration Services Console. However, you certainly don't want to perform all of these tasks manually every day. Essbase of course has a scripting alternative to automate almost any Essbase task. MaxL is the scripting language for Essbase and is installed with every instance of the Essbase server, on all operating systems. These are some of the more common actions that MaxL is used for with Planning applications:

- Load data from a text file using an Essbase load rule
- Load data from a SQL table using a SQL Essbase load rule
- Launch a calc script
- Replicate data for a partition
- View database statistics

Having a good knowledge of MaxL is absolutely essential to the smooth running of your Essbase environment. In addition to daily database updates and administration, developers can also automate repetitive tasks in order to speed up testing cycles, a trick that can save much stress when under tight deadlines.

Here is a sample MaxL script that will connect to the local Essbase server, unload the Sample application, then delete it.

```
LOGIN admin password ON localhost;
ALTER SYSTEM UNLOAD APPLICATION Sample;
DROP APPLICATION Sample;
EXIT;
```

EXECUTE MAXL

MaxL can be run in two ways: interactive and batch. Both methods use the essmsh executable (*ESS*base *MaxL SH*ell) at the command prompt. There is a visual editor for MaxL scripts in the Administration Services Console, but this is used for development only and is not normally used in production.

To run MaxL interactively, simply type **startessmsh** at the command line and the MaxL interface will then be ready to accept your commands:

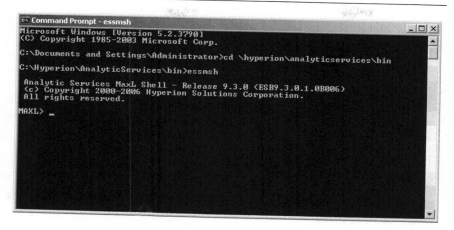

To run MaxL in batch mode, you may need to add a call or cmd /C to the line starting Essmsh. Next add the name of a script file as an argument to the command. MaxL will then read and interpret each line in succession until it reaches an EXIT command or the end of the file:

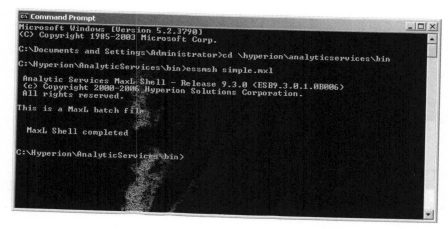

There are also MaxL interfaces for Perl and Java, but their usage is not covered in this book. More details of this can be found in the DBA Guide and Technical Reference publications.

SECURE MAXL

Beginning Essbase 9.3, the ability to secure a MaxL script using public/private key pair encryption was introduced. In prior versions, the password would either be stored as clear text in the script or passed in as a variable from the command shell, which posed a security risk.

To create a key pair, run the MaxL shell with this argument: **essmsh -gk**

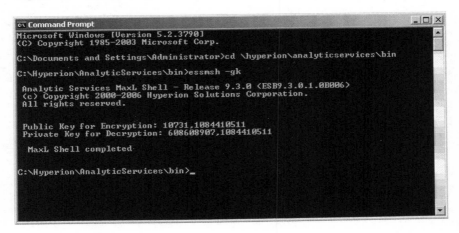

Then, to encrypt a script using this key pair, run: **essmsh -E [scriptname] [public key]** Note that this process creates a new secured script with the same name and a ".mxls" extension. To run this script you will need the corresponding private key: **essmsh -D [scriptname] [private key]**

If you try to run this script without the key you will see an error message, so don't lose the private key!

BASIC MAXL SYNTAX RULES

MaxL is neither case-sensitive nor space-sensitive, meaning you are free to format your scripts any way you see fit. The only general restrictions are that the file can only contain ASCII text, and every command must be terminated with a semicolon. Other than that, you can insert tabs, spaces, and new lines as you see fit to make the code easier to read.

Tip!

Capitalizing the MaxL keywords only will make it much easier to identify which words are your variables and which are MaxL commands.

Note!

Most objects (application names, database names, calc script names, load rule names, file paths, etc. are case-sensitive on UNIX hosts, even in MaxL scripts.

There is an important difference between single and double quotes in MaxL. Single quotes tell the engine to translate the text they enclose literally, while double quotes allow for variable translation. Consider the case where we want to output the system environment variable ARBORPATH. Here are two different MaxL statements that attempt to do this:

```
ECHO 'ARBORPATH is $ARBORPATH'

ECHO "ARBORPATH is $ARBORPATH"
```

The first statement with single quotes will output literally **ARBORPATH is $ARBORPATH**, while the second will evaluate the variable first and output the desired result of **ARBORPATH is c:\hyperion\Essbase**.

If you want to output a single quote, you need to enclose the entire statement in double quotes:

```
echo "Isn't Penny the cutest girl ever?";
```

Backslashes are considered special characters in MaxL, and need to be doubled up when specifying a Windows file location:

```
'c:\\hyperion\\Essbase\\app'
```

Even on Windows systems you can use a forward quote for path names so you don't have to use the escape character c:/Hyperion/essbase/App.

Tip!

LOGIN

The login command is used to connect to an Essbase server. The IDENTIFIED BY syntax is completely optional and was probably only included for script readability.

```
LOGIN [username] IDENTIFIED BY [password] ON
      [hostname]

LOGIN [username] [password] ON [hostname]
```

To run MaxL interactively and to easily login to the machine local to your session, type **essmsh -l [username] [password]** at the command line.

Tip!

REDIRECT OUTPUT

Most of the time, you will schedule MaxL jobs to run in the middle of the night as part of an automated process. Of course, you will want to see everything that happened when you arrive at the office in the morning.

Redirecting the output of the script is usually the first command that you will issue in a script. The syntax for this is as follows:

```
SPOOL ON TO [File Name];
```

There is no easy way to create a unique log file identifier in MaxL, but you can easily do this in most operating system command shells and pass a unique value in as a runtime variable (see the next session).

Tip!

USE VARIABLES

There are three types of variables that you can use inside your MaxL scripts.

1. Environment variables from the operating system. If you want to reference a variable set in the operating system shell, you can reference it directly by name and prefixed with a dollar sign (e.g. **$ARBORPATH**)

2. Positional variables passed in on the command line. You can add parameters to essmsh that will be translated to variables inside the script. For example, consider the script myscript.mxl that contains these commands:

```
ECHO "The third variable is $3.";
ECHO "The second variable is $2.";
ECHO "The first variable is $1.";
```

When you execute this script using this syntax:

```
essmsh myscript.mxl ten twenty thirty
```

The output will be:

```
The third variable is thirty.
The second variable is twenty.
The first variable is ten.
```

3. Temporary variables that you set inside the MaxL script. You may also want to set variables inside your MaxL scripts. To do this, use the following syntax:

```
SET myvariable = 'ten';
ECHO $myvariable;
```

MAXL ACTIONS

It can be overwhelming for first-time users to look at the large list of MaxL commands. However, everything becomes much simpler when you understand that there are only ten core actions.

The following table summarizes what each of these core actions does.

Alter	Change the state of an object.
Create	Create a new instance of an object.
Display	Show information about an object.
Drop	Delete an instance of an object.
Execute	Run a calculation or aggregation process.
Export	Output data or LRO's.
Grant	Assign security to users or groups.
Import	Load data, dimensions, or LRO's.
Query	Get information about an application or database.
Refresh	Reload partitioning information or custom Java function definitions.

SAMPLE MAXL STATEMENTS

The following sections will illustrate some of the most frequently used MaxL actions, and provide commentary on the nuances of the syntax.

Load a database from a SQL source

This statement will load data from a SQL database. You don't have to specify the ODBC data source name as that is contained within the load rule itself (named sql_load).

```
IMPORT DATABASE Sample.Basic DATA
 CONNECT AS dbadmin IDENTIFIED BY dbpasswd
 USING SERVER RULES_FILE 'sql_load'
 ON ERROR WRITE TO
      'c:\\hyperion\\MaxL_logs\\load.sample_basic.er
      r';
```

Run a Calc Script

Of course, MaxL can run a calc script that you've already saved (in this example, the calc script named "Allocate" is executed). There are two ways to do this (both of these commands have the exact same result, it's your choice which you prefer to use):

```
EXECUTE CALCULATION 'Sample.Basic.Allocate';

EXECUTE CALCULATION 'Allocate' ON Sample.Basic;
```

A nice capability that is often overlooked is the ability to send custom calc commands directly from MaxL, which is incredibly useful when you want to test different settings or commands using variable substitution.

```
EXECUTE CALCULATION
  "SET UPDATECALCOFF;
    CALC ALL;"
ON Sample.Basic;
```

Run an MDX Query

MDX queries are interesting in that they do not have an action of their own. Rather, you execute the entire MDX statement as an action itself.

```
SPOOL ON TO 'mdx_output.txt';
SELECT
  {Products.Generation(2).Members} ON ROWS,
  {Time.Level(0).Members} ON COLUMNS
FROM Sample.Basic;
SPOOL OFF;
```

To add the exit code to the exit statements, check out Cameron Lackpour's blog entry http://camerons-blog-for-essbase-hackers.blogspot.com/2011/06/no-exit-but-not-in-maxl_9756.html.

RUN AS

A new "run as" feature allows supervisors to login in as another user. This is helpful when debugging someone's security access. It was introduced for batch bursting in Financial Reporting. Type in ESSMSH –la and provide the admin id, admin password, and the user to log in as (ESSMSH –la Username, password, usernameas).

ERROR HANDLING

Error handling in MaxL is a two-stage process. The first involves redirecting the script after the error occurs so no more statements are executed. In this example, we are testing for a login failure and if not successful then there is no point in executing the load and calculate commands so we divert the MaxL script immediately to the "no_login" error handling section.

```
LOGIN admin password ON server01;
IFERROR 'no_login';

ALTER SYSTEM LOAD APPLICATION 'Sample';
EXECUTE CALCULATION DEFAULT ON 'Sample.Basic';
EXIT;

DEFINE LABEL 'no_login';
EXIT;
```

The second stage takes place in the operating system command-line environment that is called **essmsh**. The **essmsh** process will return a 0 (zero) if everything was successful, but will return a non-zero number if an error was encountered. The operating system script will then be responsible for further actions.

We want to perform hourly actual updates to our application. Write a MaxL script to clear daily data logically and perform an data load.

Try It!

We've now reached the end of the administrative and management portion of the book. Penny feels like she knows everything possible about Planning.

"Dr. Dementor can never hurt us again!" she yells triumphantly. But her wide smile falters when she sees Mr. A shaking his head.

"The last and final step to your induction as a Planning Administrator is advanced design best practices and tuning and optimization."

ADVANCED HYPERION PLANNING

Scene 9:
Application Design Best Practices

We covered the basics of building applications in *Look Smarter Than You Are with Hyperion Planning 11.1.2: Create Hyperion Planning Applications.* Now that you know the "under the covers" (get your mind out of the gutter) aspects of Planning, let's delve deeper into Hyperion Planning application design best practices. We'll build a bullet proof application that no deathray can penetrate or destroy.

THE CASE FOR MULTIPLE APPLICATIONS

First we'll cover one of the most important questions: Should you create multiple applications (potentially each with multiple plan types) or a single application with multiple plan types? Several requirements drive the number of Planning applications that are necessary for your budgeting and forecasting process. These requirements include: business purpose, user audience, user location, security, dimensionality, down time, and hardware/software limitations.

A single application results in less overall overhead and maintenance when compared to a multiple application solution. For example, having one application simplifies the maintenance of master data, because you update it in one place and then Planning pushes out updates to all the plan types (Essbase databases) in the application. One application can also be considered if the system does not have to be highly available to users in different time zones. You can further extend a single application by adding in your ASO reporting databases into the application in version 11.1.2.3.

Varying dimensionality and/or security requirements can dictate multiple applications. A single application will always be easier to maintain, but that isn't always feasible. Some planning and reporting requirements will dictate multiple Planning applications.

One example would be a global company that requires the Planning application to be available during business hours to all users around the world. In this case you might divide the system into separate regional Planning applications and create a global, consolidated view of the business in a separate Planning or Essbase ASO reporting database.

Because Planning data forms are attached to applications and plan types, you can use the form definition utility to export and import form definitions across multiple applications. If the calculation requirements are similar in all applications, the same business rules can be shared across applications and used by multiple locations. Other Essbase objects like substitution variables can be used for all the applications on the server.

If you opt for a ASO reporting database in addition to the Planning BSO plan types (within the application or outside of the application), data in the ASO database can be updated via BSO-to-ASO partitioning or the *Map to Reporting* feature available under *Administration* (we'll discuss ASO reporting in just a moment).

One of the other main reasons to split plan types into different applications is if you have user security on a dimension that will differ depending on the plan type. Let's say you have an Entity dimension and you want to do revenue planning and salary planning. The head of the sales department might be able to see all locations for revenue planning purposes but can only see his direct reports for salary planning purposes. The only way to achieve this easily is by different applications.

 Planning does not support cell level security.
Note!

There is a school of thought that says to split plan types into different applications to improve performance. This was true under 32-bit Hyperion because a single application had access to only one memory space (which under 32-bit was at most 4 GB). Every plan type in that application had to share that same memory space. While this is still true under 64-bit Hyperion, the memory spaces can now address 2 exabytes of RAM which is an amount you're not likely to reach in your lifetime. With modern hardware and well-designed applications, "splitting for performance" is no longer an issue.

It used to be difficult for users to navigate between Planning applications. Nowadays, users can simultaneously open several Planning applications and navigate among them by clicking their names on the tabs at the top of the EPM Workspace window. There is no need for end users to log out and log back in thanks to the EPM Workspace. In the same way, users can also open Financial Reporting objects that connect to Essbase or other data sources without having to leave the current Workspace session. Using task lists across applications is problematic and you can't do composite forms across applications, but for the most part, the user will not be impacted by multiple applications.

THE CASE FOR MULTIPLE PLAN TYPES

First of all, don't try to put all your planning needs into a single plan type in a single application. You will end up with a confusing, slow mess that's difficult to build, difficult to use, and difficult to maintain. While it may at first seem like one plan type with everything thrown to together might make everything easier, it will frustrate you in the end. Separate your plan types by planning need.

Note!

Different dimensions for each type of planning are an easy way to spot the need for multiple plan types. For instance, if you need an Employee dimension for salary planning and a Product dimension for revenue planning, put these in different plan types.

Utilizing multiple plan types in applications allows for planning different subject areas in a single application. Because entity, account, and custom dimensions/members are plan type specific, you can avoid inter-dimensional irrelevance for end users. Implementing multiple plan types may improve the overall performance of the Planning application by reducing the database size; it also gives you more flexibility with parallel calculations and other processes, more efficiently utilizing server resources. Calculations will execute faster when focused on specific areas and data sets; you can also aggregate each plan type separately. Beginning in 11.1.2.3 you can create both BSO and ASO plan types.

Let's analyze the standard dimensions that come with Hyperion Planning. Within a Planning application, plan types share the exact same Time Period, Year, Scenario and Version dimensions. Each plan type can have different Entity and Account dimension members. For these dimensions you can select specific members and assign them to plan types.

User defined dimensions such as Product, Operating Area and Employee can also be assigned to selected plan types, but Planning requires that the assigned plan types get all the members in the custom dimension. You can assign the entire dimension to selected plan types, but you cannot assign selected members to different plan types. That does change starting in 11.1.2.3 because you can now have different hierarchies by plan type.

A common way to define plan types within a Planning application is based on a logical segregation of the chart of accounts. Each plan type only includes the custom dimensions that are relevant to each separate group of accounts. Within a Planning application you can create up to 3 plan types for a regular Planning application and 6 plan types with the new module Project Financial Planning.

A common example of a Planning application divided based on the chart of accounts could include separate plan types for Workforce, Expense, and Revenue. In this example, the Revenue plan type can include a Customer and a Product Dimension that are not needed in the other plan types; Employee or Job Grade dimensions are only relevant to Workforce; a separate Capex application might be created with Projects and Asset Class dimensions utilizing in the Capex accounts. In Project Financial Planning, the Capex and Projects plan types are built within the main application.

Each plan type uses different sections of the chart of accounts. If we talk about data flow using the same example, the Capex plan type can have detailed driver accounts to calculate depreciation expense. Once the depreciation expense is calculated in Capex, it can be transferred to the P&L depreciation account in the Finance plan type. Because Planning data forms are attached to a plan type and separate forms are normally created by the different groups of accounts, separating plan types and forms based on the Account dimension minimizes the number of data forms that need to be created and maintained.

The picture below shows the member property window for a member of the account dimension. For accounts, you can assign individual members to different plan types.

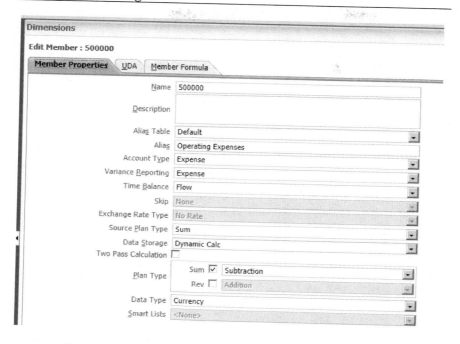

The picture below shows a property window for a member of the Entity dimension where you can assign individual members to different plan types:

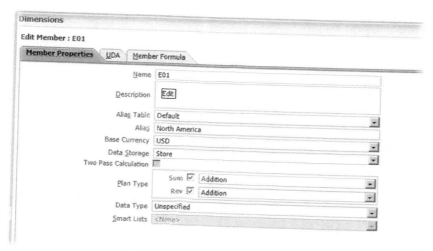

One additional consideration is that security applied to a dimension member will follow in all plan types. For example, if you assign the user "Bob" read access to the West region, he will have read access in all plan types. To address this, you can apply security by other dimensions in the specific plan types but every once in a while, you run into a "sticking" point that may prompt you to create a separate application or create different dimensionality and rollups to address how security is applied.

ASO DATABASES

Do you try to build your actuals reporting in the Planning application – block storage plan types? This answer should be NO. If the answer to this question is yes, you may likely need to revisit the application design.

Don't try to build an Actuals reporting system in your Planning block storage option plan types. Create an aggregate storage database (ASO) reporting database to perform Actuals and Variance reporting and analysis. You can store more years and more detail in the ASO database for reporting purposes (20+ dimensions and millions of members). In BSO plan types, only store the historical data that is needed for data display or calculations.

Originally, ASO was created specifically to deal with requirements for very large, read-only sparse data sets with a high number of dimensions and potentially millions of members (any one of these requirements would make a BSO database hide under the bed and whimper for its mommy). ASO utilizes a different kind of storage mechanism that allows improved calculation times from ten to one hundred times faster than BSO databases – the calculations just aren't as complex. ASO can also store up to 2^{52} dimension-level combinations. If you aren't that great at math, just know that this is a really, really big number.

Essbase ASO allows you to build different types of Essbase cubes bigger and deeper than you ever thought possible. You could do customer analysis across millions of customers, logistics analysis where we can analyze near real-time updates of product shipments, and market basket analysis where we can analyze what products are purchased along with other products.

Let's take a look at the ASOSamp.Sample outline:

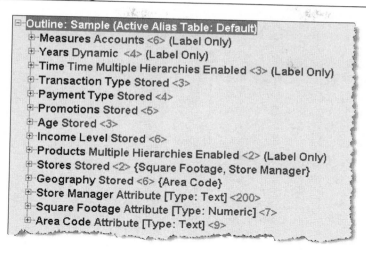

Yes, you are seeing correctly. No blurry vision. We have an outline that has 14 dimensions. Attribute dimensions in ASO databases are supported as well.

Tip!

You can easily spot an ASO database in the Administration Services Console by the red star in the box near the application name:

ASOsamp

In 11.1.2.2 you must build ASO reporting cubes as a standalone Essbase databases in EAS. In 11.1.2.3, Planning provides an interface to create ASO plan types (applications and databases) within the Planning application. These applications can be used for *both* planning and reporting!

Note!

Until Planning 11.1.2.3, Essbase BSO was the only supported cube that could sit under a Planning application. Starting in 11.1.2.3, Essbase ASO can now be a direct repository of Planning data.

You will then take advantage of the Map to Reporting feature or BSO-to-ASO replicated partitions to share data from the BSO plan types to the ASO reporting database.

ASO vs. BSO

Let's start with the most important point – what does the user see? The beauty of ASO and BSO databases is that front-end tools like the Excel Add-In, Smart View, and Financial Reporting really don't care if the database is BSO or ASO (even MaxL sees only minor differences between the two). They both seem like multidimensional databases that have Zoom In and Zoom Out and Keep Only and Remove Only and Pivot and all that nice stuff. There are some minor differences, but for the most part the database type is pretty much transparent to the end-user.

What else is the same? Both types of databases are defined by their outline. Most dimension and member properties like dimension type, data storage (store, never share, label only), consolidation tags and aliases are consistent for both ASO and BSO databases. How you build dimensions and load data is essentially the same. Certain rule files properties are database type specific but the overall interface and steps are the same.

Calculating the databases is where we really begin to see the differences between ASO and BSO. With ASO databases, after data values are loaded into the level 0 cells of an outline, *the database requires no separate calculation step*. From any point in the database, users can retrieve and view values that are aggregated for only the current retrieval. ASO databases are smaller than block storage databases, enabling quick retrieval of data. For even faster retrieval, pre-calculate data values and store the pre-calculated results in aggregations. You can add in calculated members with member formulas in ASO. The syntax for the formulas is MDX.

On the other side of the house, BSO databases have member formulas also but they use a different syntax: Essbase calc script syntax. In most cases, you will need to aggregate the BSO database after performing a data load. You will use the default calc script or one that you manually create to roll up all of the values for the dimensions in the database. These BSO calc scripts can perform complex business logic and allocations.

Write back is another differentiator. For block storage databases, users can write back to any level in the database if they have permissions while aggregate storage databases only allow write back to level zero members. Planning 11.1.2.3 allows write-back to Essbase ASO but is still constrained by ASO's limit of only allowing data to be written back to the bottom level of the database.

Under the covers, the two types of databases are radically different. ASO outlines have two types of hierarchies: stored and dynamic. BSO outlines define dense and sparse dimensions. ASO databases are stored in a series of tablespaces while BSO databases are stored in a series of index and page files. How you tune each database is very different.

Tip! General guideline – Only use BSO for applications that require complex calculations or write back capabilities to any level. .

CREATE AN ASO PLAN TYPE IN 11.1.2.3

Create the Plan Type

Planning administrators create ASO plan types during application creation or add a new plan types to existing Planning applications. You use the application creation wizard to create the Planning application in 11.1.2.3. The process is the same as 11.1.2.2 but with the new option of adding an ASO plan type.

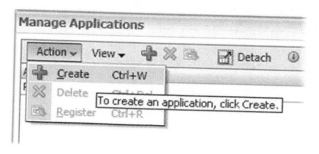

The Application Creation Wizard has a new option to add an ASO plan type. Note you must define the application name and the database name.

So what happens when you click the Create button? Planning creates the relational database tables in the underlying relational database and creates the underlying Essbase application(s); however, the Essbase databases have not yet been created. Planning will create one application which will contain all BSO databases and a separate application for ASO which will contain the ASO database.

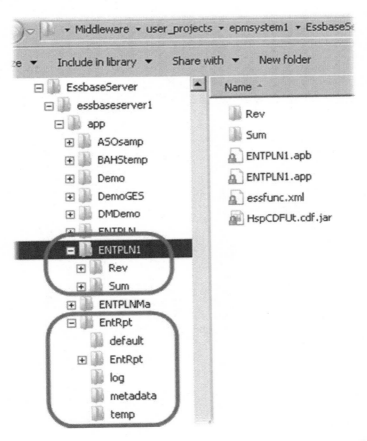

You can you only create one ASO plan type during application creation. You can add the other ASO plan types later in Plan Type Editor.

Create an ASO Plan Type via Plan Type Editor

ASO Plan types may also be added via the Plan Type Editor. Select *Administration >> Manage >> Plan Types* to access the Plan Type Editor:

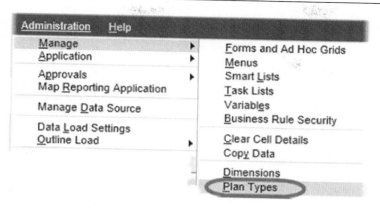

The Plan Type Editor displays:

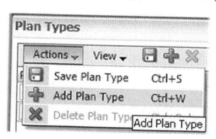

You can *Add* or *Delete* plan types from an application:

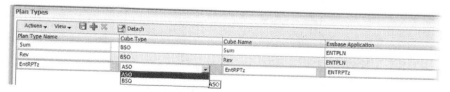

When adding a new plan type, you can choose *ASO* or *BSO*:

Plan Type Name	Cube Type	Cube Name	Essbase Application
Sum	BSO	Sum	ENTPLN
Rev	BSO	Rev	ENTPLN
EntRPTz	ASO	EntRPTz	ENTRPTz
	ASO		
	BSO		

You may create up to 3 BSO plan types within a single application (just like before) and X ASO plan types where X equals the number of BSO plan types +1.

Select *Administration* >> *Manage* >> *Refresh Database* to create the ASO application and database in Essbase. **Don't choose** *Create!*

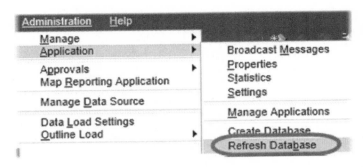

When you add a plan type click *Refresh* to create the ASO plan types. If you click *Create*, data will wipe out the BSO plan types. Only click *Create* once at the very beginning of an application's creation!

Add Dimensions and Members to an ASO Plan Type

Once the application and databases are created, plan types are selectable in the Dimension Editor so you can view all dimensions for all plan types or filter dimensions by plan type for both BSO and ASO:

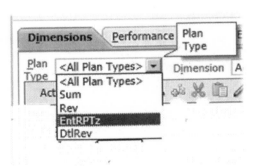

This filtering option is a great way to understand what dimensions, hierarchies and members will be built in each plan type.

Add dimensions and members to ASO plan types just have you done in the past, choosing the "Valid For Plan Type". Note a member can belong to both ASO and BSO plan types.

Dimensions

Edit Dimension Properties : FiscalYear

Dimension	FiscalYear
Description	
Alias Table	Default
Alias	
Valid for Plan Types	☑ Sum
	☑ Rev
	☐ DtlRev
	☑ DtlRev
Two Pass Calculation	☐
Apply Security	☐
Data Storage	Never Share
Display Option	Member Name

You can associate dimensions and members for ASO plan types just as you do for BSO plan types by checking the *Valid for Plan Type* check box:

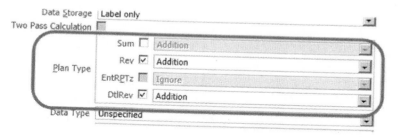

You can create dimensions that are only for an ASO plan type:

While not supported through the Planning web client, you can add MDX member formulas in EAS. You must tag the member with the HSP_UDF user defined attribute (UDA) so the formula will not be overwritten during a *Refresh*.

You can set the Hierarchy Type under Member properties.

ASO plan types support Smart Lists and Text data types. Make sure to set the Evaluation order for the plan type (just like in BSO):

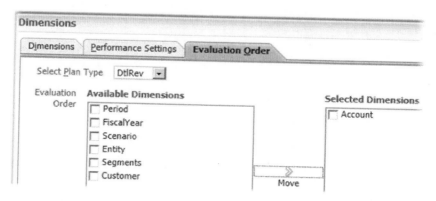

After you refresh to Essbase the ASO outline is updated with dimension and member information:

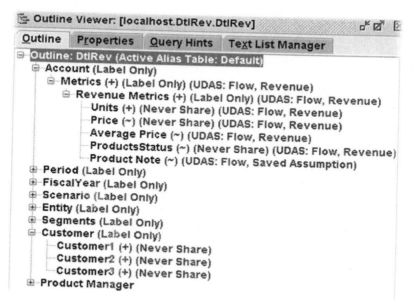

Input Data, Load Data, & Report

You load data to your ASO plan type just like the BSO plan type. The only requirement is that when loading to ASO plan types you must load to level zero members. You cannot load data to upper level members for ASO.

Once data is loaded or input, you can see the impact in data forms or retrieve and analyze data via a Smart View Planning connection or Financial Reporting documents that use the Planning ADM driver. ASO cubes require no further calculation steps.

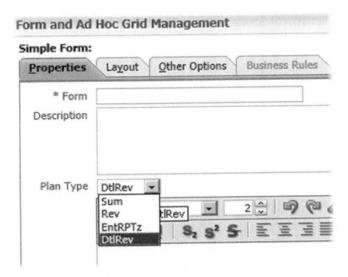

Considerations for ASO Plan Types

- ASO plan types are not supported using EPMA
- No business rule support for ASO databases
- No member formula support for ASO databases
- Planning does not generate XREFs on ASO databases
- Because Planning does not require all base dimensions on an ASO database, approvals may not apply to the ASO database if an approvals dimension is missing; If this is the case, normal security would apply
- Dynamic time series members are not supported for ASO plan types
- ^ Never consolidation tag is not supported for ASO plan types
- Solve order is not supported in the initial release; patch coming soon
- Solve order is supported in the cloud
- Must have ASO license

- Creating and refreshing security filters is not supported for ASO databases
  - This means you cannot retrieve data from ASO databases from a third party source (Smart View Essbase connection)
  - You can only retrieve data through Planning either directly or, for Financial Reporting, through the Planning ADM driver

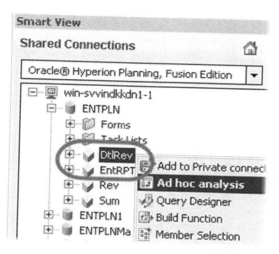

MAP TO REPORTING FEATURE

A new integration feature that was introduced in version 11.1.2 allows administrators to easily sync Planning data to an ASO reporting database. You can map Planning data to an Essbase reporting application, dimension to dimension or smart list to dimension. Both Block Storage Option (BSO) and Aggregate Storage Option (ASO) are supported in the mapping feature. The Smart List to dimension mapping feature now allows to users to slice and dice and report subtotals by Smart List in a reporting database. You can easily specify a subset of data to be pushed to the reporting application on demand or scheduled in batch via the command line utility.

To run this administrator only "push data" feature, you must first set up the mapping. The target Essbase ASO reporting database must exist. In 11.1.2.2 you create this application in Essbase Administration Services using the tools for Essbase only cubes (for more information on creating a Essbase reporting cube, check out our *Look Smarter Than You Are with Essbase: An Administrator's Guide*). In 11.1.2.3 you can also create the ASO application and database from the Planning user interface.

Try to keep member names and dimension names in sync between the Planning application and the reporting database as much as possible. This will make the mapping definition much easier.

Create a Mapping

Once the target Essbase database is in place, you'll create the mapping. To follow along with these steps, you'll need to create your own ASO reporting database.

1. Within the Planning application, select *Administration >> Map Reporting Application*.
2. Give the mapping a name (e.g. Current Budget Push) and description.
3. Select the source plan type.
4. Select the target database. (If you need to specify a different reporting Essbase server, choose the Add Server option.)
5. Select *Next*.

If the dimension names are the same between the source and target databases, the mappings will automatically match up. By default the members selected will be IDescendants (*DimensionName*). You can further refine the selected members by using the Member Selection. For example, you just want to map the Budget Scenario for the Budget Year. You can update the member selection to choose the desired slice of data to push from Planning to the reporting database. If you are pushing data to an ASO database, you can only map to level zero members in the target database.

At this point you may choose to map a Smart List in Planning to a Dimension in the Essbase reporting application.

6. Change the Mapping Type to *Smart List to Dimension*.
7. Select the desired Smart List and dimension.
8. Click *Next* once the members have been mapped.
9. In the POV section, define any point of view members for the mapping (single member for a dimension that has not been mapped in the Planning application or the reporting application).

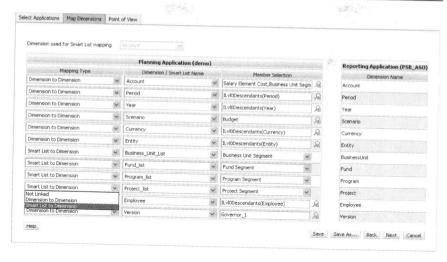

10. Click *Save* to save the mapping.

Push Data

To push data from the BSO source to the reporting target,
1. Within the Planning application, select *Administration >> Map Reporting Application.*
2. Choose the saved mapping definition on the Reporting Application Mapping page.
3. Select *Push data.*
4. Choose the desired option
   a. *Clear data on destination and push data* which clears any data for the slice before loading the current data
   b. *Push data* which will load the data to the target database, overwriting cells with the current data
5. Click *OK.*

Push Data with a Utility

You may also use a utility to push data. This is helpful when data pushes take a while or you want to run the process in off hours. The PushData utility is installed in the planning1 directory and uses the following syntax:

```
PushData [-f:passwordFile]  /U:username
/A:sourceApplication /
M:applicationMapping [/C]
```

Tip! The Map Planning Application to Reporting applications feature does not support ASO databases with duplicate members enabled, user variables, attribute dimensions, attribute member selections.

DIMENSION DESIGN

In general, good Planning dimension design follows the same principles as good Essbase dimension design. A bad Essbase application doesn't get any better when you put Planning on top (and frequently, it will just make it worse). Likewise, a bad Planning application will tend to make a bad Essbase application since, as we know, Planning uses Essbase as its underlying database. Below are some design tips that in general are applicable to both Essbase and Planning.

Minimize the number of dimensions for BSO Plan Types

Analyze your requirements very carefully and try to design applications with only the dimensions that are required for Planning. Fewer dimensions generate smaller databases resulting in better performance and less complexity for end users to find their data. Build only those dimensions that you need for the budgeting and planning process.

The general rule for the number of dimensions in a Planning BSO plan type is 6-9 dimensions. Make every one of them count! You will want to avoid dimensions that do not offer descriptive data points. This will help reduce complexity and size of database. Remember that adding a dimension increases the size and complexity of a database *exponentially*, not arithmetically. Also, adding dimensions makes your use form design and your user form experience decidedly more difficult.

Are you planning by more than 3 very sparse dimensions for a single BSO plan type? This answer should be NO. If you answered yes, then you need to seriously consider your design and the potential pitfalls that are possible. A colleague recently reviewed an Essbase cube that included dimensions for cost center, profit center, company coding structure, and legal entity. While there are many issues with this, we'll point out the two most important. The structure was too complicated and too detailed for end users to comprehend and articulate. Even if they could comprehend and navigate their way through the cube at this granular level, the performance in the application was an absolute show stopper.

"Just say no!" when your design committee says they *have* to plan by all of these dimensions. Or if on 11.1.2.3, you might respond "Just say ASO!" For BSO plan types, combine dimensions, split into different plan types, or if at all possible, change your planning process so it's not so complex to keep the number of dimensions low.

Note! Planning should not be done to the same level as actuals. Your actual data will almost always be more granular than the level at which you plan, so a good best practice is to be planning at a summarized level.

Smart Lists instead of Dimensions

Smart Lists are used to control the text a user can select in a data cell and are good alternative to adding extra dimensions to Planning. The administrator predefines a list of text values for users to review and input. Users may not type in the cell of a Smart List member. The sample below illustrates how you can classify Travel Expense line items into a "Travel Category" using a Smart List instead of using an attribute or a stored dimension of "Travel Category":

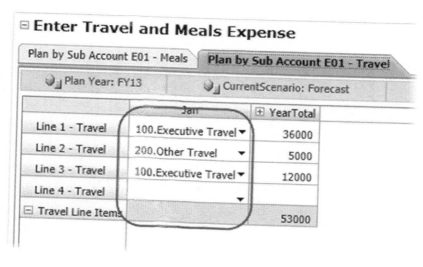

You can often create a data element as a smart list in a Planning application in place of a regular dimension (which helps with performance and database size). In the example noted earlier in the chapter, a requirement dictated dimensions for sub account, cost center, profit center, company coding structure, and legal entity. A better design might be to create Smart Lists for sub account, profit center, company code, and legal entity in the Planning application and then map the Smart Lists to dimensions in an ASO reporting database using the *Map to Reporting* feature:

Because the Smart List is a data cell, it can change over time. You cannot subtotal by a Smart List value in Planning but you can in an ASO reporting database if you map the Planning Smart List to an ASO dimension.

Dimension Order for BSO Plan Type

Here is another tuning tip related to the order of dimensions within a BSO outline. Dimension ordering within BSO outlines is critical to your overall Essbase performance. You will want to test different iterations of dimension orders to determine the optimal structure. Historically, outlines were ordered from largest dense to smallest dense and then smallest sparse to largest sparse (sometimes called the "hourglass" format). This works well when parallel calculation is not utilized. Since Essbase 6.5, though, everyone is using parallel calculation, so an improved method for ordering the dimensions was created.

First a few definitions:

Dense dimensions are the dimensions that define the internal structure of the data block. They should reside at the top of the outline.

Aggregating Sparse dimensions are dimensions that will be calculated to create new parent values. These dimensions should reside directly below the last Dense dimension in the outline. Placing these dimensions as the first Sparse dimensions positions them to be the first dimensions included in the calculator cache. This gives them an ideal location within the database for optimized calculation performance.

Non-Aggregating Sparse dimensions are dimensions that organize the data into logical slices. Examples include Scenario, Year or Version. It is not crucial for these dimensions to be included in the calculator cache because their members are typically isolated in FIX statements.

With this in mind, try the following guidelines to create an optimal outline order (sometimes called an "hourglass on a stick" which seems kinda silly, to be honest, 'cause we've never seen anyone put an hourglass on a stick):

1. Time (assuming it's a dense dimension)
2. Densest Dense Dimensions
3. Least Dense Dimensions
4. Smallest Aggregating Sparse Dimensions
5. Largest Aggregating Sparse Dimensions
6. Non-aggregating Sparse Dimensions

Example – An Employee Analysis Database:

Dimension	Type-Stored Member Count	Density After Calc	Density After Load	Data Points Created
Time Periods	D – 21	85%	85%	-
Accounts	D – 94	3 %	2%	-
Scenarios	AS – 9	22%	11%	199
Job Code	AS – 1,524	.56%	.23%	853
Organization	AS – 2,304	.34%	.09%	783
Versions	NAS – 7	19%	19%	-
Years	NAS – 7	14%	14%	-

D=Dense, AS=Aggregating Sparse, NAS=Non-Aggregating Sparse

Outlines can be ordered based on dimension stored member count or on dimension density. Ordering by stored member count is the easy option but may not be as accurate as ordering by dimension density. In the example above, the optimized outline should follow this order (assuming we order the outline based on dimension density and our other rule, Time first and then Accounts):

Original Dimension Order (Typical Hourglass)	Optimized Dimension Order (Modified Hourglass)
Accounts (D)	Time Periods (D)
Time Periods (D)	Accounts (D)
Years	Job Code (AS)
Versions	Organization (AS)
Scenarios	Years (NAS)
Job Code	Versions (NAS)
Organization	Scenarios (NAS)
Employee Status (Attr Dim)	Employee Status (Attr Dim)
Fund Group (Attr Dim)	Fund Group (Attr Dim)

Not to contradict what we just said, but ordering the sparse dimensions by density is also an oversimplification (like ordering in terms of dimension size is). In truth, we'd want the sparse dimensions ordered by the ratio of children-to-parents (lowest ratio to highest ratio). So let's say we had two sparse dimensions. "Stores" had 100 children for each parent member, on average. "Products" had 10 children for each parent member. Products would come second even if it was a smaller dimension because we want to be generating parent blocks as slowly as possible during bulk aggregations.

Of course, there are many exceptions to dimension ordering. Test iterations of dense and sparse to figure out the optimal settings for your application. For example, one customer found faster retrieval times with "Store" as dense and "Account" as sparse. Their batch calculation that was run nightly took about an hour which was acceptable because it processed after hours.

It has been noted recently that the dense dimension ordering is not as important as it once was. This is mostly because Essbase will do some internal optimization of the dense dimension order even if you can't see it directly. If you want to see what Essbase is really doing with your dense dimensions, do a column export of your database and see which dimension Essbase is putting across the columns. Internally, this is the dimension Essbase is putting first when storing the data.

Stored versus Dynamic versus Multiple Hierarchies for ASO Plan Types

Which dimensions and hierarchies should be *Stored* versus *Dynamic* versus *Enabled for multiple hierarchies* in an ASO database? Does it matter? Yes! If you tagged every dimension dynamic, you would probably have a very slow database. Tag dimensions and hierarchies as *Stored* whenever possible. Definitely use stored hierarchies for your really big dimensions (the ones with thousands and millions of members). Remember stored dimensions will perform a straight aggregation of members. Only the plus consolidation tag is allowed and no member formulas. Also note dimensions tagged "Accounts" cannot be stored.

Use the *Dynamic* hierarchy setting for dimensions and hierarchies that need to be calculated and not aggregated. Dynamic hierarchies allow multiple consolidation symbols and member formulas written in MDX. All calculations are performed at retrieval time and are not part of any aggregate view selection.

Dimensions enabled for multi-hierarchy can contain hierarchies that are either *Stored* or *Dynamic*. Multi-hierarchy enabled dimensions allow you to build alternate rollups with shared members. Non-shared members must occur in the outline before the shared members. The first hierarchy in a multi-hierarchy enabled dimension cannot contain shared members. By enabling multiple hierarchies, you can effectively use stored members and dynamic calculated members when needed.

Metadata Maintenance by the End User

As the Planning administrator, you are in charge of maintaining dimensions, member names and aliases. If a new user needs to request a new "product", you have to add it to the Planning application and refresh before the user can input their plans. Not that efficient, right? Yes, which is why Oracle added the ability for users to add new members to Planning applications for PFP, Capex and WFP starting in 11.1.2.3 (check out the What's New appendix for more information on this feature).

Since "new members on the fly" are not available for regular Planning applications, how do you build this functionality yourself? Is that possible? Sort of... using a dimension with a generic list of members and a free form text measure. The design would work as follows:

1. Under the Product dimension, create a rollup called "New Products".
2. Create children under products called "P01" – "P25" with the storage as *Never Share*.
3. Create a text measure under accounts called "New Product".
4. Create a data form that allows users to input the product name in the "New Product" text measure. Also add the appropriate accounts for users to enter the plan numbers for the new product:

		Jan		Jan		Feb		Mar	
	New Product	Product Category	Units	Price	Units	Price	Units	Price	
P01	interRelevator	Home System ▼	8.33	5000	8.33	5000	8.33	5000
P02	interRelectrode		50	41.67	50	41.67	50	
P03	adding machine	Row P04, Column Jan New Product	5	83.33	5	83.33	5	
P04		▼						
P05		▼						

Forms and Ad Hoc Grids

⊟ **Add New Products**

DynEntity: E01_101_1130

You've now placed some of the metadata maintenance into the hands of users! Now once the plans are approved, you can run some SQL in the back end to extract this data and reload the approved new products back into the application as dimension members. This is considered even too advanced for this book, but you SQL gurus in the audience can probably figure it out.

Note!

The Hyperion Planning 11.1.2.3 modules (PFP, WFP, Capex, and PSB) support the ability for end users to add new member names on the fly in all dimensions except Period and Year.

Avoid Repetition in Dimensions

Repeating members may indicate a need to split dimensions, thereby reducing redundancy. In the example below, we repeat FTE, Average Hourly Rate (AHR), and Expense dollars for every payroll account. A better design would be to split the metrics from the Accounts dimension.

Before: 1 Dimension (Payroll):

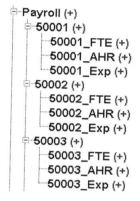

After: 2 Dimensions (Payroll and Metric):

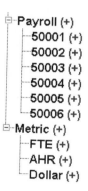

Although this rule might seem to contradict the first tip in this section about minimizing the number of dimensions, this one is really about making sure you have the *right* number of dimensions given a specified analytical requirement. Repeating members can become awkward for end-users and causes a potential maintenance nightmare for administrators.

However in the example above, if only 6 accounts are repeated, a single dimension with the repeated members will result in a much smaller database. If a large number of members are repeated, consider this "split the dimension" design practice.

Avoid Interdimensional Irrelevance

Interdimensional irrelevance is when many members of a dimension are irrelevant across other dimensions. For example, Product and Customer dimensions will probably not be needed in an employee salary planning database. Another example would be an Asset Category dimension placed in a product sales planning database.

The important point here is not to try to meet everyone's requirements in a single database. Split databases so that applications have only relevant dimensions. Your users will thank you later.

Consistent Terminology

For consistency and ease of use, it is important to keep dimensionality between your Planning applications and your reporting applications (such as stand-alone Essbase cubes) the same. Hyperion Planning requires the following:

- Separate Fiscal Year dimension
- Separate Time Periods dimension
- Scenario dimension (used for members like Actual, Budget, and Forecast)
- Version dimension (used for members like Working, Final, What-if, Sandbox)

If at all possible, keep the dimension names consistent across your Planning and reporting applications. For example, don't name a dimension in your reporting application "Version" and then put members like "Actual" or "Budget" in that dimension. This will only confuse your end users.

Use Substitution Variables

Substitution variables are global placeholders for values that change regularly, such as Current Month (&CurMth) and Current Year (&CurYr). You just need to update the value in one place and all objects using the substitution variable will take the new value. Substitution variables can be used in most Planning and Essbase items including: Data forms, member formulas, business rules, Essbase load rules and reports. The picture below shows a web form definition set to use substitution variables for the year dimension.

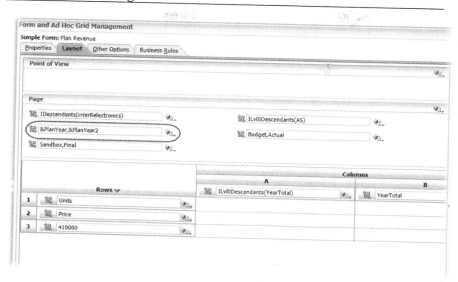

When a user opens the form, the form will take the values from the substitution variable.

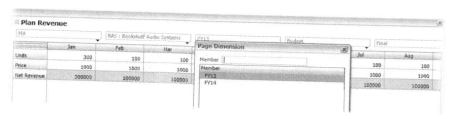

Substitution Variables are set in Planning starting with version 11.1.2.2 (in earlier versions, substitution variables were created and managed in EAS for Planning applications). Under earlier versions, the substitution values are retrieved by Planning from Essbase every 5 minutes, but you can change the update frequency in the Planning properties file HspJSHome.properties (the property is SUBST_VAR_CACHE_LIFETIME).

When selecting substitution variables in a Planning data form definition, make sure the variable matches the dimension you are trying to set. For example, if you select a substitution variable for the current month and then assign it to the year dimension, the form will error.

DIMENSION TYPE CONSIDERATIONS

Dimension Assigned as "Accounts"

Which dimension should be tagged the "Accounts" dimension? The Accounts dimension could be called many different names in your application; "Measures", "Metrics", etc. The accounts dimension typically contains the chart of accounts, statistics, and measures for the plan type and they will differ based on the type of application. Financial reporting applications will contain income statement, balance sheet, and cash flow accounts. Inventory applications will have beginning inventory, ending inventory, additions, returns, adjustments. Sales planning applications will have metrics for sales dollars, units sold, and average sales price. Workforce applications will have members called bonus, unemployment insurance, sick days, vacation days, and years of employment.

The important consideration for the dimension tagged "Account" is the built in intelligence that goes along with this assignment. The dimension tagged "Account" will have time balance intelligence (you can set the data cells to be *Time Balance Average* or *Time Balance Last)*. You can also set expense reporting tags for the proper calculation of variances.

Dimension Assigned as "Time"

The dimension tagged "Time" is typically the dimension containing the months, quarters, or custom periods for Planning. The "Time" dimension works in conjunction with the dimension tagged "Accounts" for *Time Balance* assignments.

Dimension Assigned as "Entity"

The dimension assigned as Entity is part of the Planning Unit and will be used in the "rollup" in Approvals. It is also assigned currencies if you use the out of the box multi-currency functionality (which we recommend that 90%+ of the time you *do not* use).

DESIGN BEST PRACTICES APPLIED

To pull together these concepts, let's walk through an example. The CFO has requested to budget travel and meals by sub account. The sub accounts used across the company are not standard: different departments may use different sub accounts. Users should be able to report Actual vs. Budget by Sub Account. Penny does not want to add another dimension called "Sub Account" to the BSO plan type because this will negatively impact performance. So what should Penny do?

Plan Detail Using Smart Lists

The answer might be...Implement a Planning cube that allows users to plan by Sub Account via a Smart List and an Essbase ASO reporting cube to report actual vs. budget by Sub Account. (Actuals by Sub Account would not exist in Planning).

The high level implementation steps are:
1. Build a Smart List called Sub Account.
2. Populate the Smart List using the Outline Load utility.
3. Create an account member called "Sub Account".
4. Create an "Line Item" dimension with a generic list of line item members.
5. Create data form(s) for input.
6. Create a business rule to spread Smart List value to periods (optional but saves time for the user).
7. Create a target ASO reporting cube with Sub Account as a dimension
    o For 11.1.2.2, a quick way to jump start the ASO building process is to use the EAS ASO Outline Conversion Wizard based on the Planning outline
    o For 11.1.2.3, use the Planning Plan Type Editor to create an ASO plan type
8. Setup actual data loads to the ASO reporting cube by Sub Account.
9. Create a mapping(s) between Planning and the ASO reporting cube to push Plan data by Smart List to Dimension for Sub Account.

Production steps:
10. Set up automated dimension update processes for both Planning and Essbase ASO cube.
    o For 11.1.2.2, this will be 2 step process for Planning and separate reporting database
    o For 11.1.2.3, this is a one step process through the Planning application
11. Setup automated data load processes for Planning and Essbase ASO cube.
12. Set up automation scripts to update/maintain the Sub Account Smart List (using Outline Load Utility).

13. Set up an automation script to push data from Planning to ASO cube using the defined mappings.

To see the implementation steps in more detail,

1. Build a Smart List called Sub Account (we called ours "E01SubAcct":

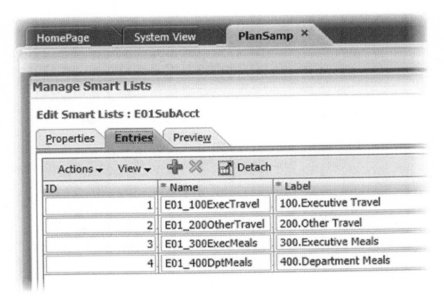

Tip!

When defining Smart List IDs, they can't start with a number; only an underscore or a letter. Essbase member name can't start with an _. So you need to add an alpha prefix to any Smart List numeric value (e.g. "100" might be "E01_100").

2. If necessary, populate the Smart List using the Outline Load utility, a faster way to populate Smart List entries.

3. Create an account member called "Sub Account":

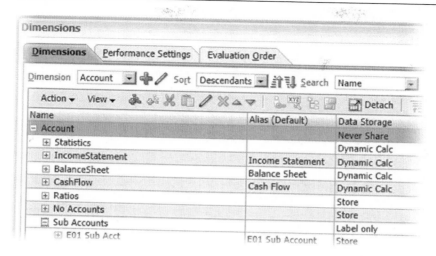

4. Create an "Line Item" dimension with a generic list of line item members:

Name	Alias (Default)	Data Storage
⊟ Line Items	Total Lines	Dynamic Calc
⊟ Travel Line Items		Dynamic Calc
⊞ Lineitem01	Line 1 - Travel	Store
⊞ LineItem02	Line 2 - Travel	Store
⊞ LineItem03	Line 3 - Travel	Store
⊞ LineItem04	Line 4 - Travel	Store
⊟ Meals Line Items		Dynamic Calc
⊞ LineItem10	Line Item 1 - Meals	Store
⊞ LineItem11	Line Item 2 - Meals	Store
⊞ LineItem12	Line Item 3 - Meals	Store
⊞ LineItem4	Line Item 4 - Meals	Store
⊞ LineItem15	Line Item 5 - Meals	Store

Make sure the evaluation order is set for Smart Lists:

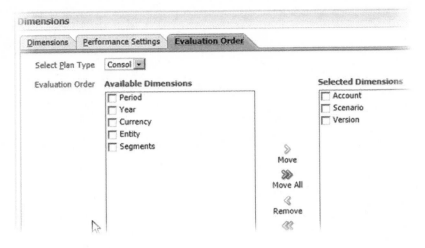

5. Create data form(s) for input.

We design the form to allow users to input the Smart List selection for Sub Account into "Jan". Later we will create a business rule that will populate the remaining values based on the "Jan" value. Notice that account is part of the columns with one segment for the Sub Account Smart List and a second column for the Account number "Meals":

The resulting data form looks as follows for end users:

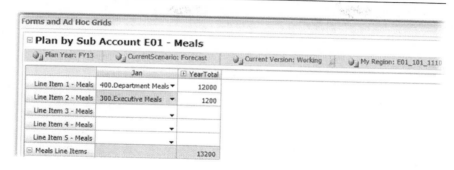

We'd then repeat the process and create a data form for planning Travel expense by sub account:

Plan by Sub Account E01 - Travel

		Jan	YearTotal
Line 1 - Travel	100.Executive Travel ▼	36000	
Line 2 - Travel	200.Other Travel ▼	5000	
Line 3 - Travel	100.Executive Travel ▼	12000	
Line 4 - Travel	▼		
⊟ Travel Line Items			53000

A design best practice would to combine these two simple forms into one composite form with a summary simple form at the bottom (more on this in the next chapter):

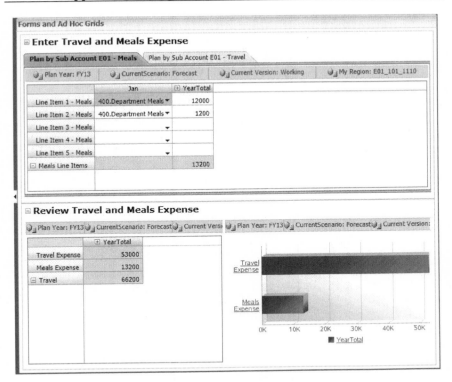

Next for Smart list data to push correctly to the Essbase ASO reporting cube, Smart List values must be by captured for each month. Unfortunately time spreading does not work for Smart Lists so users must enter Smart List values by month. Or a workaround might be to have users put Smart List values on BegBalance (the opening period in the Time Periods dimension). Then create a business rule that runs behind the scenes to copy Smart List values from BegBalance to all the months.

    6.   Create a business rule to spread Smart List value to periods (optional but saves time for the user):

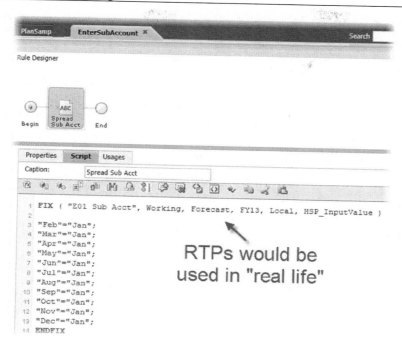

7. In 11.1.2.2, create a standalone Essbase target ASO reporting cube with Sub Account as a dimension or in 11.1.2.3, add an ASO plan type to the application.

If you created the ASO cube from the Planning outline, you would remove the "Element/Line Item" dimension from the ASO cube. You would add a new dimension called "Sub Account" that had the list of level zero members that matched the Smart List in Planning (in our example, we added the sub account members to the dimension "Segments"):

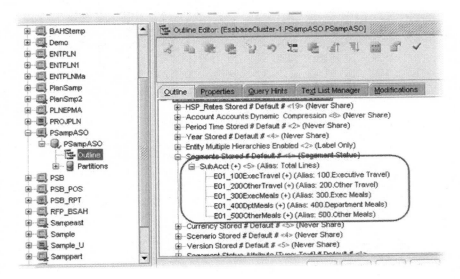

8. Create a mapping(s) between Planning and the ASO reporting cube to push Plan data by Smart List to Dimension for Sub Account.

The first step is to define the source and target database information:

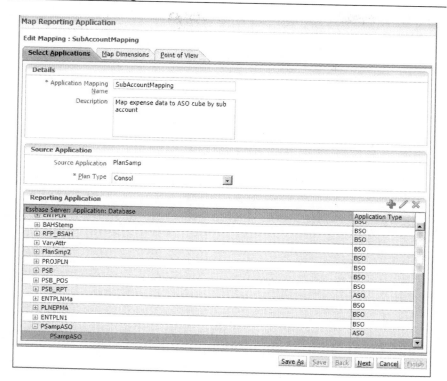

Next you define the dimension to dimension mappings or the Smart List to dimension mappings. In our case, we are mapping the E01SubAcct Smart List to the Segments dimension in the ASO reporting cube (where the sub account members exist):

We focused this mapping to only push a specific set of accounts, entities, periods, version, scenario, etc. You will likely have more than one push data mapping defined for your Planning application.

Tip! Only push level zero data to Essbase ASO cubes (data may only be loaded to level zero members and any extra data is just taking up loading time).

Once the mapping is defined, you can execute the data push (either clearing and pushing data or just pushing).

Careful! Test the mapping definitions in a development environment to make sure you don't accidently clear or overwrite unintended data.

The data is pushed to the Essbase ASO reporting cube, taking the data by Smart List in Planning and transforming it to an ASO dimension.

	A	B	C	D	E	F	G	H
			HSP_InputValue	MA	FY13	Local	Forecast	Working
1			YearTotal					
2								
3	Travel Expense	100.Executive Travel	48000					
4		200.Other Travel	5000					
5		300.Exec Meals	#Missing					
6		400.Department Meals	#Missing					
7		500.Other Meals	#Missing					
8		Total Lines	53000					
9	Meals Expense	100.Executive Travel	#Missing					
10		200.Other Travel	#Missing					
11		300.Exec Meals	#Missing					
12		400.Department Meals	13200					
13		500.Other Meals	#Missing					
14		Total Lines	13200					
15	Travel	100.Executive Travel	48000					
16		200.Other Travel	5000					
17		300.Exec Meals	#Missing					
18		400.Department Meals	13200					
19		500.Other Meals	#Missing					
20		Total Lines	66200					

Smart View
Shared Connections
Oracle® Essbase
- EssbaseCluster-1
  - ASOsamp
  - BAHStemp
  - Demo
  - ENTPLN
  - ENTPLN1
  - ENTPLNMa
  - PlanSamp
    - Consol
  - PlanSmp2
  - PLNEPMA
  - PROJPLN
  - PSampASO
    - PSampASO
  - PSB
  - PSB_POS
  - PSB_RPT
  - RFP_BSAH
  - Sampeast
- Add to Private connections
- Ad hoc analysis

Remember you will load actual data directly to the ASO reporting cube by Sub Account and now that you have pushed plan data to the same application, users can report actual vs. budget by sub account side by side.

This illustration worked well for a simple breakdown of sub account planning for a handful of accounts. What if you need to plan by sub account for a large number of accounts (e.g. 1000 accounts)? You wouldn't want to create a 1000 different data forms (one for each account member)! In this case, you may be forced to add one more additional dimension, "Element" (or maybe you can leverage an existing other dimension):

The Element dimension or section would contain at least 2 members – one that is associated with the Smart List and one that is for the "data" or facts (the Smart List is no longer associated with the account member; it is associated with the Element member):

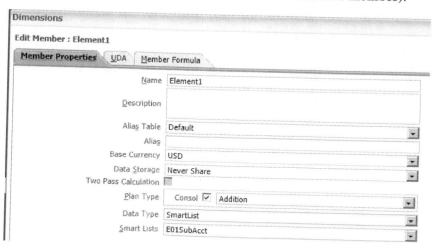

By adding Element, you can now put the account members in the rows with the line items and place the Element Smart List member and Element "Amount" member in the columns:

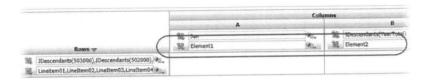

The rest of the data form definition is similar to the first examples:

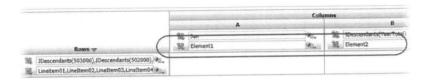

You can hide the Element dimension from users if the concept is confusing for them. The resulting form allows for the planning by sub account for multiple accounts:

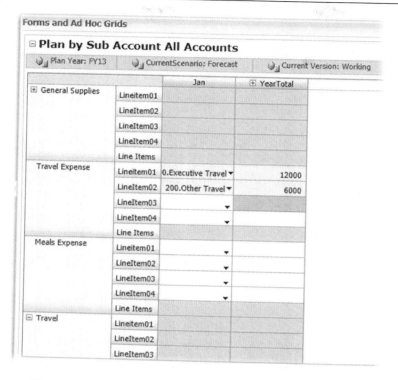

The only requirement we haven't addressed: the sub accounts may vary across departments. So one way to address this requirement is to create unique Smart Lists for each department (e.g. two Smart Lists for two departments "E01" and "E02"):

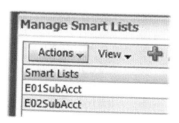

Associate the department Smart List to a departmental "Element" member (e.g. "E01_Element", "E02_Element"):

Add Sibling : Entity : E01_Element

Name	E02_Element
Description	
Alias Table	Default
Alias	
Base Currency	USD
Data Storage	Never Share
Two Pass Calculation	
Plan Type	Consol ☑ Never
Data Type	SmartList
Smart Lists	<None>
	<None>
	E01SubAcct
	E02SubAcct

Create individual department data form that selects the departmental "Element" member:

Now users see just the sub accounts that are applicable for their department.

You would also have to create a "Push to Essbase" mapping for each Smart List.

While this requires maintenance of multiple forms and Smart Lists, it beats the negative impact of adding a Sub Account dimension to the BSO plan type. This creative use of Smart Lists is also helpful even in version 11.1.2.3 when you need to plan at a more detailed level and still use Calculation Manager for more complex business rules and calculations.

Plan Detail using an ASO Plan Type

If Penny were on version 11.1.2.3, life gets a little simpler. She could just create an ASO plan type with the sub account dimension (assuming she doesn't require complex business rules and calc scripts). Benefits include reporting actuals and budget side by side in the ASO plan type, immediate rollup of budget at upper levels. The tricky part of the CFO's requirement, "sub accounts used across the company are not standard: different departments may use different sub accounts", is figuring out the best data form design for end user data entry. But let's see if we can do that!

Assuming you have the ENTPLN application created and you are on version 11.1.2.3, follow along as we add an ASO plan type.

1. Within the ENTPLN application, select *Administration >> Manage >> Plan Types* to access the Plan Type Editor:

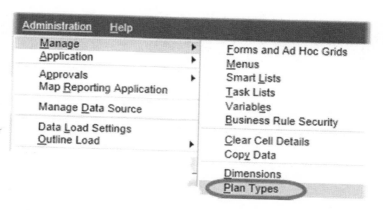

The Plan Type Editor displays:

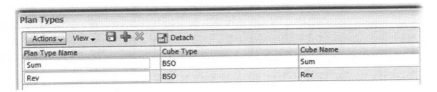

2. Select *Actions>>Add Plan Type*:

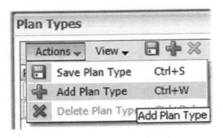

3. Enter the *Plan Type Name*: "Travel"
4. Choose *ASO* for *Cube type*:
5. Enter *Cube Name:* "Travel"
6. Enter *Essbase Application* name: "Travel":

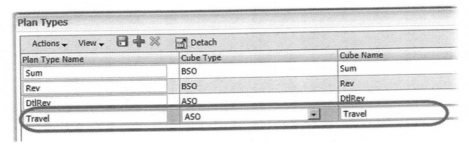

7. Click *Save*.
8. Select *Administration >> Manage >> Refresh Database* to create the ASO application and database in Essbase. **Don't choose *Create Database*!**

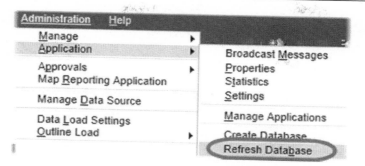

9. Navigate to the Dimension Editor.
10. Select the Account dimension member and click *Edit*.
11. Check the *Valid for Plan Type* option for the new *Travel* plan type:

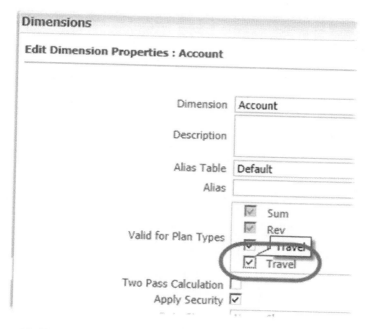

12. Repeat step 11, checking *Travel* for Valid for Plan Type for the following members in Account:
    ○ IncomeStatment, Ignore
    ○ 5000: Total Expenses, Addition
    ○ Department Expenses, Addition
    ○ Meals Expense, Addition
    ○ Travel Expense, Addition

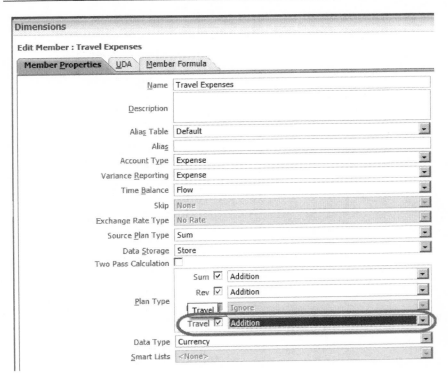

13. Repeat step 11, checking *Travel* for Valid for Plan Type for the following members for Entity:
    - Entity
    - interRelectronics, Addition
    - E05, Addition
    - E01_101, Addition
    - 301_101_2000, Adding
    - E01_101_2200, Addition
    - E01_101_2210, Addition
    - E01_101_2220, Addition
    - E01_101_2230, Addition

14. Repeat step 11, checking *Travel* for Valid for Plan Type for these remaining dimensions:
    - Fiscal Year
    - Period
    - Scenario
    - Version

15. Click the + icon to create a new dimension:

16. Create a new dimension called "SubAccount":

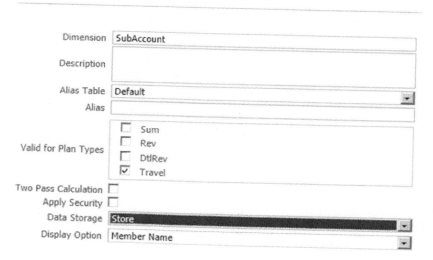

17. Make sure to only select *Valid for Plan Type*: "Travel".
18. Click *Save*.
19. Click OK to add the new custom defined dimension.
20. Add the following members to the SubAccount dimension:

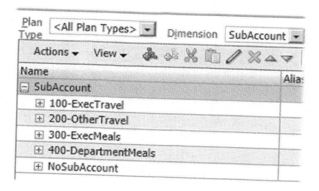

21. Select *Travel* from the Plan Type filter in the Dimension editor:

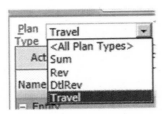

22. Review the members that are bound to the *Travel* plan type for the Entity dimension:

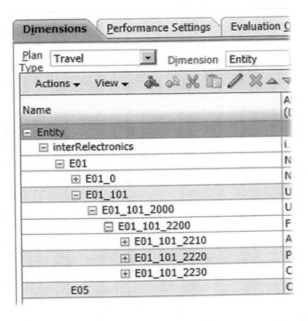

23. Review the members that are bound to the *Travel* plan type for the Account dimension:

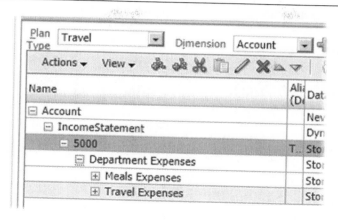

24. Review the members that are bound to this plan type for the remaining dimensions.
25. Select *Administration >> Manage >> Refresh Database* to create the ASO application and database in Essbase.

The ASO plan type is created in Essbase and ready for use!

Outline: Travel (Active Alias Table: Default)
⊕ **Account (Label Only)**
⊕ **Period (Label Only)**
⊕ **FiscalYear (Label Only)**
⊕ **Scenario (Label Only)**
⊕ **Version (Label Only)**
⊟ **Entity (Label Only)**
   ⊟ **interRelectronics (+) (Alias: interRelectronics, Inc.)**
      ⊟ **E01 (+) (Alias: North America)**
         E01_0 (+) (Alias: North America Corporate)
        ⊕ **E01_101 (+) (Alias: USA)**
        E05 (+) (Alias: Corporate HQ)
⊟ **SubAccount (Label Only)**
   100-ExecTravel (+) (Never Share)
   200-OtherTravel (+) (Never Share)
   300-ExecMeals (+) (Never Share)
   400-DepartmentMeals (+) (Never Share)

26. Create a simple data form with the ASO plan type as the source:

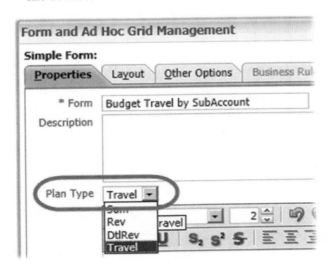

27. The layout should look as follows:

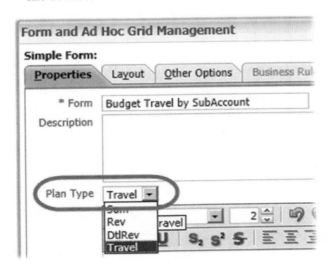

28. Hide the Scenario dimension:

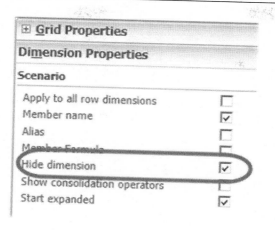

29. Save the data form.
30. Eddie can now plan travel by sub account:

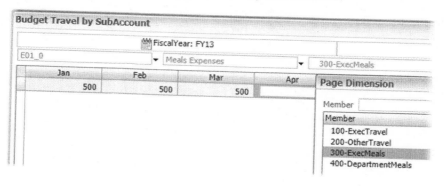

This layout meets the requirement of allowing users to plan for different subaccounts for different departments. However this design doesn't allow filtering of subaccounts by account (or department). End users could possibly choose invalid intersections to input data.

Could you add the subaccounts to the Account dimension but only have the subaccounts valid for the Travel plan type? Yes, you can!

1. Navigate to the Account dimension in the Dimension editor.
2. Add a child, "Meals-100", to Meals Expense that is applicable for Travel plan type only (accept default values for other member properties):

Dimensions

Add Child : Account : Meals Expenses

Member Properties | UDA | Member Formula

Name	Meals-100
Description	
Alias Table	Default
Alias	
Account Type	Expense
Variance Reporting	Expense
Time Balance	Flow
Skip	None
Exchange Rate Type	No Rate
Source Plan Type	Travel
Data Storage	Store
Two Pass Calculation	☐

Plan Type:

Sum	☐	Addition
Rev	☐	Addition
DtlRev	☐	Addition
Travel	☑	Addition

Data Type | Currency

3. Add a child, "Meals-200", to Meals Expense that is applicable for *Travel* plan type only
4. Add a child, "Exec-300", to Travel Expense that is applicable for *Travel* plan type only
5. Add a child, "Dpt-400", to Travel Expense that is applicable for *Travel* plan type only
6. Refresh to Essbase.
7. Review the members that are bound to the *Travel* plan type for the Account dimension:

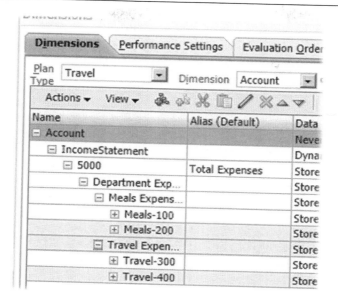

8. Review the members that are bound to the *Sum* plan type for the Account dimension and note the subaccount members do not display:

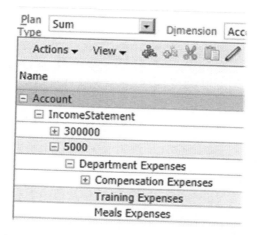

9. Create the following simple data form for the *Travel* ASO plan type:

Point of View	
"&UV_PlanYear"	"&UV_Version"
NoSubAccount	Budget

Page
IDescendants(interRelectronics)

		Columns
		A
		ILvl0Descendants(YearTotal),YearTotal
Rows ▽		
1	IDescendants(Department Expenses)	

Subaccounts are now grouped under their main account for data input:

Budget Travel by SubAccount v2

FiscalYear: FY13			Version: Sandbox

E01_0

	Jan	Feb	Mar	Apr
Meals-100				
Meals-200				
⊟ Meals Expenses				
Travel-300				
Travel-400				
⊟ Travel Expenses				
⊟ Department Expenses				

One consideration for this design (an any use of ASO for a plan type) is that XRefs are not supported. So if we needed to integrate travel subtotals to a summary cube, we'll likely have to use a report script / load rule or Essbase partitions.

Or maybe the CFO can reconsider the requirement to plan by sub account? Is it really value-add for the maintenance and complexity within the application with these different solutions?

OUT OF THE BOX MULTI-CURRENCY

Before we conclude our application design best practices chapter, we need to discuss one last topic: Planning's out of the box currency conversion design. You'll only find high level information on Planning's out-of-the-box functionality for multiple currencies in this book. Why, you may be asking. First, let's review what happens when you enable an application for multi-currency. Two additional dimensions are added to the Planning application, HSP_Rates and Currencies.

Two currency calc scripts are automatically created in the Manage Database process. The copy rates script copies the exchange rates to account members. The conversion script executes the currency conversion for accounts and entities at level zero members in the database.

With these dimensions, defined exchange rates, and currency calc scripts, you control the following:

- Which currencies an application uses
- How currencies display in reports and data forms
- How one currency is translated into another currency
- Whether a third currency (also known as a triangulation currency) is used for converting between currencies
- When currency conversions occur

While this currency conversion process certainly works, we recommend developing your own logic for currency conversion. Planning Currency Conversion has a series of problems (versus the custom XREF cube of rates method). First, two added dimensions (HSP_Rates and Currencies) are added where only one dimension is really required. Not only does this balloon the potential size of your cube, it makes it difficult for your users to do ad-hoc analysis against your Planning application.

Second, this design can be slow. The currency conversion scripts that Planning writes take much longer than custom scripts. For example, when interRel replaced the built-in HP currency conversion at a large global retail client with a custom solution, the calc times went down from over 100 hours to under 3 minutes. Yes, that's a 99.95% improvement.

Finally, the Planning multi-currency design makes it difficult to optimize your cube. The built-in method stores rates at the top member of all of your dimensions. Because of this, you can't dynamically calculate the top member of your dimensions (that would otherwise not require calculation). This can seriously affect aggregation time.

Now that said, have we ever used the built-in method? Sure. In two cases: 1) A customer had a very small application where it was going to run really quickly anyway and 2) a customer wanted to enter numbers in both local and reporting currencies in a single data form and then have the data form save action run the calculation between the currencies automatically.

In general, the drawbacks of the built-in multi-currency conversion may warrant a custom currency conversion solution unless you have a pretty small application.

You now see the fun and creativity that you'll face with designing Hyperion Planning applications. There isn't one right answer and you'll need to prototype and review design with key stakeholders to find your "best" design.

And we're not finished yet! On to Advanced Data Forms.

Scene 10:
Advanced Data Forms and Grids

Hyperion Planning data forms and ad hoc grids provide the user interface to present and collect data. Data forms use a standard structure and form to reduce end user error in data entry. Ad hoc grids provide greater flexibility for more advanced users to change the layout of dimensions in the data form and/or drill into more detailed data. Users can run related business rules from data forms, passing in members from data form selections to focus calculations.

As a data form designer you have a few main objectives:

- Make the planning process as easy as possible
- Keep it simple
- Keep them small
- Break the planning process up into easy to follow steps
  - Use all the Planning features (not just simple data forms) including right click menus, task lists, Business Rules and new ad hoc features

ROLE BASED NAVIGATION IN 11.1.2.2

In 11.1.2.2, the user interface itself is focused on role based navigation. When Planners log in they will see their Planning accordions on the left pane – e.g. Form Folders and My Task Lists:

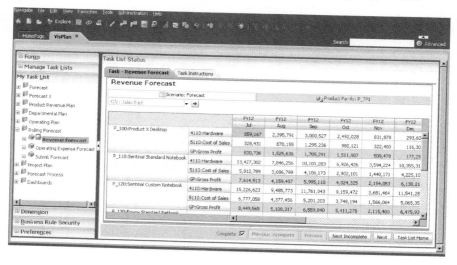

Navigation in Planning is driven by accordions on the left. The display of accordions is based on role of the user in Shared Services. Basic and Advanced modes no longer exist for Planning users in 11.1.2.2.

Bread crumb navigation allows for forms which have a right click menu navigation to other forms to be displayed using a navigation trail that is displayed above the form:

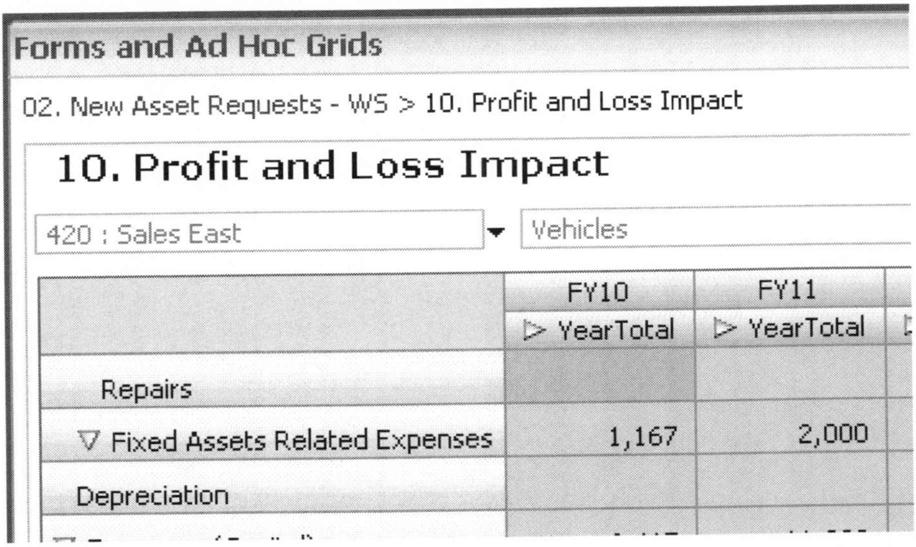

With the new role based navigation and data form designer, how you create data forms for end users will change. Let's learn how to change for the better with best practices in data form design for 11.1.2.2.

IDEAS FOR SIMPLE DATA FORMS

Don't Miss 11.1.2.1 and 11.1.2.2 Features

You must absolutely use the enhancements added over the last versions. Build validations into your data forms and/or add traffic lighting. Create calculated columns and formulas when necessary.

Design for Grid Spreader

If users are going to be using the Grid Spreader feature for Planning, make sure to include all of the members on the data form so the spreading will function properly. It's a good idea to use Descendants function and then do not check *Start Expanded* so users can enter plans at higher levels in the dimension and have the data spread properly.

Calculated Columns for Attributes

Attribute dimensions are dynamically calculated in the Planning application. It is usually the last dynamic calc that takes place. Why do you care? Many times variance calculations or ratios do not calculate properly on the data form. Now that you can build calculated columns / rows into data forms, you have a way to add a variance or ratio calculation into the data form that will calculate properly.

Custom Menus / Context Passing

Another handy set of tools that you can add to data forms are right-click menus. These objects provide users a quick way to launch related data forms, business rules, and URLs. They can even jump to workflow from a right-click menu.

Additionally you can have some of the menu items be context sensitive; dependent upon the dimension(s) listed on the data form. For example, you only wanted the "Add New Employee" menu item to show up when the user right clicked on the Employee dimension. If they right clicked on the Account or Product dimension, the right click menu item would not be relevant. Context passing allows us to build in this requirement. You can also pass the context dimension member from the source form to the target forms.

COMPOSITES, COMPOSITES, COMPOSITES

Gone are the days of navigating a long list of data form folders and simple data forms:

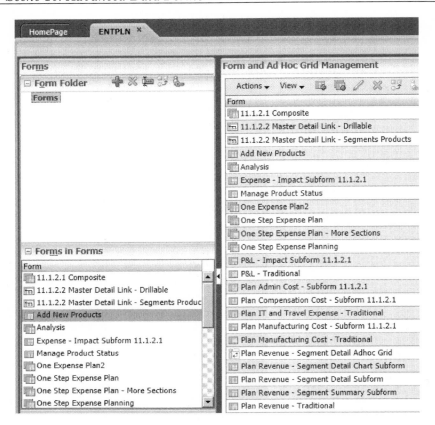

Today it is not just the "data forms" that you will build. You'll use a combination of task lists, data forms, right click menus and variables to make the process dynamic and easy to follow. In the example below, you see a right click menu with links to related data forms and business rules:

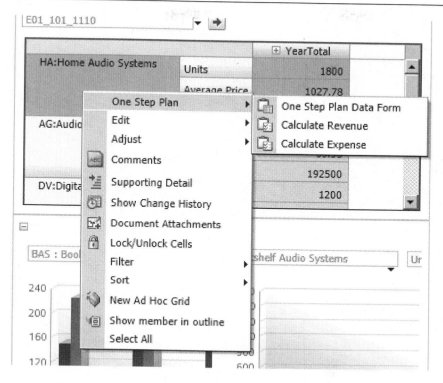

Users will likely use more composite forms than simple forms. Simple forms will be hidden from users in the list view, just showing users the forms necessary in the guided planning process. You'll try to get to a "one step" planning process that is a single composite form that contains multiple simple forms, right click menus to run relevant business rules or link to associated data forms and reports.

In this example you see one composite data form to plan expense accounts with a read only summary form in the top section and then a tabular view of planning input forms by end users. End users input factors or drivers and then save the data:

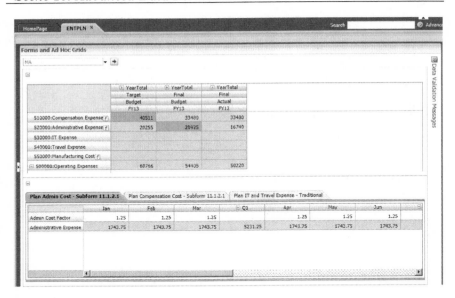

Tabular view of data forms within composite breaks data into manageable "chunks" which is easier for end users to navigate and also has performance benefits (smaller data sets are requested and returned).

You might want to create a composite form that lists the same simple data form twice, allowing users to use page drop downs to change member selections and compare plans:

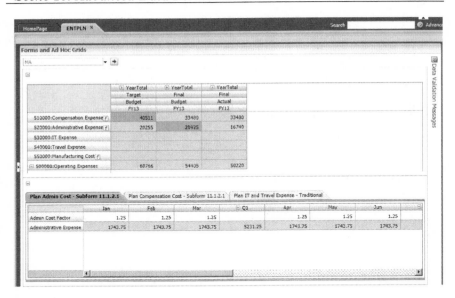

Composite forms will address a number of requirements. You can create composite forms for different plan types, presenting flash consolidated results to end users. You can create a composite form to "secure" data by year, using a simple form that is *Read only* for a selected year (that ideally uses a substitution variable) and second data form that is writable.

Composite forms work in Smart View 11.1.2.2 so don't let Smart View hold you back. Each data form within a composite displays in a separate worksheet in Smart View. The only end user feature in Smart View that is not supported is charting.

MASTER DETAIL LINKING

In 11.1.2.2, Master-Detail Composite forms were introduced. They can be used in place of right click menu navigation options for forms. These form constructs have the same pre-requisites as right click context passing. They allow you to pass the context dimension member from the source form to the target forms. The target forms need to have the dimensions for which context is being passed in the page or POV area of the target form. Master detail forms provide two significant advantages over data forms with right click menus: 1) You can visualize the source and target forms within the same content area and 2) you can see the immediate impact on several dependent forms within the same composite.

For those readers who did not purchase the *Look Smarter Than You Are with Hyperion Planning: Creating Planning Applications*, we'll share with you the steps to create a composite that leverages master detail linking and charting. We use the ENTPLN application that is created in the book.

1. Create the following simple data form called "Plan Revenue – Segment Summary Subform":

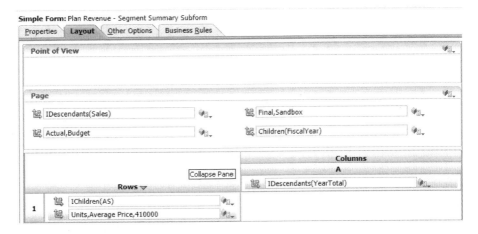

2. Set the *Dimension, Segment* and *Display* properties so the form looks as follows:

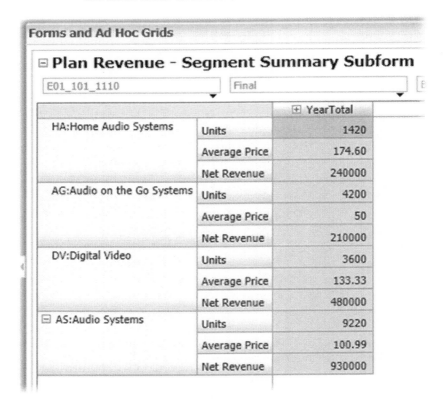

3. Create the following simple data form called "Plan Revenue – Segment Detail Subform":

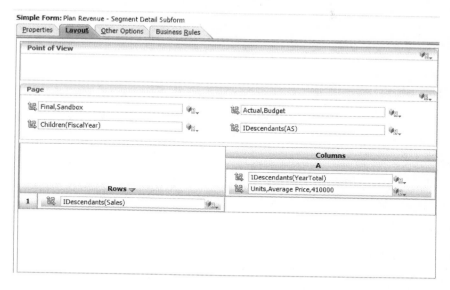

4. Set the *Dimension, Segment* and *Display* properties so the form looks as follows:

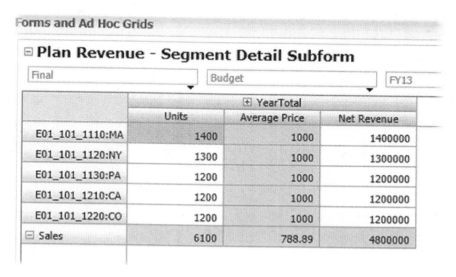

5. Create the following simple data form called "Plan Revenue – Segment Summary Subform":

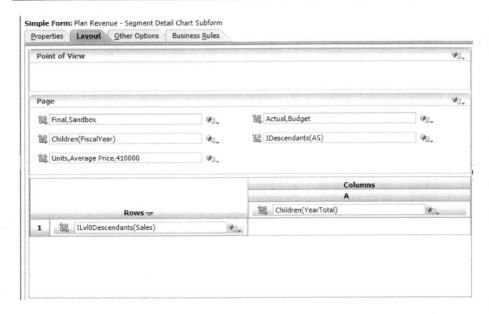

6. Set the *Dimension, Segment* and *Display* properties so the form looks as follows:

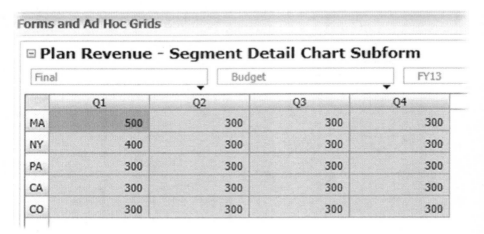

7. Create a composite data form called *11.1.2.2 Master Detail Link – Segments Products*:

Composite Form: 11.1.2.2 Master Detail Link - Segments Products

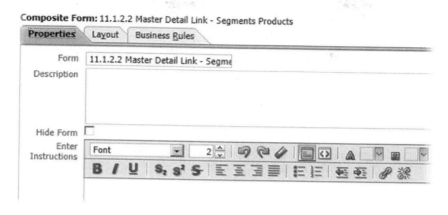

8. Click *Next*.
9. Select a horizontal layout for the composite data form.
10. Add the "Plan Revenue – Segment Summary" to the top section and the "Plan Revenue – Segment Detail Subform" and the "Plan Revenue – Segment Detail Chart Subform" to the bottom sections:

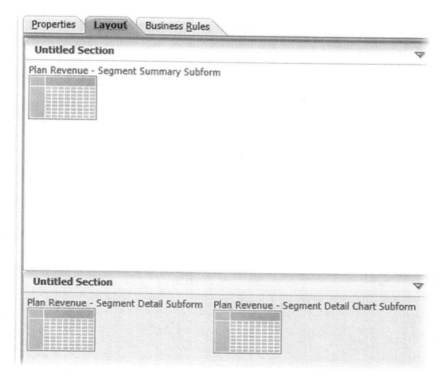

11. Check the option to *Set scope for all common dimensions as global.*

12. Right click on the "Plan Revenue – Segment Summary Subform" and choose *Tag as Master Composite Form:*

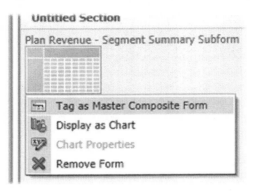

13. Right click on the "Plan Revenue – Segment Detail Chart Subform" and choose *Tag as Master Composite Form:*

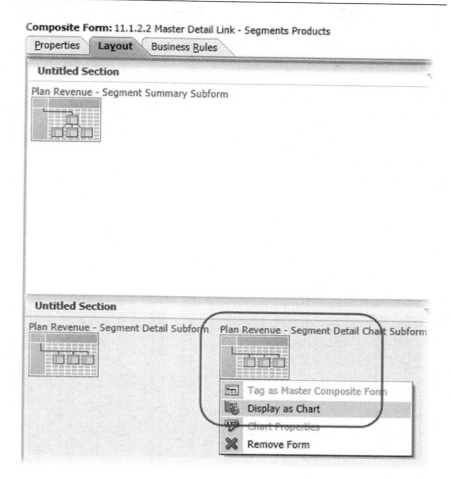

14. Choose the *Horizontal bar* option:

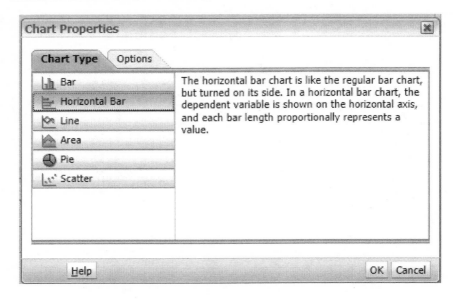

15. Click *OK*.
16. The resulting layout should look as follows:

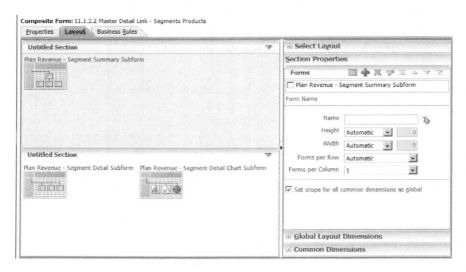

17. Click *Save*.
18. Click *Finish*.

Now you can open the data form and view the chart. To use the master detail feature, you can select a row in the master data form. Right click and select *Apply Context*. The detail forms will update the point of view to show the selected member:

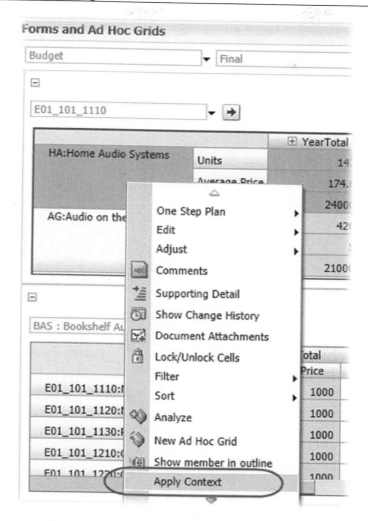

Drillable Charts

To make a "drillable" chart, insert an ad hoc grid (more on ad hoc grids in just a moment) into the composite data form and tag it *Display as Chart*:

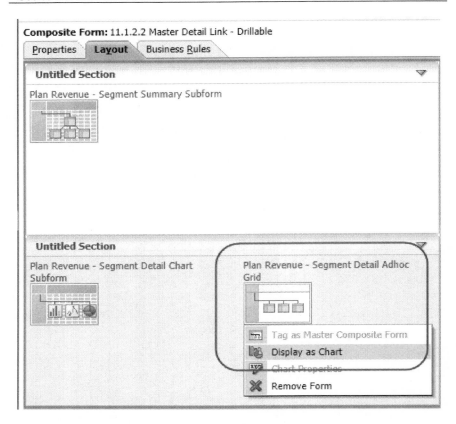

The result is a "drillable" chart within a data form that allows users to drill into the data displayed in charts:

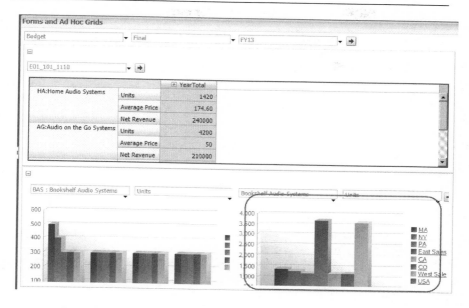

Now that you know how to make "fancy" data forms, how you make forms easy to maintain?

DYNAMIC DATA FORMS

Create Dynamic Forms with Member Functions

It is highly recommended to use member selection functions (children, descendants, level, generation) when creating data forms, calc scripts or any Planning & Essbase object that allows you to use them. Point the member functions to high-level members that are not going to change frequently. As the outline changes, your calc scripts and other objects are dynamically generated to keep in sync with the dimensions and members.

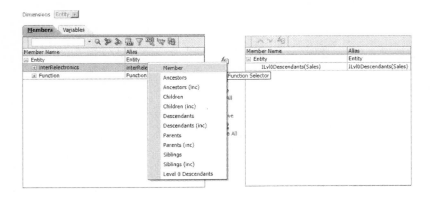

User Variables

User variables act as filters in data forms, enabling planners to focus only on the members they are interested in. In Penny's case, she can create a user variable called "My Entity" and use that variable on the data form member selection. Users set the value for their variable and are ready to plan in a data form tailored for them. Before you can associate a user variable with a data form, you must first create the user variable. Planners cannot open the data form until a value has been specified.

User variables are created by selecting *Administration >> Manage >> Variables*:

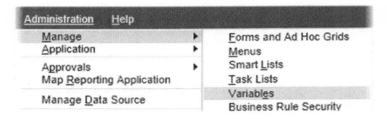

A variable is created for dimension and then is available for use in data forms. The option *Use Context* allows the value of the user variable to change dynamically based on the context of the data form:

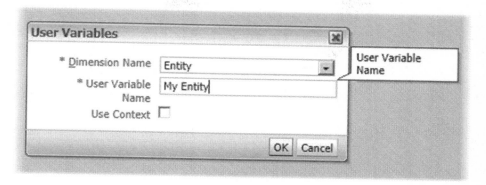

Note you could also simply choose the member or use the other available functions in the member selection. The new user variable is available for selection in the Member Selection window:

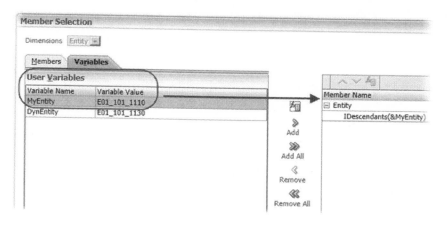

Now it's in the hands of the end users to set their user variable value under preferences.

Dynamic User Variables

In the data form definition, the data form designer can choose to enable dynamic user variables. This setting is enabled under the *Options* tab:

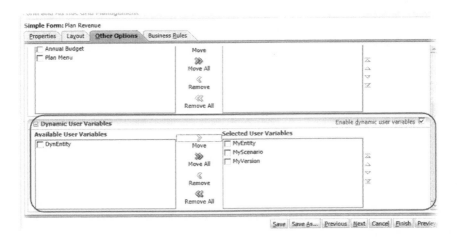

If this setting is enabled, users may change the variable value within the form (versus having to navigate to *File >> Preferences*):

In summary, user variables save the day by making one form seem tailored for their Planning experience.

Rolling Forecast Wizard

In 11.1.2.2, Planning allows you to easily set up rolling forecast forms from within the form designer using interactive components. Rolling forecasts are continuous forecasts that continue past the annual fiscal period end. The periods within the rolling forecast period should rollup together even if when they cross fiscal or annual years. Companies typically forecasts for 12 month, 18 month or 24 month cycles. The starting period shifts each month so that the forecasting window focuses on the next 12/18/24 months. Rolling forecasts are often performed by quarter.

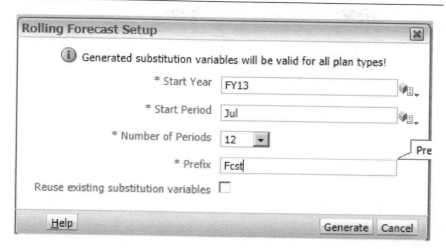

While allowing for rolling forecast forms, the required substitution variables are created on the fly and values assigned to them automatically. These and other substitution variables can be managed from within Planning web user interface directly.

When shifting rolling forecast periods, the shift is auto generated for all forms which have been set up for rolling forecast using the same variables.

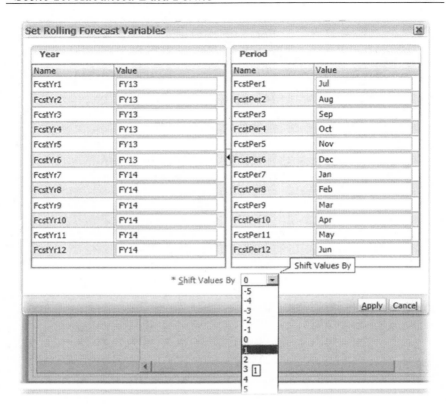

Finally let's review how to make forms fast!

FASTER DATA FORMS

Grid Size

When designing Planning forms, keep in mind that smaller forms will always perform better. Understanding the grid size for data forms will help you understand the performance. The grid size consists of the number of rows, multiplied by the number of columns. The size of the HTML is the portion of the data form that changes based on grid size. The impact on data form performance relates to grid size. The grid size doubles if an application uses multiple currencies. (So design multicurrency enabled forms carefully; in fact, consider not using built-in Planning currency functionality. Build your own and achieve easier ad hoc analysis and better performance.)

The memory usage on the client machine is found to be fairly static when the form size ranges from 200 cells to 5,000 cells.

Split a large single data form into multiple smaller data forms with fewer rows and columns. The impact on a data form's performance relates to its grid size.

Suppress Missing Data and Blocks

The Suppress Missing Data option can help you improve the time it takes a user to open a form by suppressing the rows with no data. The Suppress Missing Blocks option can help you improve performance for sparse retrievals when large sets of sparse members are on the row section of the form (this setting is also available in Financial Reporting version 11.1.1). Use caution when enabling this setting as it can degrade performance if few or no rows are suppressed. Also note you cannot display attributes in data forms when this setting is enabled. Test data forms before and after using this setting to determine if performance is improved. Both options are defined on the Row tab of the data form definition.

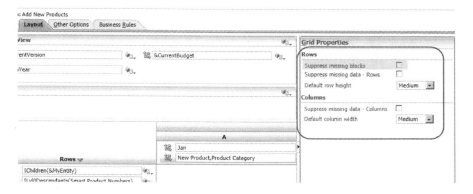

Dense in the Rows and Columns

Another important recommendation to improve performance of data forms is to place dense dimensions in the rows and columns sections of the data form definition. An example of this would be placing the dense Accounts dimension in the rows and dense Period dimension in the columns section of the data form with all remaining sparse dimensions in the Page and POV sections. This design will bring back a single block in the data form. If you place one or more sparse dimensions in the rows or columns, multiple blocks are returned and processed by the data form.

GRID DIAGNOSTIC TOOL

In 11.1.2.2, a new Grid Diagnostic tool will help you diagnose your data forms and understand how they are performing. To access the Grid Diagnostic tool, select *Tools>>Diagnostics>>Grids:*

Select the desired data forms:

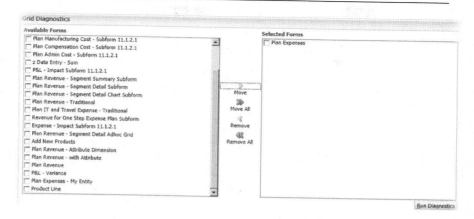

Click *Run Diagnostics*. Information related to the page load times, number of rows retrieved, and the number of rows suppressed (ideally this is not a big number) is displayed:

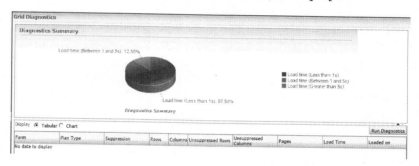

Now that we've covered some advanced concepts related to data forms, let's turn to advanced business rules and calc scripts.

Scene 11:
Advanced Business Rules &
Calc Scripts

Penny's users keep asking her, "Why does my calc script take 5 hours?" and "How can I get my calc time down?" Changing a number of the database and outline settings can significantly impact your calculation time. Some of these settings are discussed in other sections of the book ("Application Design Best Practices" and "Other Tuning Best Practices") but here are some general calculation design and tuning tips.

FASTER BUSINESS RULES

General Tips

Calculate only those dimensions requiring calculation. For example, do you need to rollup Scenario (Actual + Budget)? If all of the upper level members in your Accounts dimension are dynamic, do you need to calculate Accounts? Nope. By utilizing a lean and mean "CALC DIM" or "AGG" with only the dimensions that need to be aggregated, you'll shave valuable time from your calc scripts.

Note!

Essbase ASO cubes don't have to be aggregated though aggregating them can help retrieval performance. In this scene, we're primarily worried about Essbase BSO calculation performance.

"AGG" and "CALC DIM" are not the same. "AGG" is faster for straight aggregation of sparse dimensions with no member formulas so use this when you can. There are some cases where a sparse dimension with 7+ levels may CALC DIM faster than it AGGs, but normally AGG is faster.

Using Sample.Basic for our example, the slowest aggregation we can run is "CALC ALL;" Doing "CALC DIM (Measures, Year, Scenario, Product, Market);" would be faster, but it calculates three dense dimensions that don't need to be aggregated. The fastest possible script would be "AGG (Product, Market);" In other words, don't use CALC ALL or CALC DIM where AGG will suffice.

IF commands are extremely slow in Essbase calculations, so we want to avoid them unless we're doing different things to different dense members.   In general, use "Fix" on Sparse dimensions and use "If" on Dense dimensions if you're going to be doing different logic on different members from the same dimension. If you need to do a bunch of logic against a set of members of a dimension (dense or sparse) and you don't need to do *different* logic against different members of that dimension, use a FIX.

Simplify the calculation if possible by using unary calcs instead of member formulas and member formulas instead of logic within a calc script.   In other words, don't have a member called "Margin" with a formula of "Sales – COGS;" when you could just do Margin as a member with Sales (+) and COGS (-) rolling into it.

Avoid any stored member formulas or calc scripts that reference dynamic calcs if at all possible. You could find performance issues and will likely need to increase the dynamic calc cache.

Make sure to turn on the normal headings at the top of your calc scripts that will boost performance.   In the example below, we're telling the calc script to launch 40 threads which is probably on the high side, but we wanted to make sure you remembered to set it:

```
SET CALCPARALLEL 40;
SET UPDATECALC Off;
SET CACHE High;
SET AGGMISSING On;
```

Minimize the number of passes through the database for calculations. Try to bring in a set of blocks once and then perform all of the necessary calcs. Multiple passes will happen but try to reduce them as much as possible.

Add comments to your business rules and calc scripts. This is a no brainer yet we sometimes get lazy and do not complete this step. It's not for performance but rather for maintenance later: take the few extra seconds to add an "English" description of what your calc syntax is performing. Document and add comments as you go so others (or your own self after a period of time) can understand the logic.

Make upper members Dynamic in dense dimensions

Consider setting the storage property to Dynamic on all upper-level members in your dense dimensions. This reduces the size of the data block and eliminates the need to execute business rules on those dense dimensions when saving data.

Let's assume the Periods and Accounts dimensions are dense, upper level members are set to "Dynamic Calc," and most data forms have Periods on the columns and Accounts on the rows. When users enter data into these forms or refresh the forms, all totals will be dynamically calculated without running any business rule. In the example below, "Total Orders" is an upper level account that is dynamically calculated. The form does not need to execute business rules to display the "Total Orders" result.

⊟ 400000	Gross Profit	Dynamic Calc
⊞ 410000	Net Revenue	Store
⊞ 420000	COGs	Store

Forms and Ad Hoc Grids	
⊟ **P&L - Traditional - Read Only**	
Final ▼	Budget ▼	FY13 ▼	E01_101_1110 ▼ ➔

	⊞ YearTotal
410000:Net Revenue *f*	930000
420000:COGs	1065000
⊟ 400000:Gross Profit	-135000
510000:Compensation Expense *f*	
520000:Administrative Expense *f*	
530000:IT Expense	
540000:Travel Expense	
550000:Manufacturing Cost *f*	
⊟ 500000:Operating Expenses	
⊟ 300000:Net Income	-135000

Aggressive Use of Dynamic Calc Member Tags

We discussed the benefits of using dynamic calcs (which result in smaller block size). However, an aggressive use of the dynamic calc tag can create a large difference between the size of the block in the dynamic calculator cache and the size of the block in the data cache. If you use a large number of Dynamic Calc tags, you will probably need to tune the Dynamic Calculator cache.

Also watch out for business rules and calc scripts that reference or require dynamically calculated blocks. These can slow down performance as it calculates those members and blocks in memory

When tuning business rules and calc scripts, first ask yourself. "Is this a batch process or something the end user will run?" Some tuning elements may differ between these two types of calculations.

Consider Turning Off RTP Storage

By default, the values for processed runtime prompts in the application are stored in the database and available for viewing from the Job Console (select *Tools >> Job Console*). If many users are running business rules with runtime prompts, tracking these values consumes significant system resources.

To improve performance, you can turn off the tracking and storage of runtime prompt values. Select *Administration >> Application>>Properties.* Click the + icon and add the CAPTURE_RTP_ON_JOB_CONSOLE property to the listing and set the value to FALSE:

TUNING FOR BATCH CALCULATIONS

During batch calculations, users are typically disconnected from the system, and all user initiated processing is halted. Data is then loaded to cubes, calculated and/or moved between cubes as appropriate. Once complete, the applications are released back to users.

The batch process assumes complete control of the environment. This permits the Admin to allocate 100% of Server resources to the process if desired or required, effecting maximum use of server resources and parallelism.

Parallel Calculation - CALCPARALLEL

The CALCPARALLEL setting (which can be set in the Essbase.CFG or at the calc script level) should be set for batch calculation scripts. This setting tells Essbase to use multiple processors for the calculation. How effective Essbase is at parallelizing a calculation is cube dependent on a few factors, including the task list set for the parallel calc defined in the CALKTASKDIMS setting. Essbase will evaluate the specific outline to determine a task list that can be worked through in parallel.

Note!

While we generally want to be increasing CALCPARALLEL substantially for batch calculations, be careful about setting it high on business rules initiated by users during the planning process. Since multiple users can be kicking off multiple calculations simultaneously, a high CALCPARALLEL setting can result in that number times the number of users running it to be used.

Parallel Calculation - CALCTASKDIMS

This setting tells Essbase how many sparse dimensions (from the bottom of the outline upwards) to consider when determining a task schedule for parallel processing of cube aggregations. The default value is one, which means that Essbase will only consider the last sparse dimension for defining a task list.

It is a common strategy to move non-aggregating sparse dimensions to the bottom of the outline in an attempt to optimize calculation times. Testing needs to determine what the best CALCPARALLEL and CALCTASKDIM settings are for a given calc script.

The objective is to enable Essbase to devise a task list that it can use to parallelize the calculation without having to stop parallelism at the end to add values together at the top of a sparse dimension. Performance degradations can occur when configuring the calc to evaluate too many CALCTASKDIMS.

An adjustment might have to be made when using CALCPARALLEL in combination with moving non-aggregating sparse dimensions to the bottom of the outline. For example, if the last three dimensions in the outline are non-aggregating dimensions, and parallelism is required, then start testing setting the CALCTASKDIMS at four, five and/or six to ensure that Essbase will consider appropriate dimensions to create its task list.

Essbase 11.1.2.2 provides enhancements for the CALCPARALLEL command/setting. The maximum number of threads that can be made available for parallel calculation has been increased:

For block storage databases:
- Running on 32-bit platforms: 64
- Running on 64-bit platforms: 128

For aggregate storage databases:
- Running on 32-bit or 64-bit platforms: 128

Setting the number of CALCTASKDIMS to high values can have a negative impact depending on your hardware. Essbase calc performance can be greatly reduced by asking it to analyze too many dimensions when determining a task list.

Note! In 11.1.2.2 Essbase will dynamically set the **CALCTASKDIMS** setting so you may want to try *not* defining this setting and review calc performance impact.

TUNE THE CALCULATOR CACHE

Warning – this topic is confusing. We'll give you the background information related to calculator cache but when all is said and done, use this cache when the database has at least two sparse dimensions, and either you calculate at least one, full sparse dimension OR you specify the SET CACHE ALL command in a calculation script. Be prepared to read this section at least two or three times for full comprehension.

The best size for the calculator cache depends on the number and density of the sparse dimensions in your outline. First let's review a few terms:

The bitmap is a highly efficient mechanism that is used to very quickly tell the Essbase Calculation Engine whether a block exists or not at a given location. As the engine will not have to perform this lookup by reading the index file (which is relatively slow), and large Essbase databases can have a massive number of potential blocks, this little time saving for each potential block location can save a very large amount of time overall.

The bitmap dimensions will be the sparse dimensions from the database outline that Essbase fits into the bitmap until the bitmap is full. Each member combination of the sparse dimensions placed in the bitmap occupies (wait for it) 1 bit of memory. There must be enough space in the bitmap for every member combination of a sparse dimension for it to be placed in the bitmap, so we will need to make sure we size the cache to be large enough for what we want to load into the bitmap.

The anchoring dimensions are the remaining one or more sparse dimensions in the database outline that do not fit into the bitmap.

The calculator cache controls the size of the bitmap, therefore controlling the number of dimensions that can fit into the bitmap.

In case you found that section too simple, here are some equations:

- Calculator cache = Bitmap size in bytes * Number of bitmaps
- Bitmap size in bytes = Max ((member combinations on the bitmap dimensions/8), 4)
- Number of bitmaps = Maximum number of dependent parents in the anchoring dimension + 2 constant bitmaps
- Minimum bitmap size is 4 bytes

There are a few different ways to define the calculator cache. The default calculator cache size is set in the Essbase.CFG. You can also choose the size of the calculator cache (based on values set in the Essbase.CFG) within a calculation script, at which time the setting is used only for the duration of that script.

This is definitely one of those settings that you will want to test to get the maximum performance from your calc scripts, but be prepared to spend a lot of time tweaking the settings to get it just right.

TUNE THE DYNAMIC CALCULATOR CACHE

This cache is used to perform dynamic calculations. The dynamic calc tag was developed to enable designers to delay certain member calculations to query time. This assumes that the amount of time to compute the values dynamically will be transparent to the user at runtime and does not affect batch or script driven calculation times. When a database calculation is coded to invoke dynamic calc members in a script, the purpose of the dynamic calc tag is completely defeated, and Essbase is forced to expand blocks fully in this cache during script/batch processes.

All dynamic calculator cache settings are configurable at the database level. Oracle strongly recommends that they be tuned per database to ensure optimal use of server resources. The amount of memory available to an application is determined by the OS and it is important not to over-allocate memory beyond that limit.

Tuning the dynamic calculator cache to handle dynamic calculations is a non-trivial task and strictly speaking depends on your database configuration. You should attempt to limit the use of dynamic calc tags to dense dimensions to defray the impact of unexpected resource requirements. It is just as important to ensure that no dynamic calc references occur during business rule processing. If dynamic calc tags on sparse members are necessary, it is equally necessary to study end user query behavior in-depth and configure the dynamic calculator cache appropriately.

Dynamic Calc Cache usage information is recorded in the application log.

```
[Thu May 14 16:14:27 2009]Local/Sample/Basic/admin/Info(1020082)
Spreadsheet Extractor Big Block Allocs -- Dyn.Calc.Cache : [90] non-Dyn.Calc.Cache : [0]
```

Dynamic calc processing of sparse members are not recorded in log entries, so the cost of their computation is not easily determined beforehand.

To tune the dynamic calculator cache, you will use the following settings in the Essbase.CFG file:

DYNCALCCACHEMAXSIZE

This setting determines how much memory (20 MB default) a database will reserve for dynamic calculations. By default, if more memory is required, Essbase asks the OS for more RAM. Underestimating and overestimating this cache setting can cause overall poor system performance: Too many requests from the OS are expensive, and allocating too much memory to the buffer can starve the application of memory.

Essbase records the usage of the dynamic calculator cache in the application log.

It is important to note that dynamic calc processing of sparse members are not recorded in log entries, so the cost of their computation is not easily determined beforehand. A cube with an outline that uses dynamic calc tags on sparse members, and has business rules that reference dynamic calc members (dense or sparse), can seriously degrade overall system performance. In extreme cases, this can lead to application or even server-wide instability. This is the result of the unexpected resource demand for Essbase to process the dynamic calculations concurrently for the business rules and query requests.

DYNCALCCACHEONLY

This setting is used to restrict Essbase from making OS level requests for resources. If the Server Admin decides in favor of this restriction, then it is important to specify what Essbase needs to do when there is not sufficient memory in the dynamic calculator cache.

DYNCALCCACHEWAITFORBLK

This setting instructs Essbase to wait for memory to be freed within the dynamic calculator cache. If the setting is set to true, and the DYNAMICCAHCEBLKTIMEOUT setting has been exceeded, Essbase generates an error message. You can instruct Essbase to create a DYNCALCCACHECOMPRBLKBUFSIZE buffer to store blocks temporarily when the timeout has been reached. Overall application memory limits need to be respected.

DYNCALCCACHEBLKTIMEOUT

This setting specifies how long Essbase waits for memory to be freed within the dynamic calculator cache before generating an error message.

DYNCALCCACHECOMPRBLKBUFSIZE

Use this setting to specify an area of memory for Essbase to temporarily compress and store blocks to make room in the dynamic calculator cache. Essbase temporarily stores compressed blocks from the dynamic calculator cache into this buffer.

DYNCALCCACHEBLKRELEASE

Enables Essbase to create a temporary buffer for dynamic calculations in cases where the wait for space in the dynamic calculator cache has exceeded the specified wait time.

Balance dynamic calculations and stored members

While the dynamic calculator cache helps performance on dynamic calculations, you still want to watch out for:
- Complex formulas on dense dynamically calculated members
- Sparse dynamic calc members
- Dynamic calculations that reference other dynamic calculations
- Dynamic calculations referenced in calc scripts or stored member formulas

BUSINESS RULE DIAGNOSTICS

If you are on version 11.1.2.3, Calculation Manager has a feature called the Business Rule Diagnostic tool to help review your logic and provide feedback on ways to improve design and performance.

In the Calculation Manager editor for a business rule, select the *Errors & Warnings* tab. Click the green arrow icon to *Run script diagnostics:*

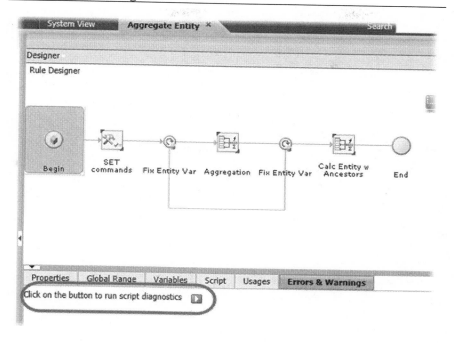

Feedback will display after evaluating the business rule:

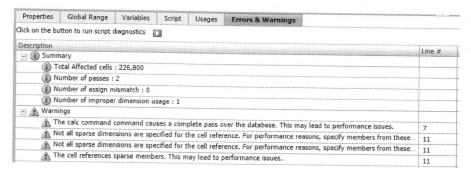

TUNING FOR END USER CALCS

Use Calc on Save / Calc on Load only when necessary

You can attach the Calculate Data Form business rule or custom business rules to data forms. The Calculate Data form rules are automatically created for every form and it calculate data for the members on the data form. Custom Business Rules can be added to forms and set to "Run on Save" and "Run on Load". These options run the business rule when the user clicks the Save button on the data form or when the user opens the form.

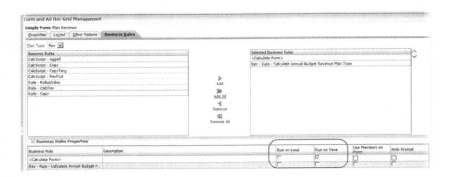

While this is a powerful feature, to the end user it looks as if the data form is taking a long time to open or save. Only use these features when needed. If your data form requires no additional calculation (possibly all members on the data form are dynamic), do not enable Calculate Data Form or other custom business rules. Add any business rules to a right-click menu or task list so the end user understands the rule may take a few seconds or minutes to execute. If you use this feature, communicate to end users the expected form save and/or open times.

Focus Business Rules

Focus Business Rule logic on only those members that need to be calculated. For example, if you need to roll up a specific section of the entity dimension, don't aggregate the entire Entity dimension. Use a runtime prompt to focus the calculation on the desired member(s). Members available to users for runtime prompts are limited by security and specific limitations that can be established when creating the runtime prompt. You can prompt for single or multiple members, numeric value, Smart List value, or text value.

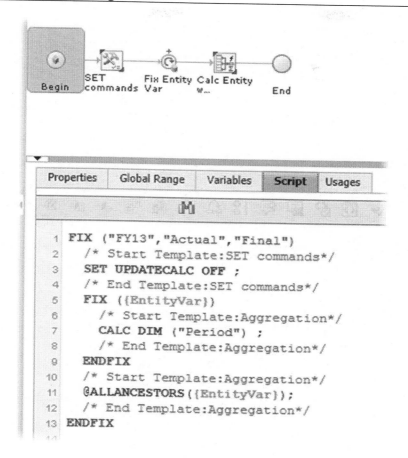

```
1  FIX ("FY13","Actual","Final")
2    /* Start Template:SET commands*/
3    SET UPDATECALC OFF ;
4    /* End Template:SET commands*/
5    FIX ({EntityVar})
6      /* Start Template:Aggregation*/
7      CALC DIM ("Period") ;
8      /* End Template:Aggregation*/
9    ENDFIX
10   /* Start Template:Aggregation*/
11   @ALLANCESTORS({EntityVar});
12   /* End Template:Aggregation*/
13   ENDFIX
```

DYNAMIC BUSINESS RULES

Use Member Functions

Just like data forms, it is highly recommended to use member selection functions (children, descendants, level, generation) when creating calc scripts or any Essbase object that allows you to use them. Point the member functions to high-level members that are not going to change frequently. As the outline changes, your calc scripts and other objects are dynamically generated to use the current outline structure.

Create Dynamic Business Rules

Use variables and runtime prompts when creating Business Rules to dramatically reduce the number of redundant rules in the system. With runtime prompts you can create a business rule once and then use runtime prompts to filter the logic for user selected members.

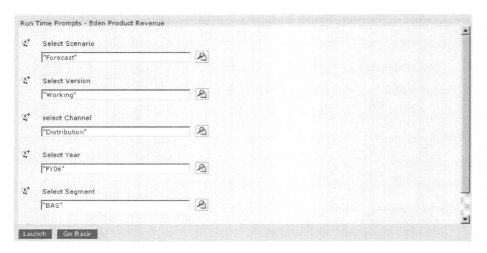

Place Variable Value Setting in Hands of the User

Never hard code "numbers" within the business rule. If business rule logic calculates plan as last year's actual with a 30% increase, do not hardcode ".3" into the business rule. What if the increase % changes? The user can't make the change. The Planning administrator must make the change. The design best practice is to create this as a measure that can be entered by users via a data form. That measure can be used in the business rule instead of the hard coded value.

REDUCE MAINTENANCE

Calculation Manager provides one interface to create Business Rules for HFM, Planning and Essbase. You can design a rule in a graphical environment, toggle to a script ("enhanced calc") view, and back to the graphical display, a feature not available in Essbase Administration Services business rules. We covered the fundamentals of Calculation Manager in *Look Smarter Than You Are with Hyperion Planning 11.1.2: Creating Hyperion Planning Applications*. Now let's review a few additional Calculation Manager features that help with business rule maintenance.

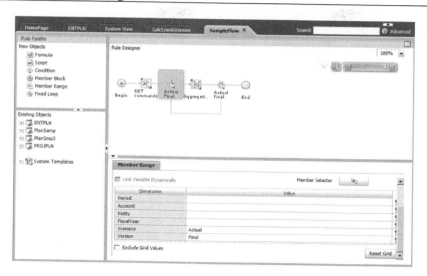

You want to reduce the amount of coding and logic that you perform across your business rules. Often times you might have the same logic set that is used across a number of business rules. Is there a way to create the logic once and then use in multiple business rules? Yes! The feature is called Reusable Formula Components.

Reusable Formula Component

A reusable formula component is a specific set of business rule logic or syntax that can be used across multiple business rules. When an update to the logic is required, you can change the logic in one place and updates flow through automatically.

Note!

The steps below assume you are created the ENTPLN application, business rules and variables from the Look Smarter Than You Are with Hyperion Planning 11.1.2: Creating Hyperion Planning Applications book.

To create a reusable formula component,

1. Select *File >> New >> Formula Component* or in the System View of Calculation Manager and right-click on Formulas and click *New*:

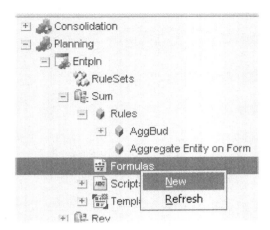

2. Enter the formula name "Calculate Revenue Forecast".
3. Select *Planning* as *Application Type*.
4. Select *Entpln* as *Application*:
5. Select *Rev* as *Plan Type*:

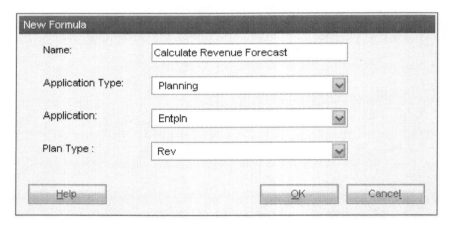

6. Click *OK*.
7. Enter the formula for calculating revenue "411100" = Units*Price":

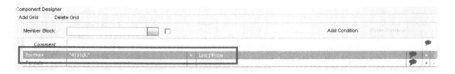

8. Save and validate the Formula component.
9. Close the Formula component.

Now let's create a rule that uses the Calculate Revenue Forecast formula component.

1. Select *File >> New >> Rule*.
2. Enter the name "Calculate Forecast by Entity on Form".
3. Select *Planning* as *Application Type*.
4. Select *Entpln* as *Application*.
5. Select *Rev* as *Plan Type*:

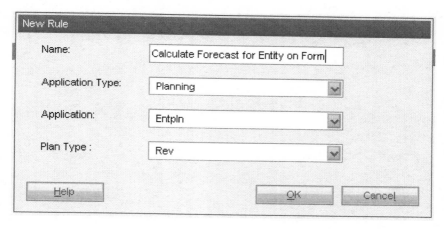

10. Click *OK*.
11. Set the following members (and variables if you have them defined) for the Global Range of the Business Rule ("VersionVar", "Forecast", "FiscalYearVar"):

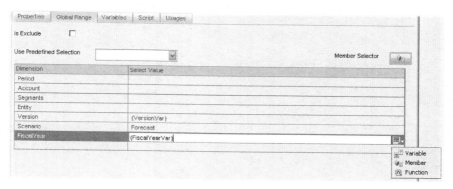

12. Drag a *Member Range* component into the Flow Diagram.
13. Select "EntityVar" for the Entity dimension in the Member Range component:

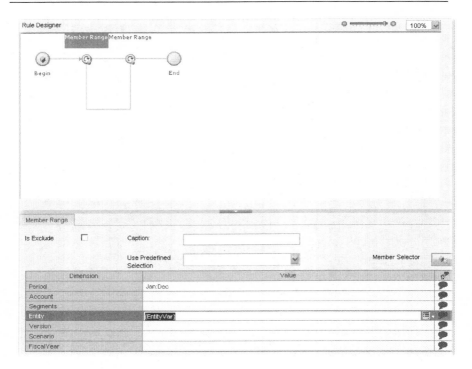

14. Drag another *Member Range* component into the Business Rule within the "EntityVar" Member Range component.
15. Set the range for this component to *Jan:Dec* for Period.
16. Navigate to the Calculate Revenue Forecast component under Existing *Objects>>Entpln>>Rev>>Formulas*.
17. Drag this component within the *Jan:Dec* Member Range component:

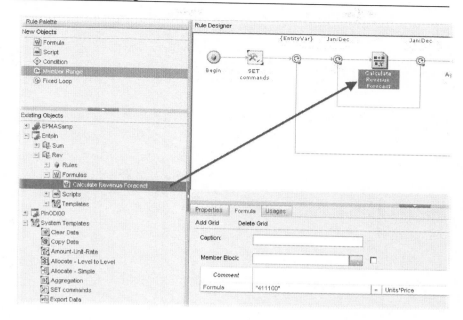

18. Add in an aggregation to rollup the Period dimension for the fixed entity after the *Jan:Dec* Member Range Component.
19. Add in an *Aggregation* to rollup the Entity and it's ancestors after the *EntityVar* Member Range Component:

The resulting rule and script should look as follows:

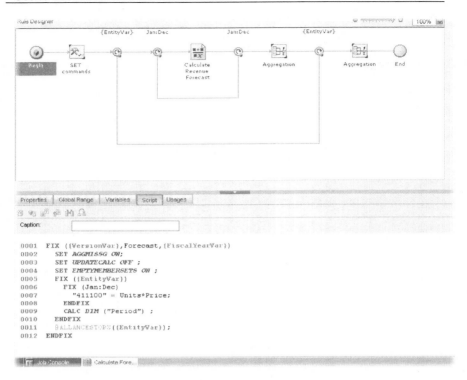

20. Don't forget to rename captions to help make the flow diagram more readable.

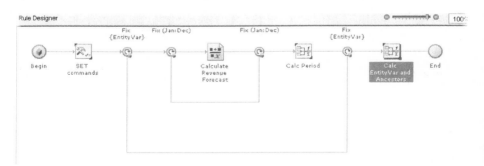

Rule Sets

A rule set is a grouping or sequence of business rules that are run together in a defined order. Grouping componentized business rules allow for efficient business rule design and rules sets let you combine combinations of rules to achieve a desired requirement.

For example, you have one business rule that performs an allocation that is run on a monthly basis when specific drivers are entered. You have another business rule that calculates the database on a nightly basis. You can create a rule set for the monthly process that runs the allocation rule first and then the calculation business rule (versus including the same nightly calculation logic in the allocation rule).

To create a rule set, select *File >> New >> Rules Set* or in the System View of Calculation Manager and right-click on RuleSets and click *New*. You can then drag and drop the desired rules into the Ruleset Designer:

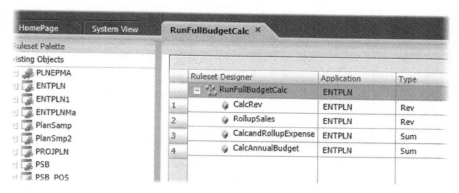

After the ruleset has been saved, validated and deployed, it may be attached to data forms (just like a regular business rule) or run via *Tools>> Business Rules*. Optionally filter to only view a type of ruleset:

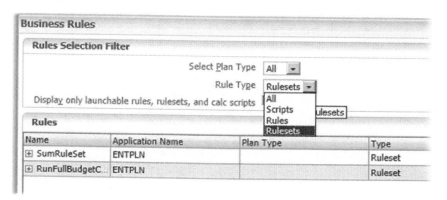

Help Debugging

Version 11.1.2.2 delivers increased help in debugging. The key new functionality in this release is the 'Interactive debugging mode.' Interactive debugging provides following features to the end user:

- Ability to insert the break points
- Ability to Remove/Disable the break points
- Ability to add a condition to the break point
- Ability to view the members of the intersection
- Display before value and after value of the execution of all the intersection(s) for member(s) in a statement.
- Display all execution variable values (present in the statement) before and after statement execution.

Compare Business Rules Feature

In 11.1.2.3 you can compare the scripts of business rules using *Compare Scripts*. Shift click the desired business rules and right click. Choose *Compare Scripts:*

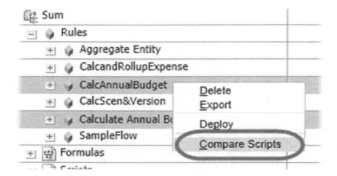

The script will display side by side for review and comparison:

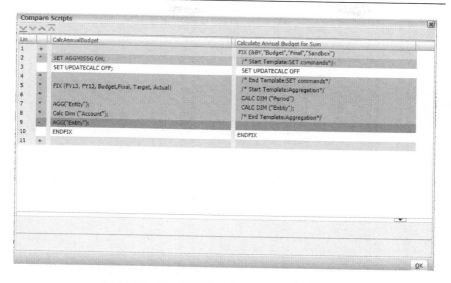

BLOCK CREATION ISSUES

A common issue in Hyperion Planning calculations involves the creation of blocks. Calculations often need blocks that do not exist as example when performing allocations where the target blocks are not there. Calculations may not calculate properly because the blocks do not exist. In addition, if too many blocks are created, performance may suffer. You need to make sure the blocks are created when needed and not too many block are generated. Only create the blocks you need.

A colleague once told us about a administrator with a member formula that set the member to a constant. The formula set "count" to 1 since the idea was to be able to do a count and then aggregate that member. It was not dynamic, but stored. He ran a calculation to aggregate the database and had to kill the calculation when it was at about 30 page files (60 GB) as he was running out of disk space. This took about 15-20 minutes. Basically the formula was creating every block in the database. Definitely *not* the way to create blocks.

There are several methods to create blocks:
- Load data
- Calculate the database
- Use the DATACOPY calculation command
- Place a sparse member on the left side of an assignment statement
    - You must not set equal to a constant

- o SET CREATEBLOCKONEQ ON; must be in the calc script or create blocks on equations must be turned on at the database level.
- Use SET CREATENONMISSINGBLK ON;
  - o This will create blocks based on dense equations.
  - o This generally is very slow and will create more blocks than you need.
- Use @CREATEBLOCK
  - o This function became available in 11.1.2.3 and works in a calc script or business rule.

OUT OF THE BOX ALLOCATIONS – MASS ALLOCATE

Why is this in the business rules section you may be asking? This handy out of the box feature will actually create allocation business rules for you.

The *Mass Allocate* end user feature is similar to Grid Spread in that you can spread data across one or more dimensions, but Mass Allocate is far more powerful. Unlike Grid Spread where the spreading is limited to what you see on the form itself, Mass Allocate creates a Business Rule that runs behind the scenes on the Essbase server.

Data will automatically spread (no chance to view ahead of time before saving). The grid is reloaded and the result is presented to the end user. Allocation options available for Mass Allocate include: Proportional, Relational spread, Fill, and Even Split.

So instead of creating your own complicated allocation business rules, see if the Mass Allocate feature will perform the allocation for you.

To use Mass Allocate:
1. Put the cursor in the source cell containing the value you wish to allocate to lower level cells.
2. Select *Edit >> Mass Allocate*.
3. Options:
   a. Increase or decrease values by a specified amount with Adjust.
   b. Increase or decrease values by a specified percentage with Adjust.
   c. Replace values with a new value by entering it in the Spread Value text box.
4. Choose Spread Type - *Proportional, Relational, Evenly split,* or *Fill*:

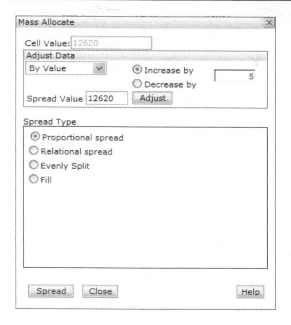

5. Click *Spread*:

Like Grid Spread, Mass Allocate is also enabled on a form by form basis:

We enabled Mass Allocate for the "Plan Operating Expenses" in the Planning Sample allocation data form and assigned the Mass Allocate role for the Planning Sample application (you can do the same to follow along with us; for the detailed steps check out the appendix).

To spread data using Mass Allocate,

1. Open the "Plan Operating Expenses" data form.
2. Set your page options to the members "MA", "Working", "Plan", "FY012".
3. Select the cell for "Consulting Services", "Jan".
4. Select *Edit >> Mass Allocate.*
5. The first item we see, "Cell Value: 10,000" shows us the cell that we selected prior to opening the Mass Allocate option.
6. Type "8000" directly in the Spread Value text box.
7. Select *Relational Spread.*

In real life we would most likely choose Actual, Final, FY12 as the relative members for spreading.

Spread Type

Currency	Local	Local	
Segments	NoSegment	NoSegment	
Entity	E01_101_1110	E01_101_1110	
Version	Working	Final	
Scenario	Plan	Actual	
Year	FY09	FY08	
Account	506100	506100	
Period	Jan	Jan	

○ Evenly Split

Sadly, the sample data in the Planning sample application contains just a sample of the data we need to allocate correctly. To make the spreading actually work, we're going to have to choose some other members to run through the steps.

   8. Select the relative members for spreading ("Plan", "Final", "FY13").

   9. Click *Spread*.

The data is automatically spread and saved to the underlying Essbase database:

Page	MA					Working	Plan		FY09	Go

	Jan	Feb	Mar	
Individual Contractors	2527	2367	1404	
Consulting Firms	5473	5201	2786	
Consulting Services	8000	7568	4190	

Before we conclude our advanced planning scenes, we have one last big finale song to cover other important tuning tips!

Scene 12:
Other Tuning Best Practices

Disclaimer: **There simply isn't one right answer when it comes to optimization and tuning.** Some of the tuning guidelines can contradict other tuning guidelines. Optimizing can have different perspectives: are you tuning for calculations or retrievals or both? In some databases these tuning tips will have significant impact and in other databases they won't. Make sure you test, test, test. Did we say that tuning wasn't an exact science?

FACTORS IN TUNING PLANNING APPLICATIONS

Tuning for Planning applications has different considerations than reporting-only Essbase databases. In a Planning environment, data is loaded to the cubes in several ways. Data can be loaded into Essbase in batch processes (using data loads, replicated partitions, etc.). Calc scripts are executed to allocate and aggregate the data in offline batch processes. End-user data, however, is input online to the cube via the Planning interfaces and is calculated by Business Rules. During peak time, data is continuously and concurrently being moved between caches and disk to accommodate query requests, database updates from the data forms, and end-user business rule executions. Needless to say it is a very busy processing environment. So keep this in mind as you tune your Planning applications.

OPTIMIZE DATA LOAD RULES

Make sure the columns of your data file (or SQL load) follow the reverse order of the outline: Non-aggregating sparse dimensions, aggregating sparse dimensions, and finally the dense dimensions (assuming your outline follows the optimized dimension ordering model we mentioned earlier). The file/table should then be sorted from left-to-right.

Outline Order	Data File Order and Sort
Time Periods (D)	Scenarios (NAS)
Accounts (D)	Versions (NAS)

Job Code (AS)	Years (NAS)
Organization (AS)	Organization (AS)
Years (NAS)	Job Code (AS)
Versions (NAS)	Accounts (D)
Scenarios (NAS)	Time Periods (D)
Employee Status (Attr Dim)	
Fund Group (Attr Dim)	

Tip!

If you ever forget the order for an optimal data load file, do a columnar export. Look at the order of the dimensions in the file (and the dense dimension across the columns). Match your input file to the order of the dimensions in the export file.

Other tuning tips for faster data loads include using the first dense dimension members as the columns of your data so you can avoid using the single "data field" with only one column of numbers in it. For example, an optimized data file with columns for each period will load much quicker than a file with only one data value per line and the periods going down the rows.

Avoid unnecessary columns (such as attribute dimensions or roll-up levels) in the source data file. For example, your data file has columns for period, account, product, sales manager, product description, and product introduction date. Unless your rules file updates the product dimension and loads data, take out the extraneous columns like sales manager, product description, and product introduction date. For large data loads, every little bit counts.

Copy data load files directly to the Essbase server if you're not loading from a relational sort. It is faster to load from the server than the client where the network can sometimes become a bottleneck.

And lastly, pre-aggregate records before loading instead of accumulating them at level-0 as you load. Here is a data file where the Jan records will have to be added together during the load process:

```
01/01/2007, Jan, California,Caffeine Free Cola, Sales, 145
01/02/2007, Jan, California,Caffeine Free Cola, Sales, 123
01/03/2007, Jan, California,Caffeine Free Cola, Sales, 132
01/04/2007, Jan, California,Caffeine Free Cola, Sales, 145
01/05/2007, Jan, California,Caffeine Free Cola, Sales, 102
01/06/2007, Jan, California,Caffeine Free Cola, Sales, 116|
```

Here is an optimized data file with records pre-aggregated by month. This is a very simple task for any relational database.

```
Jan, California, Caffeine Free Cola, Sales, 762
Feb, California, Caffeine Free Cola, Sales, 775
Mar, California, Caffeine Free Cola, Sales, 862
Apr, California, Caffeine Free Cola, Sales, 700|
```

OPTIMIZE RETRIEVALS

You *can* speed up data retrievals by increasing the value of two retrieval-specific buffer settings, *Buffer Size* and *Sort Buffer Size*. These buffers hold extracted row data cells before they are evaluated or sorted. If the buffer is too small, retrieval times can increase with the constant emptying and re-filling of the buffer. If the buffer is too large, retrieval times can increase when too much memory is used as concurrent users perform queries. The default buffer is set to 10KB for 32-bit platforms and 20 KB for 64-bit. As a rule, don't exceed 100KB for either buffer though we have seen this exceeded on Exalytics and other high-powered 64-bit servers.

To set the retrieval buffers,

1. Right-click on the Database and select *Edit Properties*.
2. Go to the *General* tab and set the *Data retrieval buffers*:

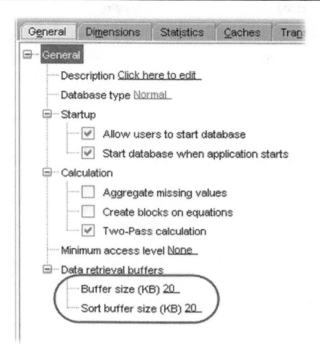

FRAGMENTATION

Fragmentation is often a crippling side-effect of frequently updated databases. Let's assume that we have a very simple block with only eight cells:

100	#Missing	#Missing	#Missing
#Missing	#Missing	#Missing	#Missing

Any one of Essbase's compression methods would work well for this example, but let's assume Run-Length Encoding is used and is able to compress the data storage component to 32 bytes (8 Bytes for the 100 and 24 Bytes to compress all the #Missing values together). Then, a user writes some budget data to this block:

100	150	200	#Missing
#Missing	#Missing	#Missing	#Missing

This block will now require 48 Bytes to store (8 Bytes for each number, and 24 Bytes for the #Missing values). Fragmentation happens because Essbase can't fit 48 Bytes back into the original 32 Byte location and it is written to the end of the file. The original block still remains in the file, but there is no corresponding pointer in the index file so it is lost forever but still taking up space. Actually, it's not quite forever. Essbase tracks empty space in the database directory in another file, so it's really only extra space until Essbase finds a block to put there that fits.

Now that you understand fragmentation, an alarm should be going off for all budgeting application administrators. Budgeting not only involves frequent updates which add more data to previously smaller blocks but also calc scripts that expand the data in each block. Fragmentation also runs rampant when data load rules aren't sorted properly and blocks are written to the .PAG file then updated later in the load and re-written to a new block location.

To eliminate fragmentation, you can export the data from the database to a file, clear all data from the database and reload from the export file (see the Backup and Recovery scene). This workaround (and various other unseemly workarounds like adding "dummy members" to dense dimensions) was the only method to defragment an Essbase cube until a few years ago. Newer versions of Essbase MaxL support a command called **alter database [database name] force restructure** which removes all fragmentation from the database. You can now also just right-click on a database in EAS and choose "Restructure."

TUNE THE INDEX CACHE

The index cache is a reserved set of memory that is used to store all or a portion of the index file for quick access. You want to try and place as much of the index file into memory as possible to help with performance.

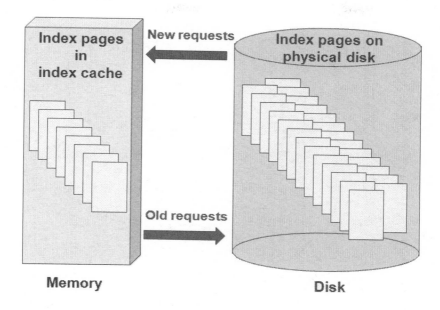

Here is a guideline for setting the index cache:

Set the index cache equal to the combined size of all essn.IND files, if possible. If you can't do that, then size the index cache as large as possible. Do not set this cache size higher than the total index size, as no performance improvement will be realized and you'll be consuming memory that other processes might need to use.

It is possible for the index to be too large: Essbase will spend more time looking in the index cache than it would use by giving up and reading from the hard drive. In other words, if your index is 1,750 GB, don't set your index cache to 1,750 GB. Start by setting the index cache to the size of all the index files and then tune downward from there. Also the index cache is consumed when the database starts and is not released until the database stops so if your index cache it too high, you waste system resources.

Here's an example: the index size for ENTPLN.Rev is 8024 KB. We have enough memory on the server, so we will increase the index cache to 8024 KB.

To set the index cache, select the database, right-click and select *Edit >> Properties*. Select the *Caches* tab:

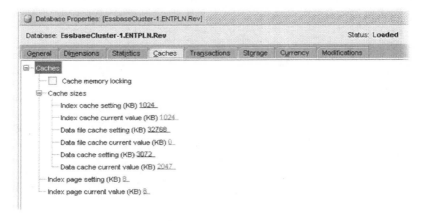

Enter the new index cache value.

TUNE THE DATA CACHE

The data cache is the memory set aside to hold data blocks once read from the hard drive. Blocks in the data cache are fully expanded, decompressed blocks, so if you have 100 Mb of data in your page file, it will take more than 100 Mb of RAM to load it into the data cache. You'll want to place as many blocks in memory as possible, but with the caveat that too much places a management burden on the system and can hurt overall performance.

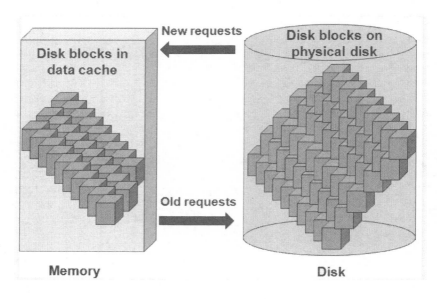

A starting guideline for setting the data cache is to set it to 0.125 times the combined size of all ess*n*.PAG files with a minimum value of about 307,200 KB (the default is only a miserly 3 Mb, and we're forcing back another diatribe on stupid defaults that never get increased). Consider increasing this value even further if you have a high number of concurrent users and they're complaining about retrieval times during peak times. Another time to further increase the Data Cache is when you have calculation scripts that contain functions that operate across sparse ranges and the functions require all members of a range to be in memory; for example, when using @RANK and @RANGE.

Here's an example of the recommended initial setting: the page size for your database is 3 GB. We have more than enough memory on the server, so we will increase the data cache to .125 * 3072000 KB or 384,000 KB which is about 384 MB.

To set the data cache, select the database, right-click and select *Edit >> Properties*. Select the *Caches* tab:

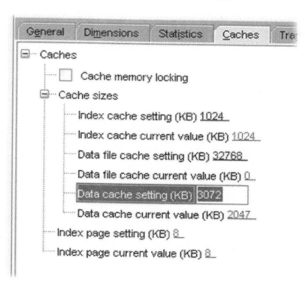

Enter the new data cache value.

The priority for cache tuning is as follows:
1. Index Cache
2. Data File Cache (when using Direct I/O which shouldn't be 99% of the time)

3. Data Cache

The new cache settings will not take effect until the database is restarted.

Cache hit ratios will tell you how well your caches are being utilized. The ratio will tell you the percentage of time that a requested piece of information is available in the cache. As a general rule, the higher the ratio, the better. The goal for the index cache ratio should be close to 1. The goal for the data cache ratio should be 1, but values as low as 0.3 are acceptable. Why so low for data cache ratio? Your page files are a lot bigger than the index file. The chances that you can fit all of the page files or data into memory is pretty slim to impossible and if the Data Cache is too big, you will encounter reduced performance.

To view the cache ratios, right-click on the database and select *Edit >> Properties*. Select the Statistics tab to view hit ratios:

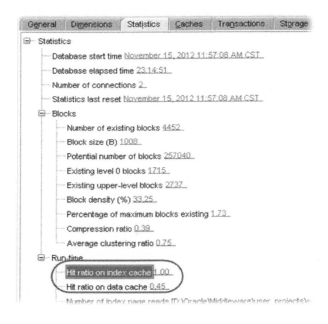

In 11.1.2.2 64-bit Essbase, you can define larger index, data, and data file cache sizes (cache sizes larger than 4 GB) without setting a scaling factor (more on this in a few pages).

OTHER TUNING SETTINGS FOR THE ESSBASE.CFG

As we discussed earlier in the book, the Essbase.CFG file is the main configuration file for Essbase, and it is simply a text file stored in the BIN directory with the Essbase binaries. Administrators may add or change parameters and values in this file to customize Essbase functionality. Most of these settings apply to the entire Essbase Server. Essbase reads the configuration file at startup of the Essbase Agent and every time an Application is loaded. Be aware of the potential requirement to restart the system or an application when you are making changes to this file.

To update the Essbase.CFG,

1. In the Administration Services console, right click on the Essbase server and select *Edit >> Properties*.
2. Choose the Environment tab.
3. Update the parameters by typing directly in the Essbase.CFG.
4. Restart the Essbase server for settings to take effect.

So what are the common configuration settings to include to help with performance? A sample config file may use the following settings (NOTE: The settings for your environment are dependent upon hardware and other factors. Test to find your optimal settings.):

```
CALCOPTFRMLBOTTOMUP        True
CALCCACHEHIGH              190000000
CALCCACHEDEFAULT    50000000
CALCCACHELOW        20000000
CALCLOCKBLOCKHIGH          15000
CALCLOCKBLOCKDEFAULT       10000
CALCLOCKBLOCKLOW    5000
DATAERRORLIMIT             65000
DYNCALCCACHEMAXSIZE        500 M
EXCEPTIONLOGOVERWRITE      False
LOCKTIMEOUT         120
MAXLOGINS           50000
NETDELAY                   2000
NETRETRYCOUNT              2000
DIRECTIO            FALSE
SSPROCROWLIMIT             500000
SSLOGUNKNOWN              False
SUPNA                     On
TIMINGMESSAGES            False
UPDATECALC          False

;Added for timeout issues on large queries
AGENTTHREADS 40
AGTSVRCONNECTIONS 30
SERVERTHREADS 40
```

CALCOPTFRMLBOTTOMUP

This setting can optimize the calculation of complex formulas on large flat sparse dimensions in large BSO database outlines, speeding up the CALC ALL or CALC DIM statements in calc scripts. If enabled, Essbase performs a bottom-up calculation on formulas that would otherwise require a top-down calculation. A warning though that in some calculations, this setting can cause inaccurate results.

CALCLOCKBLOCK

When a block is calculated, Essbase fixes on the block along with the blocks containing the children. Once the block is calculated, it is released along with the children. The default setting is 100 blocks (which works in most cases). You may need to increase if you have large number of children in a calculation. The settings you'll define are CALCLOCKBLOCKHIGH | CALCLOCKBLOCKDEFAULT | CALCLOCKBLOCKLOW n where n specifies the maximum number of blocks that Essbase can fix when calculating one block.

CALCLOCKBLOCKHIGH is the maximum number of blocks that a user can choose to fix concurrently when one data block is calculated. CALCLOCKBLOCKDEFAULT is the default setting and CALCLOCKBLOCKLOW is the minimum number of blocks. You'll use this setting with the SET LOCKBLOCK command in calc script.

MEMSCALINGFACTOR

This setting applies only to 64-bit environments in Essbase versions up to 11.1.2.1. It affects performance only to the extent that using it enables you to take advantage of the increased memory space available to 64-bit applications by increasing the cache.

The Essbase server only allows a 4GB limit on data cache settings. MEMSCALINGFACTOR allows you to allow more than 4GB. Cache settings are multiplied by the factor of n set in MEMSCALINGFACTOR . For example, if the cache setting in Essbase in 500 MB, and in Essbase.CFG MEMSCALINGFACTOR Sample Basic 10, the data cache would be 500 x 10 = 5 GB

In 11.1.2.2 and later, you do not need the MEMSCALINGFACTOR setting to increase the cache.

DLTHREADSPREPARE & DLTHREADSWRITE

The DLTHREADSPREPARE setting tells Essbase how many threads it may use in the data load preparation stage (to organize source data in memory in preparation of storing the data in blocks). The DLTHREADSWRITE sets how many threads Essbase may use in the data load process that writes blocks on disk.

You'll want to use multiple threads in parallel to improve performance. The setting is DLTHREADSPREPARE [appname [dbname]] n where N is the number of threads (which can go as high as 128 on 11.1.2.2+ Essbase on 64-bit). Watch carefully as this setting can saturate resources pretty easily.

NETDELAY

You may need to increase the NETDELAY setting if you're operating on a network with a great deal of latency. This is the amount of time Essbase waits after an unsuccessful operation to retry the operation. The minimum value (in milliseconds) is 100 and the default setting is 200.

NETRETRYCOUNT

The NETRETRYCOUNT n tells Essbase the number of times Essbase will retry the operation before it fails and reports an error. The minimum setting is 300 and the default is 600.

AGENTTHREADS & AGTSVRCONNECTIONS

Only change these settings if you are having performance issues. You can control the maximum number of threads that the Agent creates to perform the initial connection to Essbase Server using AGENTTHREADS and AGTSVRCONNECTIONS. Increasing the maximum number of possible threads between Essbase Server and the Agent allows more than one user to log on and connect to an application and database at a time. With the setting, you define the maximum number of threads that can be spawned by the Agent.

```
AGENTTHREADS maximum_number_of_threads
```

```
AGTSVRCONNECTIONS maximum_number_of_threads
```

The AGTSVRCONNECTIONS sets the maximum number of threads that the server can spawn to communicate with Agent for initial connection and disconnection.

Keep the value of maximum_number_of_threads for AGTSVRCONNECTIONS equal to or less than that value for AGENTTHREADS to avoid wasting resources. Each connection requires one thread each from server and Agent, so there is no need for higher values for AGTSVRCONNECTIONS. The default value for each setting is 5, the minimum is 1, and the maximum is 500.

Query Management

You can control query size that may slow overall performance or fail using QRYGOVEXECTIME and QRYGOVEXEBLK. QRYGOVEXECTIME limits the length of time Essbase Server allows a query to run before terminating the query. QRYGOVEXECBLK limits the number of blocks a query can access before terminating the query.

```
QRYGOVEXECTIME [appname [dbname]] n
QRYGOVEXECBLK [appname [dbname]] n
```

You can apply these settings to all the applications and databases on Essbase Server, to all the databases on a single application, or to a single database

As Essbase processes requests, the requested grids consist of the number of cells requested and sent from the target to the source. If too many cells are requested, response time can be slowed. This is where limiting the request grid size and splitting grids into multiple data slices can be useful.

```
MAX_REQUEST_GRID_SIZE [appname [dbname]] n
MAX_RESPONSE_GRID_SIZE [appname [dbname]] n
```

PERFORMANCE IMPROVEMENTS IN ESSBASE 11.1.2.2

In 11.1.2.2 Essbase you will find some big "under the covers" performance improvements and the ability to take advantage of more processors and memory that comes with hardware today..

Block storage parallel calculations (discussed earlier) are more effective, able to use an increased setting for task dimensions (sparse dimensions used to identify tasks). The task dimensions can either be selected dynamically by Essbase or can be overridden by specifying a value for CALCTASKDIMS in the Essbase.CFG file

Block storage parallel restructuring allows more restructuring threads to be used when setting the RESTRUCTURETHREADS setting.

Block storage parallel data exports are supported using the **export data** MaxL statement which exports data from a BSO database in parallel. You can specify a comma-separated list of export files (up to a maximum of 1024 filenames). This results in a more even distribution of data blocks between export threads. The EXPORTTHREADS configuration setting has been enhanced to support block storage parallel data export.

Block storage parallel data loads are possible, loading multiple data files concurrently. This approach uses multiple parallel pipelines on the server and multiple threads on the client. To control the number of pipelines or threads spawned by a data load request, you set the limit using the max_threads grammar in the **import data** MaxL statement

64-bit Essbase Server can now accommodate larger index, data, and data file cache sizes without setting a scaling factor (cache sizes larger than 4 GB).

New in Essbase 11.1.2.2, we can throttle the total number of active transactions. Each allotted server thread for an application may create child threads for tasks such as parallel calculation, parallel data load or export, or parallel restructuring. To take advantage of this feature, use the use the MAXTOTALACTIVETRANSACTIONS and MAXACTIVEUPDATETRANSACTIONS Essbase.CFG settings.

If the total number of running threads is too high, threads may lose efficiency while contending for server resources.

DEFINE COMPRESSION METHOD FOR BSO

Attention readers: this last section is for the IT geeks in the audience (OK, maybe this entire chapter is for the IT geeks). When Essbase stores blocks to disk, it can compress the blocks using one of several different algorithms to save space. When a compressed block is requested, Essbase will uncompress the block before sending the data into the main engine for further processing. Luckily this is all happening behind the scenes, so you can just make your choice and Essbase will handle all these details for you. Compression options include:

- No compression
- zLib
- Index Value Pair
- Bitmap
- RLE

No compression is an option, but you should only use it in production if your average block density is around 90%.

zLib compression is good for very sparse data.

Index value pair (IVP) is good for large blocks with sparse data though you don't directly assign this compression type. Use index value pair when your blocks are very large, say more than 1Mb and you have just a few values loaded per block.

Bitmap is the default and is good for non-repeating data. Behind the scenes, each block has a hashtable of bits for each potential cell in the block: if the bit is set to 1 then that says that cell in the block has a value, but if it is set to 0 then that cell is #Missing. It uses that hashtable to index to a series of values stored in the block. Both the block's hashtable and the values are stored in the block itself (not in the index file) If bitmap compression is chosen, then Essbase can choose between bitmap and index value pair compression types for the best fit. If bitmap compression is chosen, then Essbase can choose between bitmap, index value pair, and "no compression" compression types for the best fit.

RLE or run length encoding compression type is good for blocks with many zeroes or repeating values. RLE works by keeping track of repeating values and then saying essentially "there are X number of value Y at this spot in the block." For instance, if there are 17 zeros in succession in the block, RLE would compress that down to "17,0." If RLE compression is chosen, then Essbase can choose between RLE, bitmap, index value pair, and "no compression" compression types for the best fit.

To set compression:
1. Select the database.
2. Right click and select *Edit Properties*.
3. Select the Storage tab.
4. Select the desired compression type:

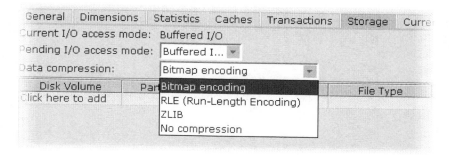

5. Click *Apply*.

Note!

The storage tab will tell you the size of your database (both index and page files):

Dimension order within your outline will make a difference with respect to optimizing compression. If you think of a block on disk like a spreadsheet, the first dense dimension determines the columns in the page file (though new versions of Essbase sometimes ignore your dimension order and decide internally which dimension to put first). Compression then works from left to right, top to bottom. Historically, people said that Accounts should be the first then Time the second dense dimension:

	A	B	C	D	E	F	
1		Budget					
2		Sales	COGS	Margin	Exp	Profit	
3	Jan	100	50	50	30	20	
4	Feb	100	50	50	30	20	
5	Mar	100	50	50	30	20	
6	Apr	120	50	70	30	40	
7	May	120	50	70	30	40	
8	Jun	120	50	70	30	40	
9							

For the last few years, we recommended using RLE compression assuming you could make a dense dimension with repeating values be first in the outline. When you used RLE compression, you could switch the order of dimensions, listing Time as your first dense dimension, then Accounts, so that Essbase would take advantage of the high probability of values repeating in successive periods (especially in budget scenarios).

	A	B	C	D	E	F	G	
1		Budget						
2		Jan	Feb	Mar	Apr	May	Jun	
3	Sales	100	100	100	120	120	120	
4	COGS	50	50	50	50	50	50	
5	Margin	50	50	50	70	70	70	
6	Exp	30	30	30	30	30	30	
7	Profit	20	20	20	40	40	40	
8								

Based on recent testing on 11.1.2.2 versions, Essbase internally determines the optimal dense dimension order (ignoring the outline order) and hence, not necessarily taking advantage of the dimension you told it had all the repeating values. We also found in some cases while RLE does reduce the PAG size but it doesn't necessarily reduce calc time. In some cases, it seemed to be slowing it while it chooses for each block the optimal type of compression. Lessons learned? Test different compressions settings for each database to find the optimal setting and don't assume that your first dense dimension is necessarily the one along which it compresses.

Penny's head is buried in her arms on the desk, fast asleep, a pile of drool forming under her chin. The Translator gently taps Penny on the shoulder, waking her.

Penny sits up, a bit groggy.

"Penny, that's it. We've covered all of the Tuning topics. Granted you slept through the last scene but that's why you have this book. You can come back and review this information when you need it," The Translator says.

"It's time to call Eddie," says SuperManager. That wakes Penny up.

"I don't know if I can. What if I can't defeat Dr. Dementor next time? Am I ready?"

"You are ready," says Aquaman.

"We're here for you," says Mr. Anachronism.

(Lights dim. Disco ball and wild colored lights start up. Spotlight goes on The Consultants. EVERYONE including BAND dons wild disco wigs and puts on bling and sings the reprisal set to I Believe in Miracles.)

I BELIEVE THAT PENNY, CAN WIN OVER EDDIE!
(LIKE CONSULTANTS DO)
BUT I THINK TO DO IT, PENNY WILL NEED,
HYPERION PLANNING!

YOU'RE GOING TO HELP EDDIE.
IT'S SO GREAT THAT HE NEEDS YOU.
IT'S GREAT THAT HE NEEDS YOU SO BADLY.
BECAUSE BY NEXT WEEK, HE'LL HAVE FALLEN
BACK IN LOVE MADLY.

YESTERDAY, YOU WERE A PATHETIC IT GEEK
NOW YOU'VE GOT A WEEK TO SINK OR SWIM, NO
PRESSURE YOU SEE, CAUSE
I BELIEVE IN PENNY, SHE CAN DO, ANYTHING
(ANYTHING IT'S TRUE)
I BELIEVE IN PENNY, AND ORACLE HYPERION
PLANNING...

"OK," Penny says and picks up the phone.

EPILOGUE

You can plan on the web, plan in Excel, approve plans, and set preferences. We've reached the end of our computer books / musical.

Our musical ends with the CFO giving himself a big bonus when actuals exceeded the plan numbers. Aquaman received a promotion when he proved he could be really useful. And most importantly, despite attempts by Dr. Dementor, Eddie and Penny finish the plan and reunite and are married in Las Vegas at the Annual Budgeteer's Conference.

We'd like to dedicate our last song to our fearless leader at Oracle, Larry Ellison. Sing along if you know the lyrics (parody of *Mickey Mouse Club Theme*).

ALL

WHO'S THE LEADER OF THE CLUB
WHO MAKES THIS MERGER A WIN WIN?

L A R R Y E L
L I S O N

LARRY!
ELLISON!
LARRY!
ELLISON!

HE'LL TAKE THIS COMPANY HIGHER THAN JOHN GLENN! (GLENN, GLENN, GLENN)

COME ALONG AND SING THE SONG
WE'LL SAY WE KNEW HIM WHEN,

L A R R Y E L
L I S O N

(Signs held up spelling letters as each word is sung.)

ORACLE!
EPM!
ORACLE!
EPM!

SINGLEHANDEDLY
YOU'LL KILL S.A.P.!

HEY THERE, HI THERE, HO THERE,

WHAT A GREAT RIDE IT'S BEEN

L A R R Y E L
L I S O N

(Ending theme, much slower.)

NOW IT'S TIME TO SAY GOODBYE
TO OUR DEAR HY-PER-I-ON.

L A R
(Spoken by Penny) ARE WE SURE THIS ISN'T A BIG
MISTAKE?

R Y E L
(Spoken by Eddie) 'ELL IF I KNOW, BUT IT'LL BE FUN.
L I S O N

Appendix A:
Introduction to EPMA

As you begin to rollout Oracle EPM / Hyperion, the number of applications required to meet performance management needs is likely to grow. With a growing environment, you encounter many challenges in developing and maintaining a number of different dimensions and data sets across applications. The result is duplicate efforts and higher development and maintenance costs which are never a good thing.

Does your dimension maintenance process look like the following?

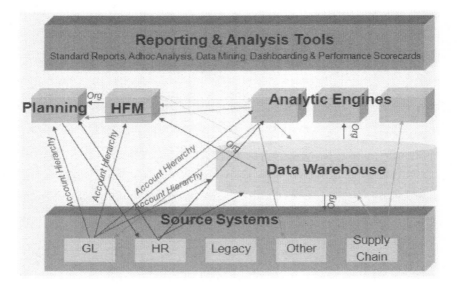

For example, the Accounts dimension is sourced from the GL system and shared with the data warehouse, Essbase, Planning and Financial Management. The Organization dimension is sourced and maintained in the data warehouse to all Hyperion applications. Other dimensions may be maintained in Essbase or other applications, resulting in a hodge-podge of dimension maintenance processes.

Enterprise Performance Management Architect is a solution that can address some of these concerns and issues. Enterprise Performance Management Architect (EPMA) provides a single interface to build, deploy, and manage all financial applications for

Planning, Financial Management, Essbase and Profitability and Cost Management. EPMA uses a visual interface to manage, link, and synchronize applications for Hyperion administrators.

EPMA contains the following components:

- Dimensions Library – one place to create and maintain dimensions across Hyperion applications
- Applications Library – one place to manage Hyperion applications
- Data Synchronization View – synchronize data across Hyperion applications
- Application Upgrade – upgrade Planning and FM applications from previous releases
- Job Console – view a summary of Dimension Library and Application activities like imports, deployments and data synchronizations

The basic architecture for EPMA contains a number of underlying EPMA services and a backend relational repository.

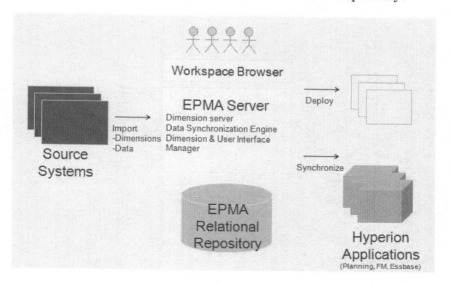

Do you have to use Enterprise Performance Management Architect? No. You can continue to use Planning "Classic" if desired.

Note!

If you are on version 9.3.1, stop reading now. Revisit EPMA when you upgrade to version 11. EPMA was introduced in version 9.3 and while you can get it to work, it will be a long, painful, buggy process. Version 11 addressed a number of different items that make the deployment process a much smoother sailing effort.

Note!

The content in this appendix is based on 11.1.2.2.

At a very high level, the process is as follows: Dimensions are imported into or manually created in EPMA via the Workspace browser and then grouped together to create EPMA applications. The EPMA application is deployed to the specific solution like Planning, Essbase or Financial Management. The easiest way to learn EPMA is to create an EPMA deployed application, so let us jump head first into your first EPMA application.

Access EPMA

Test question: Where do you access EPMA? This should be an easy one, The Workspace, of course. You get to practically everything via the Workspace.

1. Log into the Workspace.
2. Select *Navigate icon >> Administer* and then the desired EPMA module: Dimension Library, Application Library, Data Synchronization, Transform Classic to EPM Architect, Library Job Console, and Configure Interface Data Source.
3. To get started, we'll select *Dimension Library*.

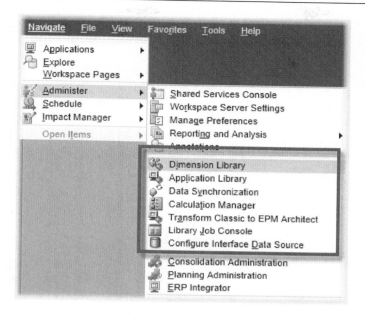

DIMENSION LIBRARY

The Dimension Library will open and may or may not have dimensions listed in your environment (this depends on if others have created dimensions):

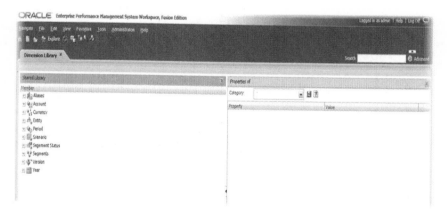

The EPMA Dimension Library provides one place to create and maintain dimensions across Oracle EPM / Hyperion applications. You can maintain the hierarchies for the dimensions as well as global and application specific properties. Dimensions can be used in multiple applications. For EPMA deployed applications, you will maintain dimensions here and not in the web clients for Planning and Financial Management. You can still view dimensions in the Classic applications but you can't change them.

Within the Dimension Library you can have two types of dimensions: shared dimensions and local dimensions. Shared dimensions are dimensions that can be used by multiple applications. Local dimensions are detached, independent dimensions that exist in only one application. Dimensions can be switched from shared to local and local to shared as well synchronized in applications.

Create a Dimension

To create a dimension in the Dimension Library,
1. Select *File>> New>>Dimension*:

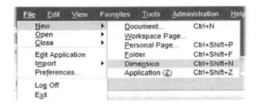

2. Type in the *Dimension name* and *Description*.
3. Select the *Dimension type*. To follow along choose *Generic*:

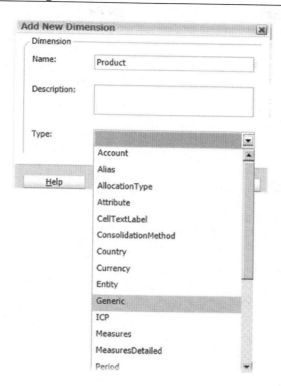

A number of dimension types exist for EPMA dimensions and not all of those types are applicable to Planning. For example, Financial Management will use dimension types like Security Class or Consolidation Method.

The dimension types that you could possibly use in Planning include:

- Account
- Alias
- Allocation Type
- Attribute
- CellTextLabel
- ConsolidationMethod
- Country
- Currency
- Entity
- Generic
- ICP
- Measures
- MeasuresDetailed

- Period
- Scenario
- ScenarioClass
- Smart List
- Time
- UDA
- Value
- Version
- View
- Year

By selecting the dimension type, the appropriate properties will be created (e.g. Time Balance properties only apply to Accounts dimensions). These dimension types and elements are covered throughout the main content of the book so we're going to assume that you know and understand these concepts.

4. Click *OK*.
    The Product dimension is created in the Shared Library:

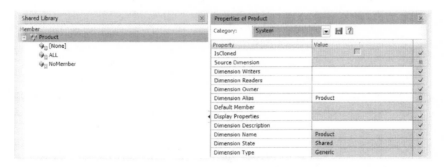

Now all you need to do is create the members and hierarchies.

5. Right-click on "Product" and select *Create Member >> As Child:*

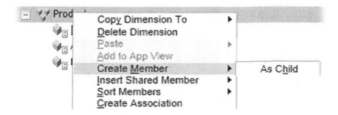

6. Type in the member name "Colas":

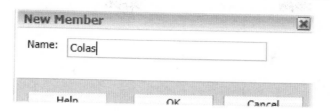

7. Click *OK*.
8. Repeat the same *Create Member* steps to build the following hierarchy under Product:

9. Select the member "Colas".
10. From the property drop down box, select *Planning*:

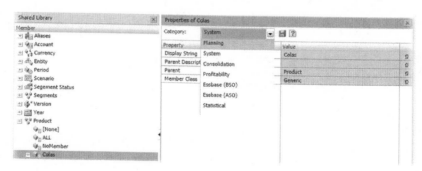

11. The Planning properties will display:

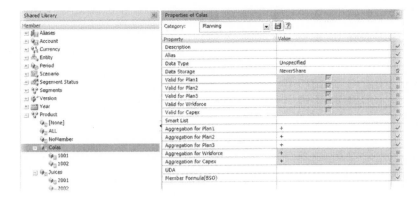

Notice the plan type options are grayed out. This is because those are application specific properties. You can define an alias, consolidation tag, UDA, data storage and other Planning properties.

12. Change the Data Storage property from *NeverShare* to *StoreData*:

Data Type	Unspecified	
Data Storage	NeverShare	▼
Valid for Plan1	StoreData	
Valid for Plan2	DynamicCalcAndStore	
Valid for Plan3		
Valid for Wrkforce	DynamicCalc	
Valid for Capex	NeverShare	
Smart List	LabelOnly	

The Data Storage property is changed to yellow to highlight that a change has been made but not saved.

13. Click the *Save* icon:

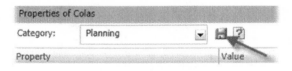

14. Click in the *Alias* text box and select the *ellipses* icon to define an alias:

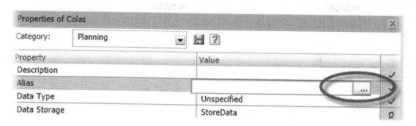

Did you get an error message?

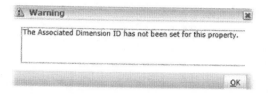

Create an Associated Dimension

Dimension associations are used in EPMA to relate dimensions within the Shared Library and applications. A dimension association is created for all properties where the property value refers to a member of another dimension.

The alias property requires an associated dimension. So your steps are to: 1) create an alias dimension and 2) associate it with the Product dimension. Once you pull the Product dimension or any other dimension with dimensions associations into an application, you must activate the dimension associations.

1. Select *File >> New >> Dimension*.
2. Type in "Aliases" for the *Dimension name* and choose *Alias* as the dimension type:

3. Click *OK*.

4. The Aliases dimension is created in the Dimension Library.
5. Right-click on the Product dimension and select *Create Association*:

6. Select *Existing Property*.
7. Choose the property *Alias*.
8. Choose the dimension *Aliases* (the new Aliases dimension you just created):

9. Click *OK*.
10. Navigate back to the "Colas" member and its Planning properties.
11. Click in the *Alias* text box and select the ellipses icon to define an alias.
12. Enter an alias in the *Default* text box:

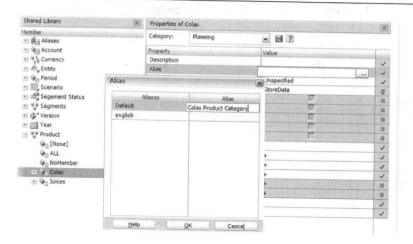

13. Click *OK*.

The alias is added though you can't see it in the property window:

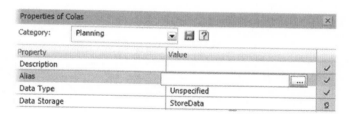

14. Click the *Save* icon to save the alias.

You can perform the following actions on dimensions within the EPMA Dimension Library:
- Copy local dimensions to the Shared Library
- Copy dimensions to an application
- Delete dimensions
- Create and view associations
- View application membership and deployment status
- Find members and orphan members

You can perform the following actions on members within the EPMA Dimension Library:

- Cut and copy
- Create members
- Insert shared members
- Sort Members
- Remove members
- Delete members
- Collapse Parent
- Rename member
- View application membership (in which applications does the member exist)
- Find members
- Reorder a members children

Import File Format

For most dimensions with a large number of members, you will want to import the dimension (versus manually typing the members into EPMA). You may import the dimension once and then maintain the hierarchy in EPMA going forward or you may run dimension imports on a periodic basis from other sources to keep the hierarchy current.

EPMA supports dimension imports using a specific flat file format or user interface tables. In this appendix, we will cover the flat file method. Within the flat file, five sections are possible:

- Dimensions
- Dimension Associations
- Members
- Hierarchies
- Property Array

Additionally there is a header that must be included:
FILE_FORMAT = ADS
VERSION=1.0

The Dimensions section lists the dimension contained in the import file along with any defined dimension properties:

```
!FILE_FORMAT=ADS
!VERSION=1.0

!Section=Dimensions
'Name|DimensionClass|DimensionAlias|DimDataStorage|DimTwoPassCalc|Plan1Density|P
Active-Inactive|Attribute|Active-Inactive||||||Boolean||||||||||||||||
Account|Account|Account|NeverShare||Dense|Dense|Dense|||1|0|0|||Y|N|N|N|2|1|1|
Currency|Currency|Currency|NeverShare||Sparse|Sparse|Sparse|||2|0|0|||Y|N|N|N|
Entity|Entity|Entity|NeverShare||Sparse|Sparse|Sparse|||3|0|0|||Y|N|N|N|3|7|7|
Period|Period|Period|NeverShare||Dense|Dense|Dense|||4|0|0|||Y|N|N|N|2|2|2|2|
Scenario|Scenario|Scenario|NeverShare||Sparse|Sparse|Sparse|||5|0|0|||Y|N|N|N|
Segments|Generic|Segments|StoreData||Sparse|Sparse|Sparse|||6|0|0|||Y|N|N|N|4
Version|Version|Version|NeverShare||Sparse|Sparse|Sparse|||7|0|0|||Y|N|N|N|8|
Year|Year|Year|NeverShare||Sparse|Sparse|Sparse|||8|0|0|||Y|N|N|N|
S1_Sales_Risk|SmartList|Sales_Risk|||||||||||||||||ID|Grid|Y|Sales Risk|
S1_Test_SmartList|SmartList|Test_SmartList|||||||||||||||||Pick One|NAME|
Alias|Alias|Alias|||||||||||||||||||||

!Section=DimensionAssociations
'BaseDimension|Property|TargetDimension
Active-Inactive|Alias|Alias
Account|Alias|Alias
Currency|Alias|Alias
Currency|TriangulationCurrency|Currency
```

The DimensionAssociations section lists the base dimension, the property to be mapped using an associated dimension, and the associated dimension itself:

```
 Scenario|Scenario|Scenario|NeverShare||Sparse|Sparse|S
 Segments|Generic|Segments|StoreData||Sparse|Sparse|Spa
 Version|Version|Version|NeverShare||Sparse|Sparse|Spar
 Year|Year|Year|NeverShare||Sparse|Sparse|Sparse|||8|0
 sl_Sales_Risk|SmartList|Sales_Risk||||||||||||||||||
 sl_Test_SmartList|SmartList|Test_SmartList||||||||||||
 Alias|Alias|Alias|||||||||||||||||||||||||||||
```

```
!Section=DimensionAssociations
'BaseDimension|Property|TargetDimension
Active-Inactive|Alias|Alias
Account|Alias|Alias
Currency|Alias|Alias
Currency|TriangulationCurrency|Currency
Entity|Alias|Alias
Entity|Currency|Currency
Period|Alias|Alias
Scenario|Alias|Alias
Scenario|StartPeriod|Period
Scenario|EndPeriod|Period
Scenario|StartYear|Year
Scenario|EndYear|Year
Segments|Alias|Alias
Segments|Active-Inactive|Active-Inactive
Version|Alias|Alias
Year|Alias|Alias
```

```
!Hierarchies=Active-Inactive
'Parent|Child|DataStorage|IsPrimary|Alias=Default
#root|True||Y|Active
```

The Hierarchies section defines the hierarchy in parent child format along with any defined properties for the child:

```
!Hierarchies=Active-Inactive
'Parent|Child|DataStorage|IsPrimary|Alias=Default
#root|True||Y|Active
#root|False||Y|Inactive

!Hierarchies=Account
'Parent|Child|DataStorage|IsPrimary|MemberValidForPlan1|MemberValidForPlan2|Memb
#root|Statistics|DynamicCalc|Y|Y|N|N|||~||||NonCurrency|Plan1|SavedAssumption|N
Statistics|CapitalExpenditures|DynamicCalc|Y|Y|N|N|||~||||NonCurrency|Plan1|Sav
CapitalExpenditures|CapExLand|StoreData|Y|Y|N|N|||+||||NonCurrency|Plan1|SavedAssu
CapitalExpenditures|CapExBuildings|StoreData|Y|Y|N|N|||+||||NonCurrency|Plan1|Sa
CapitalExpenditures|CapExLsholdImprov|StoreData|Y|Y|N|N|||+||||NonCurrency|Plan1
CapitalExpenditures|CapExMfgMach|StoreData|Y|Y|N|N|||+||||NonCurrency|Plan1|Sav
CapitalExpenditures|CapExOffFurn|StoreData|Y|Y|N|N|||+||||NonCurrency|Plan1|Sav
CapitalExpenditures|CapExCompEquip|StoreData|Y|Y|N|N|||+||||NonCurrency|Plan1|S
CapitalExpenditures|CapExCompSftwr|StoreData|Y|Y|N|N|||+||||NonCurrency|Plan1|S
CapitalExpenditures|CapExVehicles|StoreData|Y|Y|N|N|||+||||NonCurrency|Plan1|Sa
Statistics|OtherDrivers|DynamicCalc|Y|Y|N|N|||~||||NonCurrency|Plan1|SavedAssum
OtherDrivers|NI|StoreData|Y|Y|N|N|||~||||NonCurrency|Plan1|SavedAssumption|Average
OtherDrivers|EBITDA|StoreData|Y|Y|N|N|||~||||NonCurrency|Plan1|SavedAssumption||
OtherDrivers|InventoryDays|StoreData|Y|Y|N|N|||~||||NonCurrency|Plan1|SavedAssu
OtherDrivers|PayablesDays|StoreData|Y|Y|N|N|||~||||NonCurrency|Plan1|SavedAssum
OtherDrivers|ReceivablesDays|StoreData|Y|Y|N|N|||~||||NonCurrency|Plan1|SavedAs
OtherDrivers|WorkingDays|StoreData|Y|Y|N|N|||~||||NonCurrency|Plan1|SavedAssump
```

Depending on what you need to do, you may not need all sections. If you are creating a new dimension, the Dimension, Dimension Association, and Relationship sections are required. If you are updating a dimension, only the Relationship section is required. The Members and PropArray (alias property) sections are optional.

EPMA File Generator

Creating the import file can be the trickiest part of EPMA. To jump start the process, you can create an EPMA import file from an existing Planning application (or other) using the EPMA File Generator. This utility generates import files from existing applications from existing Planning and Financial Management applications, Financial Management metadata files, existing EPMA applications and even Excel.

To create an EPMA import file from the EPMA File Generator,

1. On the EPMA server, select *Start Programs >> Oracle EPM>>Foundation Services>>Performance Management Architect>>Start EPMA File Generator.* (Your start menu structure may vary).

The EPMA File Generator will launch:

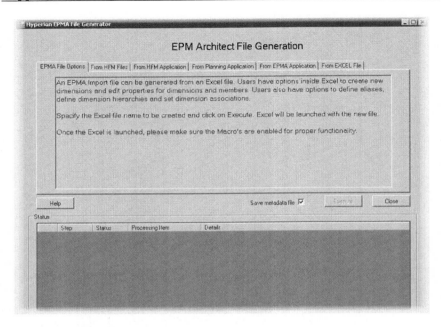

2. Select the *From Planning Application* tab.
3. Enter the Planning administrator user name and password.
4. Enter the *Workspace URL*.
5. Enter the *Planning Web URL*.
6. Enter the *Planning application name* and *Application server*. To follow along, choose the Planning Sample application (we are using a slightly modified version of the Planning Sample application).
7. Specify the directory where the file should be placed and the file name for the .ads file:

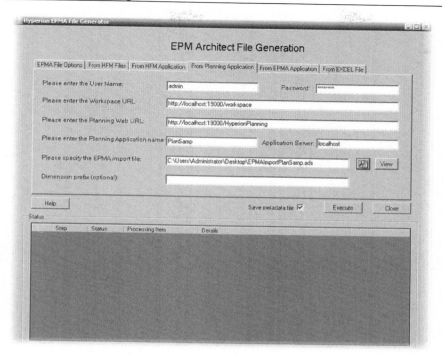

8. Optionally add a prefix to all of the dimensions.

Note!   Above entries may differ,
- Port 19000: may need to be modified depending on your environment
- localhost: modify, as needed, for your environment

For example, the EPMA Dimension Library already contains an Entity dimension. You want to import the Entity dimension from the Planning application that may be different than the one already in EPMA so you'll need to create it as its own dimension. You could add a prefix of "NewSamp" that will be added to the Entity name so that the 2 dimensions can coexist separately. (If you are testing this in a development EPMA environment, consider adding a prefix of your initials so that you won't run into issues with other administrators who have tested this same process.)

9. Click *Execute* and the file will generate.

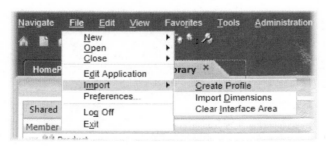

```
EPMAImport.ads - Notepad
File  Edit  Format  View  Help
!FILE_FORMAT=ADS
!VERSION=1.0

!Section=Dimensions
'Name|DimensionClass|DimensionAlias|DimDataStorage|DimTwoPassCalc|Plan1Density|Plan2Density|Plan3Density|wo
Introduction Date|Attribute|Introduction Date||||||Date||||||||||||
Active-Inactive Products|Attribute|Active-Inactive Products|||||Boolean||||||||||||||||
weight|Attribute|weight|||||||Numeric||||||||||
Account|Account|Account|NeverShare||Dense|Dense|Dense||||1|0|0|||Y|N|N|N|N|2|1|1|2|2||||
Currency|Currency|Currency|NeverShare||Sparse|Sparse|Sparse||||0|0|0|||Y|N|N|N|N|6|6|6|6|6||||
Entity|Entity|Entity|NeverShare||Sparse|Sparse|Sparse||||0|0|0|||Y|N|N|N|N|3|7|7|3|3||||
Period|Period|Period|NeverShare||Dense|Dense|Dense||||0|0|0|||Y|N|N|N|N|2|2|2|2|2||||
Scenario|Scenario|Scenario|NeverShare||Sparse|Sparse|Sparse||||2|0|0|||Y|N|N|N|N|7|4|4|7|7||||
Segments|Generic|Segments|StoreData||Sparse|Sparse|Sparse||||0|0|0|||Y|N|N|N|N|4|8|8|4|4||||
Version|Version|Version|NeverShare||Sparse|Sparse|Sparse||||4|0|0|||Y|N|N|N|N|8|5|5|8|8||||
Year|Year|Year|NeverShare||Sparse|Sparse|Sparse||||0|0|0|||Y|N|N|N|N|3|3|3|3|3||||
Alias|Alias|Alias|||||||||||||||||||||

!Section=DimensionAssociations
'BaseDimension|Property|TargetDimension
Introduction Date|Alias|Alias
Active-Inactive Products|Alias|Alias
weight|Alias|Alias
Account|Alias|Alias
Currency|Alias|Alias
Currency|TriangulationCurrency|Currency
Entity|Alias|Alias
Entity|Currency|Currency
Period|Alias|Alias
Scenario|Alias|Alias
Scenario|StartPeriod|Period
Scenario|EndPeriod|Period
Scenario|StartYear|Year
Scenario|EndYear|Year
Segments|Alias|Alias
Segments|Introduction Date|Introduction Date
Segments|Active-Inactive Products|Active-Inactive Products
Segments|weight|weight
Version|Alias|Alias
Year|Alias|Alias

!Hierarchies=Introduction Date
```

Now that we have an EPMA import file ready to go, let's create an import profile.

Create an Import Profile

An import profile tells EPMA how to handle the import file including whether or not to create dimensions, what columns should be mapped to what properties, and how merges should take place.

To create an import profile,

1. Select *File >> Import >> Create Profile*:

2. Define the *Profile Name*.
3. Select the *Import Type*; in our example choose *Flat File*:

You can import dimensions from a flat file, the EPMA interface tables or directly from Data Relationship Management.

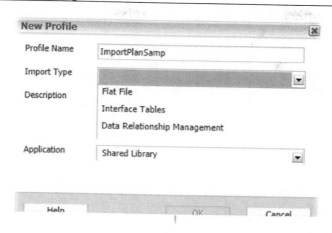

4. For Application, select *Shared Library*.

If EPMA applications exist, you can alternatively import metadata directly into an EPMA application as a local dimension.

5. Browse to and select the import file. Click *Open*:

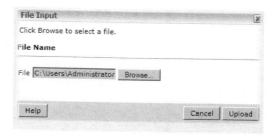

6. Click *Upload*.
7. Click *OK*.
8. Define the appropriate File Properties to match the import file: *Column Delimiter, Remove Double Quotes on Strings, Remove White Space,* and *Suppress Transaction logs*:

In most cases for imports, you will want to turn off transaction logging.

9. Click *Next*.
10. Map each dimension in the flat file to a dimension in the Shared Library.
11. Optionally check the option to *Create Dimensions for non-mapped dimensions*.
12. Optionally check the *Reorder Existing Members*:

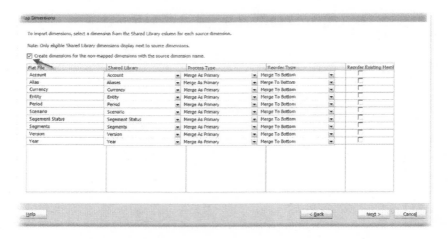

13. Click *Next*.
14. For each dimension in the import file, map the properties in the file to the properties in the Shared Library.

The Account dimension properties should match as follows: (No checks for Shared Library)

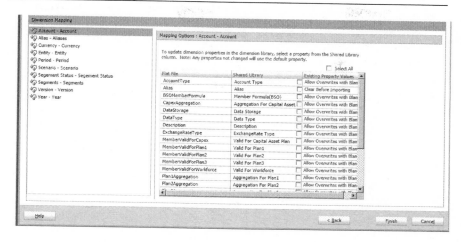

The Entity dimension properties should match as follows:

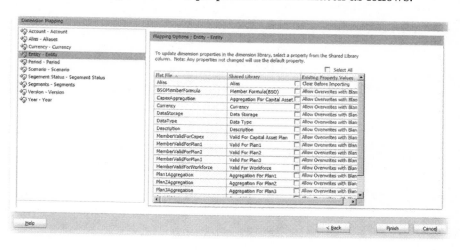

The Period dimension properties should match as follows:

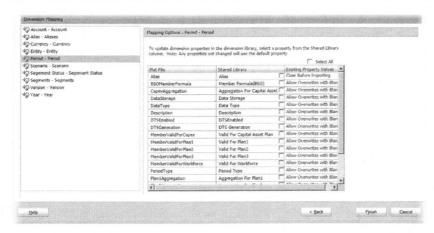

The Scenario dimension properties should match as follows:

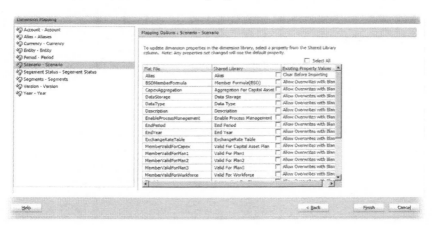

The Version dimension properties should match as follows:

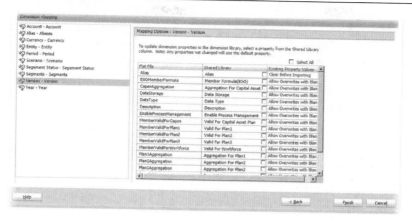

15. Once the properties have been mapped for all
dimensions, click *Finish.*

The import profile will be created and you'll be prompted to
execute the profile (a.k.a. run the import process).

16. Click *Yes* to run the import.

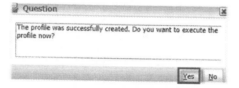

A message will display informing you of the Job ID. If
desired, you can click on the link to navigate to the Job Console and
view the status. Otherwise click *Close.*

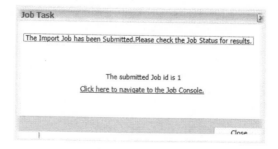

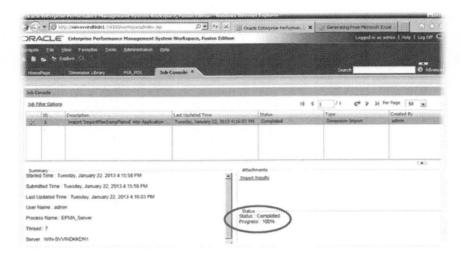

The dimensions should import successfully into the Dimension Library upon completion of the import:

Now that the import profile is created, you can rerun the import process with new data files (as long as the sections and mappings are the same).

To import dimensions with an existing import profile,

1. Select *File>>Import>>Import Dimensions*:

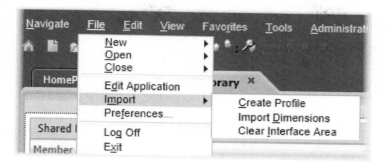

2. Select the *Import Profile.*
3. Select the Import Type: *Flat File, Interface Tables or DRM.*
4. Browse to the import file.
5. Click *Upload:*

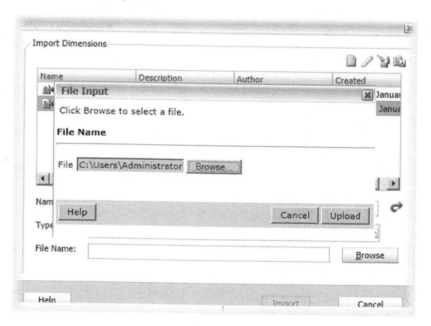

6. Click *Upload*
7. Click *Import.*

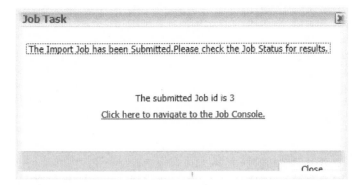

Edit Properties

Once you have imported dimensions or created them manually, you are ready to set the properties. EPMA supports the following properties:

- System
- Planning
- Consolidation
- Hyperion Profitability and Cost Management
- Essbase (BSO)
- Essbase (ASO)
- Statistical

Some of the properties are maintained by EPMA. Others are set to a default but can be overridden by an administrator and some properties are blank, ready to be defined. These are the same properties that you have worked with in the Planning web client:

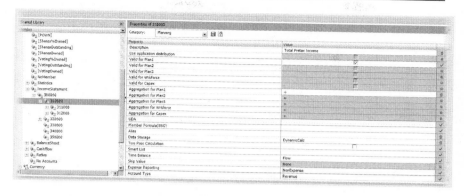

Notice in this Shared Library view, we can only view properties one member at a time. Is there another way to view the properties for multiple members at once?

In the Planning web client, no. In EPMA, yes, with the Grid Editor.

Grid Editor

The Grid Editor is an option within the Dimension Library that allows you to view, manage, and update many members and properties at the same time in a grid display. This is one of the convincing factors for migrating from Classic to EPMA.

To use the Grid Editor,

1. Right-click on the dimension (or member) and select *Grid Editor*:

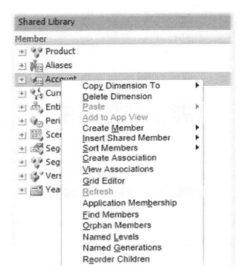

2. Select the desired member or members. In our example, choose *IDescendants of NetRevenue*.

Note you can use the member selection functions to select a dynamic list of members:

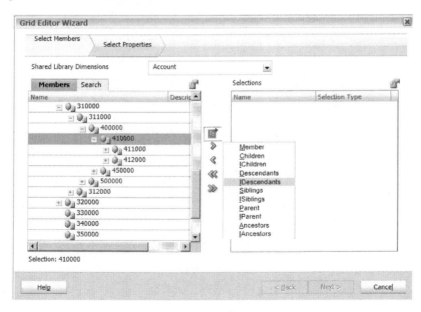

3. Click *Next*.

4. Select the property (or properties) that you want to display by property category. In our example we chose all of the Planning properties:

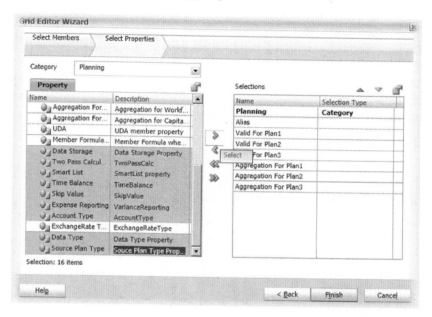

5. Click *Finish*.

The Grid Editor will display with the selected members and the properties. From this window you can view and update properties. You can add or remove members from the dimension or copy and paste members.

Now that we've taken you through the basics of the Dimension Library and created some dimensions, let's create an EPMA application.

APPLICATION LIBRARY

An application in EPMA is a grouping of dimensions (either Shared or Local) that will ultimately be deployed to create an application in Planning or other Hyperion solution. With EPMA's drag and drop interface, the application creation process is simple. Let's create one now.

Create an Application

To create an application,

1. Select *File >> New >> Application*:

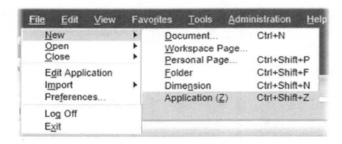

2. Enter the *Application Name*; for our example, we entered "PLNEPMA".
3. Select *Planning* for the *Application Type*:

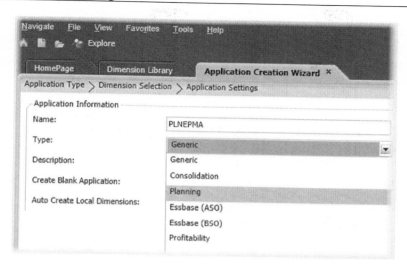

At that point the Planning Application Creation Wizard will display. Define the same application information as you do in Classic Planning: Plan types, Currency and Calendar information.

4. Because we are "recreating" the Planning Sample application and we know the properties are defined correctly for Planning Sample structure, set the information as follows (one plan type named Consol, Yes-Multi-currency, Default currency, 12 months, Jan, Even):

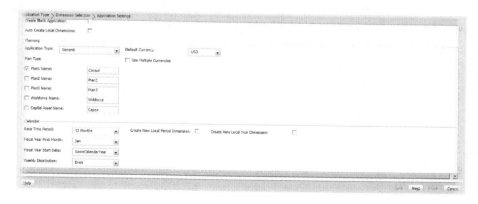

If you wanted, you could have chosen a new local period and year dimension. For our example we will use the shared dimensions in the Dimension Library.

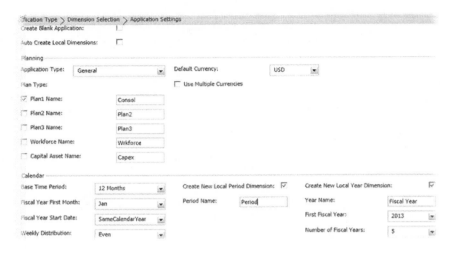

5. Click *Next*.
6. Select the dimensions to be added to the application:

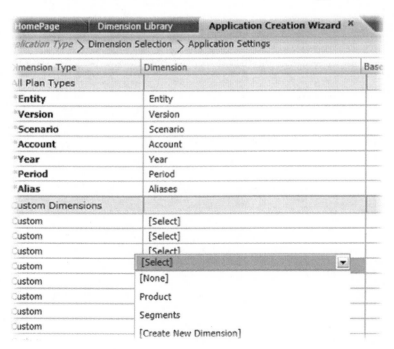

If your Dimension Library contains a single Account, Entity, Version, and Scenario dimension, they will automatically associate. If more than one exists, you can choose the specific dimension for the application.

7. Click *Next* once the dimensions are defined. The EPMA application is created:

8. The next step in the wizard driven process is to define any application specific settings or properties (those that may vary from the Shared Library):

For example, you can right-click on a member and select Exclude to filter the member (and its descendants) from the application. In this portion of the Application definition, you can also define the outline order of dimensions.

9. Right-click on the application and select *Performance Settings*:

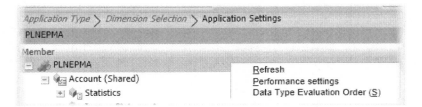

10. Update the dense and sparse settings and move the order of dimensions to achieve optimal performance in the deployed application:

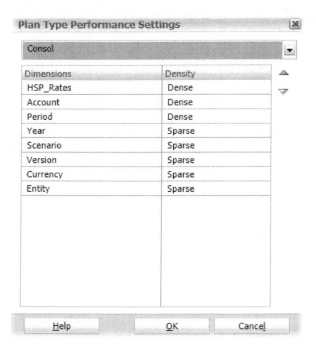

11. Click *OK*.

You can also set the Data Type evaluation order (important when you define Smart Lists across multiple dimensions).

Remember earlier in this appendix when we created a dimension association we said "Once you pull a dimension with dimensions associations into an application, you must activate the dimension associations." We're at that step now.

12. Right-click on the application and select *Activate All Associations*:

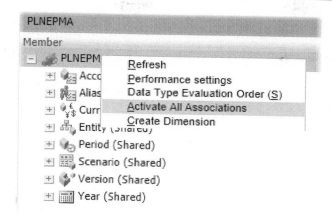

13. Click *Finish*. (Optionally you can click *Deploy* when finished but let's hold off with deployment for now.)

Manage Applications in the Application Library

The application has now been created in the Application Library. The Application Library displays all of the applications that have been created within EPMA.

To access the Application Library,

1. Select *File >> Administer >> Application Library*:

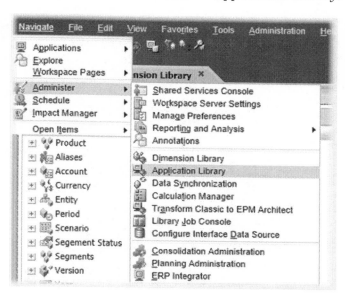

The applications can have the following statuses: *Not Deployed* means the application has been created, but has not been deployed to an environment and *Deployed* means the application has been created and deployed to an environment.

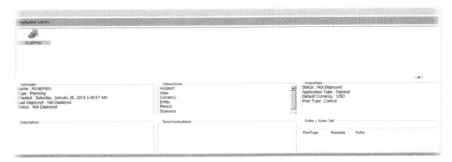

When an application icon is selected, the summary information that is available for this application is visible. The summary information includes:

- Summary – Name, type, created, deployed, synchronization status
- Description – Application description that was entered when the application was created
- Dimensions – A listing of all dimensions that are available within the application
- Application Properties – Organization by Period, Deployed, Default Currency
- Synchronizations – displays all data synchronizations that contain the application

You can perform a number of actions on EPMA applications.

Edit	Allows the end user to edit the EPMA application
Duplicate	Allows the end user to make a copy of the application's dimensions and hierarchies
Delete	Deletes the application from EPMA and, if previously deployed, from the deployed environment
Open	Allows the application to be opened in the Planning web client and the administrator to begin working within the deployed application
Validate	Validates dimensions and their properties to ensure the application can be deployed correctly
Reregister	Reregisters the application with Hyperion Shared

	Services
Data Flow	Displays the inputs and outputs related to this application
Synchronize	Allows the creation of data synchronizations for this application
Migrate	Allows the application to be moved from one environment to another (e.g. development to production)
Compare	When an application has been deployed and the library has been updated, the end user can compare the deployed application to the library and accept or reject the library changes.

If you edit the application, you can now view dimensions in the Application as well as the Shared Library:

Validate and Deploy the Application

Now that we've created the application, we need to perform a validation to make sure it is deployment ready.

Before deploying, the application needs to be validated (with any issues corrected and then re-validated) and then deployed Planning/FM/Essbase. Validation can be executed separately from the right mouse click menu or if not run separately, the validation will be executed as part of the deployment process. (While you think the validation will catch all possible issues, this isn't necessarily the case. You could still encounter errors during deployment.)

New in version 11.1.2.2, you can validate and deploy Calc Manager rules, application metadata or both. A number of issues between validation commands and deploy commands have been resolved in the 11.1.2.2 release. New validations have been added for the application creation wizard, DTS, Calculation Manager rules, shared members, UDAs, member formulas, and alternate hierarchies. Validation results are saved in Job Console.

To validate an application,
1. Right-click on the application in the Application Library and click *Validate*.

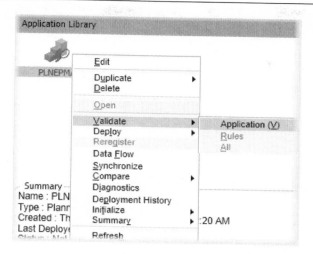

2. A job will be submitted and you can view the status in the Job Console.

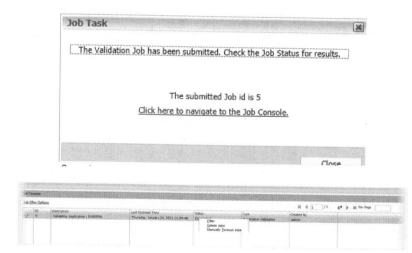

Note!

Did you know you can filter the jobs in the Job Console by user, job ID, job type, job status or submitted time? Click on Job Filter Options to search for a specific job.

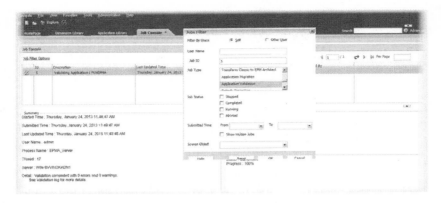

Once the application has been validated you are ready to deploy! Deployment is required to push EPMA application information to the target solution. This will actually create the Planning application and the underlying Essbase database (in Classic Administration, this is performed in two steps; in EPMA, just one step). A prerequisite step to deploying a Planning application is creating the underlying relational repository. We assume this has been done in our example.

To deploy an application,
1. Right-click on the application in the Application Library and click *Deploy>> Application*.

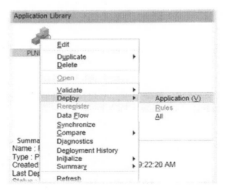

2. Select the *Planning Instance, Application Server, and Shared Services project* (probably Planning).
3. Select an existing data source or click the *New* icon to create a new data source (in our example, we click the New icon).

4. Enter the *Data Source Name* and *Description*:

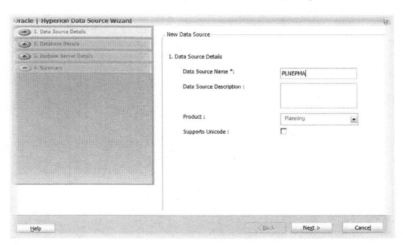

5. Click *Next*.

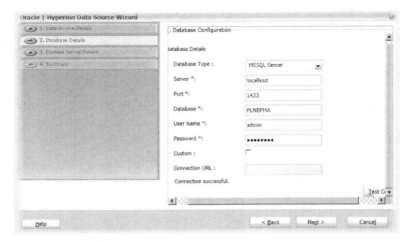

6. Enter the relational database information:
7. Click *Test Connection* to verify a successful connection.
8. Click *Next*.
9. Enter the Essbase database information (make sure to use an Essbase supervisor ID):

10. Click *Test Connection* to verify a successful connection.
11. Click *Next*.

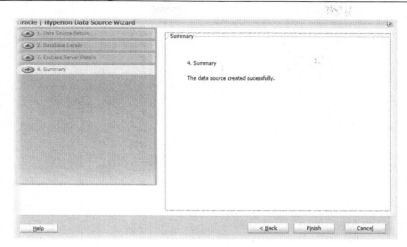

12. Click *Finish*.

If message "data source not created successfully" Go back to 2. And 3. Test connections again and resolve any connectivity issues.

13. Check the option to *Create Outline* (you will check Create Outline the first time and check *Refresh Outline* all other times):

Deploy	⊠

Application Name	PLNEPMA
Description	
Notes	
Web Server	WIN-SVVINDKKDN1
Application Server	PLANNING_LWA ▼
Shared Services Project	Planning ▼
Data Source	PLNEPMA ▼
Create Outline	☑
Refresh Outline	☐
Create Security Filters	☐
Shared Members Security Filters	☐
Validate Security Filter Limit	☐
Full Deploy	☑

Help	Deploy	Cancel

14. Click *Deploy*.

The deployment process will begin and the job will be submitted to the job console:

To view the status, select the link *Click here to navigate to Job Console*:

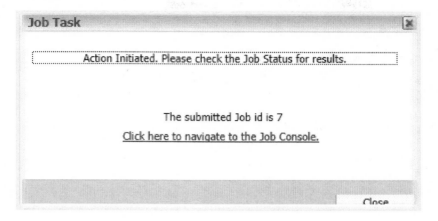

Ideally the job will complete successfully with no errors:

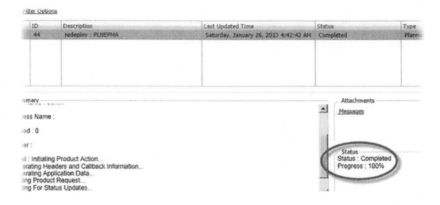

But that is not always the case. Let's look at one example. The following deployment resulted in a number of issues related to member formulas:

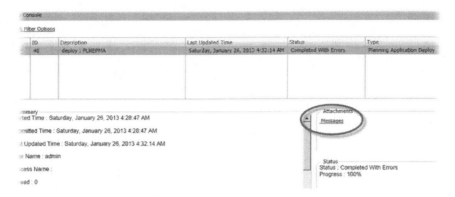

Click on *Messages*, the transaction log file opens:

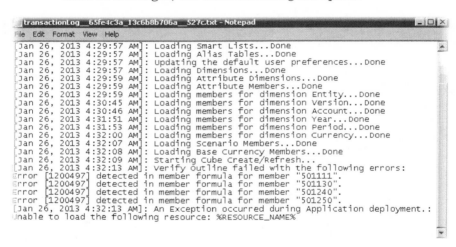

To investigate further, we search for the member in the Dimension Library by right-clicking in the dimension and choosing *Find*. You can then search by *Name* or other property:

The member is quickly found and now we open the member formula property. Do you see any issues? The double quotes are missing from the members with spaces. How did that happen?

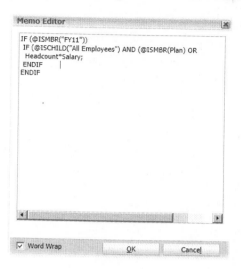

Do you remember back to the beginning of the appendix when we created the import profile? In the Import Profile definition we specified the option to *Remove Double Quotes on Strings*:

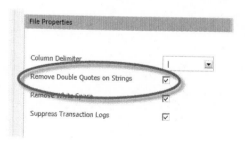

Be careful checking this option because, as you can see, in some cases you want to keep double quotes.

Access an EPMA Deployed Application

The application has now been created and is ready for further development; items like data forms, task lists, and business rules.

To access the application,

1. Select *Navigate* >> *Applications* >> *Planning* >> *Refresh.*

2. Select *Navigate icon>>Applications* >> *Planning* >> *PLNEPMA.*

3. Select *Administration* >> *Manage* >> *Dimensions* and notice that the dimensions cannot be edited within the Planning web client.

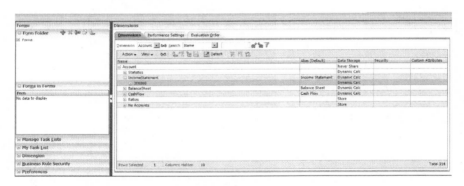

Sync / Redeploy an Application

As you make updates to the dimensions in the Dimension Library, your application will be come out of sync with deployment.

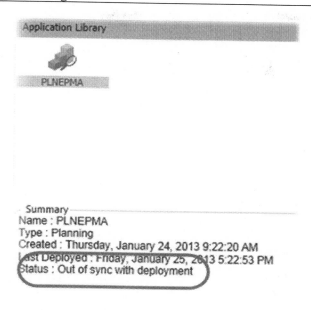

Follow along with our example to update a dimension and then sync the changes to the deployed Planning application.

1. Add a new member to the Segment dimension, "SP" for Support services in the Shared Library under "Seg02".
2. The new member is also added in the EPMA application:

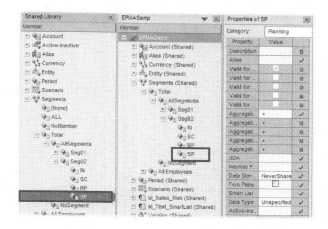

Next we have to redeploy to push this member to Planning and Essbase.

3. In the Application Library, right-click on the application and click *Deploy >> Application.*
4. Select the option to *Refresh* the outline.
5. Additionally if you have security filters that require refreshing you could check this option as well:

6. Click *Deploy*. The application and underlying Essbase database should now be in sync.

Summary
Name : PLNEPMA
Type : Planning
Created : Saturday, January 26, 2013 3:48:57 AM
Last Deployed : Saturday, January 26, 2013 4:42:42 AM
Status : In sync with deployment

Now that we've covered the basics of dimension and application creation and maintenance, we will conclude this introduction to Enterprise Performance Architect with two last concepts: the data synchronizations and EPMA batch client.

DATA SYNCHRONIZATIONS

Data synchronization in EPMA enables you to synchronize and map data between Hyperion applications, interface tables, and external files. With data synchronizations you can share data from applications in Financial Management, Planning, and Essbase as well as external source flat files and interface tables to Financial Management, Planning, Essbase, and HPCM applications. Filters and default members are possible when creating data synchronizations. Basic mapping tables are also possible. Note: EPMA data synchronization is not a full blown ETL tool (see Oracle Data Integrator).

BATCH CLIENT

We've been working with EPMA in the Workspace but a command line interface is also available for scripting EPMA tasks. Via the batch client you can perform incremental changes to data objects like applications, dimensions, members, and properties. You can run jobs for imports, deployments and synchronizations. Recent versions of EPMA introduced several new commands in the batch client to further support automated EPMA tasks.

We've jump started your EPMA process with this appendix. This tool is certainly worth testing if you have a large number of Planning, Essbase, HPCM or HFM applications.

Appendix B:
PFP, WFP, & Capex

The nice developers at Oracle have put in some additional efforts to help customers quickly and easily plan for your people, projects, and capital expenses with add on modules for Project Financial Planning (PFP), Workforce (WFP) and Capital Expenditure (Cap Ex). And of course, with an additional price tag.

Are these modules new software? No, in fact they are plain old Planning applications with prebuilt dimensions, calculations, business rules, data forms, and more designed for workforce planning and capital expenditure planning and projects planning.

Let's look in more detail at each one of these add-on Planning modules.

PROJECT FINANCIAL PLANNING

Key features of Project Financial Planning include the ability to perform Planning for Indirect, Capital, and Contract projects. End users can perform expense planning at the detail or account level (labor, material, equipment), allocate workforce resources and capital assets to projects, calculate driver-based overheads for projects, and perform different types of revenue planning and revenue recognition based on the type of Contract projects (Time and Material, Fixed Price, or Cost Plus).

Project governance committees and executives can view the impact on financial statements from a project level or an entity level including Profit and Loss, Cash Flow, and key performance indicators [KPIs]. They can rank and approve projects based on a project score using financial measures and subjective measures like net present value [NPV], return on investment [ROI], payback, lifetime investment, risk assessment, strategic assessment, business assessment, organization missions, and in 11.1.2.3 earned value management.

Other features include planning and reconciliation for intercompany projects, data forms and flows to request funding, and track project approval flow.

PFP comes with prebuilt components to support this project financial process including data forms, right click menus, task lists, business rules and more:

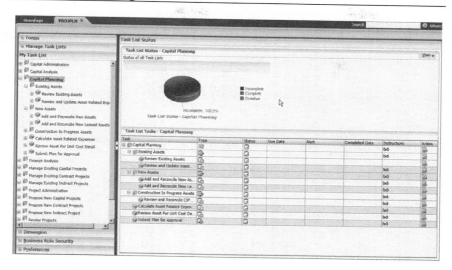

Business Rules with Prompts (along with Task Lists and Data Forms) are used to input information in for new projects:

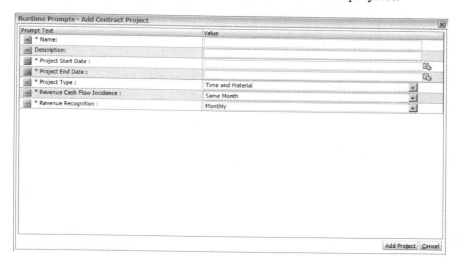

Three additional plan types are created in a Project Financial Planning application: Capex plan type, Workforce plan type, and Project plan type.

Project Financial Planning is equipped with extra dimensions in addition to the ones Oracle Hyperion Planning provides (Entity, Scenario, Version, Year, and Period). The PFP dimensions are Account, Project, Project Element, Job, Employee, Asset Class, and Asset Detail.

Project Classifications

Project Financial Planning classifies Indirect projects as internal or administrative projects that impact expense planning but generate no revenue. For Indirect projects, you can only budget the expense of the project and cannot budget revenue for the project. An example of an Indirect project would be if you created internal training on how to use Hyperion Planning.

Capital projects on the other hand, are long-term investment projects for the construction of a capital asset like a building or road. For Capital projects, you only plan expenses for the project. Expenses are tracked as Construction in Progress (CIP) on the Balance Sheet while the asset is developed. Once in service, the CIP asset must be reconciled with the existing assets.

A project is classified as a Contract project when work is completed for a client and the client reimburses the company. For Contract projects, expenses and revenue are both generated based on the underlying contract. Contract projects supported by Project Financial Planning include Time and Materials, Fixed Price, Cost Plus and Other. 11.1.2.3 supports revenue planning for Contract projects.

Implementation Steps

1. Install and configure
2. Create and initialize the application
3. Load the Entity dimension
4. Review and update Smart Lists (AssignmentLocation, Customer, FundingSource, PhysicalLocation, etc.)
5. Load existing positions to the Job dimension
6. Load the existing employees to the Employee dimension
7. Load the Asset Class with any specific assets
8. Load the Asset Detail dimension with your assets (group assets to scale – e.g. single "Laptop" member with units = 1000)
9. Load Project dimension with projects
10. Refresh to Essbase
11. Load data – project, workforce, and capital
12. Set the substitution variables
13. Specify global assumption defaults
14. Users set their user variables

Project Financial Planning works to facilitate all financial phases within the project lifecycle. Companies can now forecast a project based off of long range financial models and manage financial performance of ongoing projects using interactive financial forecasts and what-if scenarios. Targets like plan, propose, fund, approve, and initiate can be established on a project timeline. The project approval process is focused on key decision criteria that impact approval and funding of anticipated projects. Project managers also have full visibility of revisions to approvals for ongoing projects to gain better insights into the financial impacts of proposed projects.

Project Financial Planning provides the following benefits:

- Reduced reliance on spreadsheets and manual processes
- Provides full visibility of the impacts on company financials when project approval and funding decisions are being made
- Improved insights into the financial impacts of proposed projects
- What-If impact and feedback loop analysis of financial considerations for projects is immediate
- Accurate reporting and forecasting of financial results for ongoing projects
- Improves the reporting and tracking of the financial results helping managers more accurately forecast future results of projects and project portfolios
- Streamlined project planning with financial planning and forecasting
- Keeps track of project-related revenue and expenses in real time due to the integration with the financial planning and approval system
- Leverage investments in existing project management and ERP systems
- Integrates project data from ERP and Project Management applications ensuring consistency and eliminating the need to rekey data across systems.
- Improved management of projects and project portfolios
- Fully documents all costs and revenues associated with projects so managers can gain insight into the financial impacts of proposed projects and improve the evaluation and funding process

WORKFORCE PLANNING

The Workforce Planning (WFP) module provides out-of-the-box functionality for the most common workforce and workforce-related expense planning activities facing any organization. Built-in components address budget headcount and workforce expenses, forecasts for total compensation, variance analysis and more. WFP assumes planning at the employee level of detail. You can also directly link the WFP plan type to main planning applications for real-time impact analysis.

Workforce planning comes with over 100 prebuilt accounts, 60+ prebuilt member formulas and prebuilt business rules, data forms, right click menus, and more. Employees can manage employee status within workforce planning via a data form or business rule. For example, when an employee takes leave or is terminated, salary and total personnel expense are impacted. Workforce Planning is redesigned in version 11.1.2.3.

CAP ASSET PLANNING

Planning for capital expenses isn't an easy thing to do, coping with uncertain projections for unusual activities. The Capital Expenditure (Capex) module for Hyperion Planning assists you in the management of assets and provides a process for creating capital expense plans for submission and approval. CapEx establishes global assumptions for each asset class and provides driver based calculations. A structure for timing and cost adjustments to capital expenses and functionality for asset transfers across departments are all features of CapEx. Like its cohort WFP, it can easily integrate the capex plan with other Hyperion Planning applications.

End users can set assumptions like the useful life of assets, depreciation methods, depreciation conventions, amortization methods and more. Capital Asset Planning is redesigned in version 11.1.2.3.

BENEFITS & CONSIDERATIONS

Before we conclude the appendix, let's re-cap the benefits and considerations for these Planning modules. The prebuilt modules provide a number of benefits to you: less time to setup, reduction in planning cycle time, increased visibility into drivers, and improved accountability, accuracy and predictability in these plans.

When it comes to development, these modules can help you achieve faster implementation time (hey, everything is already built, right?). But remember, if you have a very specific workforce and/or capital expenditure planning process, carefully evaluate whether the PFP, WFP and/or CapEX predefined processes and objects meet your requirements. We've seen about a 50/50 split in our client base where for about 50% of clients, it made more sense to design a custom Planning solution. For the other 50% of clients, the prebuilt modules worked beautifully. While you can customize these modules, depending on the customization, it could actually take longer to customize than developing an application from scratch.

And also note that while a number of objects are already built, you still have steps to complete after initialization (e.g. build dimensions like the Organization, Employee dimension, Asset dimension and other custom dimensions, update Smart Lists, integrate with existing account structure, setup and assign security, create reports, and create aggregation calc scripts).

Note!

You can customize anything but edit with care and make sure to understand the model completely and dependencies between all of the data forms, member formulas and rules.

Out of the box functionality to ...	**PFP**	**WFP**	**Capex**
Plan Workforce expense	Y (by project if desired)	Y	N
Plan Capital Asset	Y (by project if desired)	N	Y
Plan by project	Y	N	N

You could build "by Project" planning into WFP or Capex but why would you when it comes out of the box with PFP?

We've only had time in this appendix to provide a glimpse of PFP, WFP and CapEx. For more information, training classes from interRel or Oracle are your best bet for getting into the details. Your friendly Oracle sales rep or partner (nudge, nudge interRel Consulting) can also provide demos and more information.

Appendix C:
What's New in Planning

WHAT'S NEW IN 11.1.2.1?

Version 11.1.2.1 of Hyperion Planning focused on enhancing the End User Experience by adding enriching features, such as context sensitive right-click menu options, Ad hoc Grids, Sorting & Filtering options, and complete Planning End User Parity in Smart View. In addition, a new Data Form Designer was introduced along with functional enhancements for Process Management and Data Validation, ASO Integration from Planning, and improvements under the Public Sector Budgeting module.

Context Sensitive Menu Options

In order to boost the end user experience, new pre-built and easy to use context sensitive right-click menu options not only provide Planners the options to perform operations such as Sorting and Filtering, but administrators can create Custom menu items as well.

	14518	20277	40000
	74	73	73
+)	1079309	1483341	2903600
ns (+)	Revenue Assumptions / Cost of Sales Rate	-91041	-169893
ints (+)	Filter ▶	Filter...	
Allowances	Sort ▶	Hide rows with no data	
	Show member in outline	Hide rows with zeros	
)	964663	Hide rows with zeros and no data	
	624967	872878	1721908

Ad Hoc Grid Options

In 11.1.2.1, users having appropriate permissions and assigned roles are given an option to create, personalize, and dynamically alter the focused data slices that are frequently used from both Planning and Smart View. This removes the restrictions imposed by the data form definition, and users can now change the data intersection and layout of the ad hoc grids – provided they have appropriate access to the members.

With the new Ad Hoc Grid feature, users can general actions, such as selecting which alias table is used by the ad hoc grid, specifying the number of decimal places to display for numerical data, and specifying the text to be displayed for cells having no or missing data. Planners have the flexibility to set ad hoc analysis action options within the Data Form to control which members are selected when actions such as, Zoom In/Out, Keep Only, and Remove Only operations are executed, and have the ability to choose whether to refresh data when carrying out ad hoc actions such as Pivot To, Move, Zoom In etc.

Planning End User Parity in Smart View

Smart View now has full parity from an end user perspective for Hyperion Planning. From the new Connection Manager that services direct connections between Smart View and Planning. The supported Smart View features for Planning include: Task List in Excel, Task List in Outlook, Data Validation / Traffic Lighting, Composite Forms, Process Management/Workflow, Dynamic User Variables, User Preference Settings, Copy Version option, access to Job Console, Task List Reports, Context Sensitive Right Click Menus on Forms, Document Attachment for Data Cells and Process Management, and Cell Level Launch Menus.

New Module Specific Ribbons are introduced:

The availability of Task Lists in Smart View was one of the welcomed features as Planners are now able to carry out Planning tasks directly from Excel.

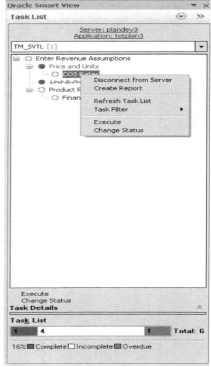

Additionally, the Task List view provided Context Sensitive right-click menus and execution steps including the option to view/change Task list status.

In addition to MS Excel, this version integrated Task Lists under MS Outlook.

The integration with Outlook allowed Planners to use the familiar Outlook functionality and perform actions such as Mark Complete, Execute, review Due Dates, and view/change Status etc. to facilitate the planning process.

Data Form Designer

With 11.1.2.1, a new interface & grid layout was introduced as part of the Data Form Designer enhancements that helped reduce the time needed to create forms. The new design provides an all in one layout view where the Properties are displayed to the side based on the selected section, and within the data form list, icons now distinguishes whether data forms are Simple, Composite, or Ad hoc grids.

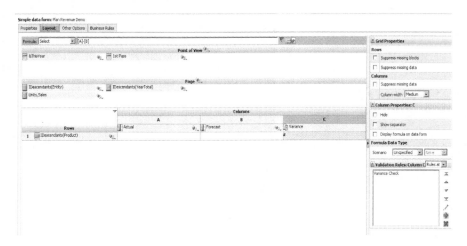

The new rows and columns design replaces the "segments" from earlier versions. Users can now utilize Multiple Rows and/or Columns with different properties such as Read vs. Write, Rows or Columns used in calculations, Hidden rows or columns, and adding separators.

Moreover, the new Member Selection tool provides improved member search and member selection capabilities including enhanced search capabilities and filter criteria in the member selector, a new properties pane that reveals display, grid, column, and row properties. In addition, user can now filter by Attribute, Generation, or Level with the flexibility of placing the selections in separate columns or rows.

Formulas in Rows

Much like Financial Reporting, Formula rows or columns can now be added as a separate segment, Formula rows can be used to create blank rows, and Formula rows and columns can be utilized to set Validation rules.

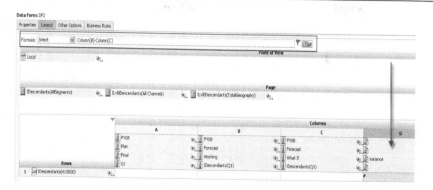

Composite Form Designer

Simple data forms and composite data forms are unified under the new Data Form Designer.

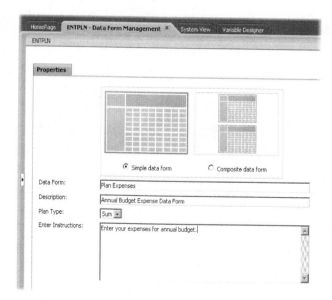

Process Management / Approvals

With 11.1.2.1, the Planning Process Management module has many great enhancements that support simple to complex submission processes.

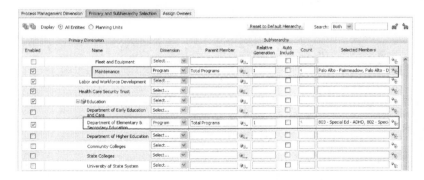

At any point in time users can view the Promotional Path and approvals status:

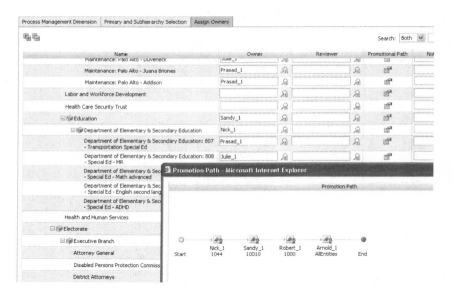

Data Validation

Validation rules are supported for data forms.

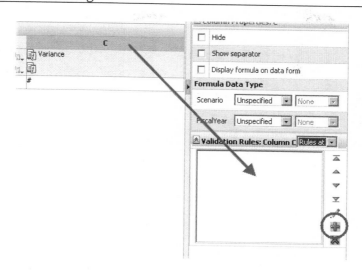

Validation rules (with its traffic lighting and validation messages) provide better guidance for data entry.

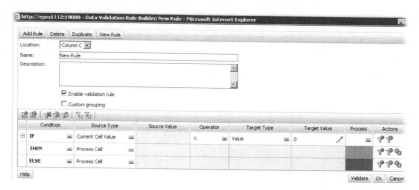

Push To Reporting Feature

Planning provides a built-in integration tool to map Planning data to ASO and BSO reporting databases. One of the great features this integration provides is that it allows users to map Smart Lists to Dimensions in ASO database so that you can report on the Smart Lists.

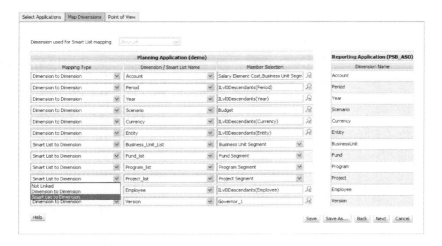

Public Sector Budgeting

Public Sector Budgeting (PSB), a pre-built Planning application with direct integrations to ERPs for HR data, was introduced to overcome common challenges of public sector organizations and healthcare institutions. Government budget requirements dictate proper accountability, adequate levels of review in the budgeting process, precise regulatory oversight, emphasis on better use of resources for managing time intensive processes, and support for complex programs, committees and agencies.

The PSB solution provides packaged application for public sector organizations that was built using Hyperion Planning as the supporting technology. Addressing planning and budgeting needs for public sector organizations, this new module introduced support management of complex budgeting processes including budgeting books, position budgeting capabilities, integration with ERP sources via ERPI to load data as well as provide drill-back capability, and the option to leverage all of the Planning 11.1.2 features.

In order to accelerate Position & Employee Budgeting, this new module provided out of the box configurable & expandable position and employee expense budgeting capabilities that allow Planners to project and evaluate impact of employee compensation and benefits, forecast impact of new positions, introduce powerful workflow and process management for budgeting and forecasting, evaluate workforce reductions, and review contract proposals.

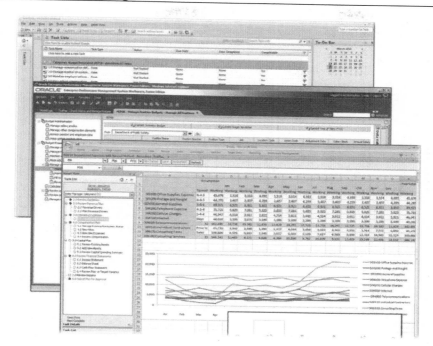

WHAT'S NEW IN 11.1.2.2?

From the new navigation and layout improvements to the increased functionality, this version of Planning has made it easier to use for both planners and admins. In 11.1.2, the Public Sector Budgeting module debuted, but in 11.1.2.2 Project Financial Planning makes its appearance.

New User Interface Developed in ADF

Planners now experience a role-driven navigation flow with the new accordion-style expandable left pane. Security defines each users access privileges, while the system displays the appropriate level functionality.

Navigation in Planning 11.1.2.2 is driven by the accordions in the left pane. Although the top navigation menus still exist, they will be removed in a follow up patch release once all the top navigation menus are included within the left navigation accordion.

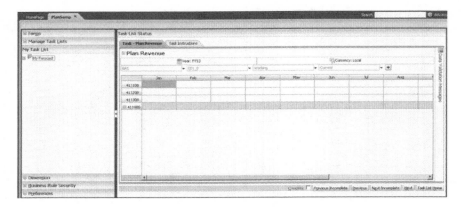

When a planner logs on to an application, they see the *My Task Lists* panel and a graphical or tabular depiction of the current status of their tasks. The previously supported options of Advanced and Basic views are no longer available in Planning 11.1.2.2.

When a user highlights a task list in the left navigation pane, the content page shows the task list home page which gives the user a current status of their task. The pie chart is interactive and clicking on it allows the user to filter the list of tasks based on their status.

In the bottom section of the task list the user can review instructions or other attributes of the task and start acting on the tasks using the action icon.

On completion of executing a task, the user can select the complete check box and then use the 'Task List Home' button to navigate to the Task List Home Page. Here the user can see the updated status of the tasks belonging to that task list.

Master Detail Composite Forms

To help planners see the relevant context when working with multiple forms, administrators can now create a new form type called the *master composite form*. The master composite form has one master form and can have multiple simple forms. This allows the selection of members in the master form to flow through and automatically filter the members in the simple forms.

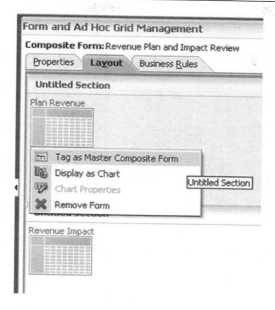

Master-Detail Composite Forms can be used in place of the right-click menu feature for data forms. These form constructs have the same pre-requisites as a right-click context passing. They allow you to pass the context dimension member from the source form to the target forms.

The target forms need to have the dimensions for which context is being passed in the page or POV area of the target form. There are two significant advantages of creating master-detail forms in place of forms with right-click menus: 1)You can visualize the source and target forms within the same content area and 2)You can see the immediate impact on several dependent forms within the same composite.

Breadcrumb Navigation

Breadcrumb navigation allows for movement to other forms to be displayed using a navigation trail. Administrators can set up forms so that planners can invoke them from shortcut menus. Invoking such forms using right-click (shortcut) menus, you can navigate among them by:

- Clicking the hyperlinked form names at the top of the page.
- Clicking the tab named for the form.
- Right-clicking and then selecting the form to move to.

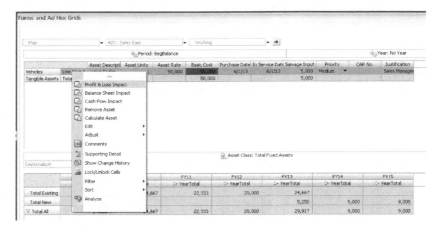

Bi-Directional Language Support

Languages, like Arabic, that flow right to left are now supported by Planning, Calc Manager, Financial Reports, Workspace and Web Analysis. The Regional Locale selection sets the language preference - change the browser language and then restart the browser.

Dimension Name of Page Axis of Form

In 11.1.2.2, users can visualize the dimension names of page members in a form by selecting *View >> Show Dimension Name on Page*:

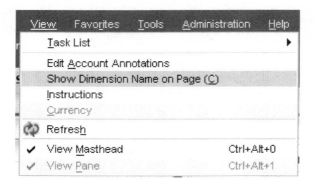

Voila! That's the Year dimension:

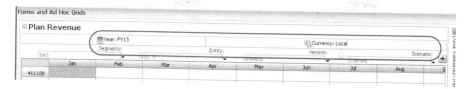

Rolling Forecast Wizard

Administrators can now easily set up forms to include a rolling forecast window. Rolling forecasts differ from traditional forecasts in that they are continuous - they are not tied to a fiscal year. The periods in a rolling forecast roll along based on how the administrator defined them when creating the form.

Planning allows you to easily set up rolling forecast forms from within the form designer using interactive components. The substitution variables needed for the rolling forecast are created on the fly and values are assigned to them automatically. These and other substitution variables can be managed from within the Planning web UI directly.

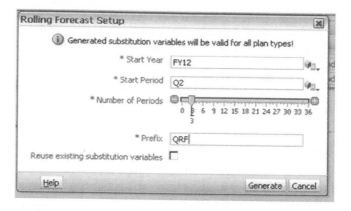

All Years Parent

You can now create an All Years parent member that includes all years. The All Years parent member in the 'Year' dimension can be chosen during application creation to facilitate aggregations and calculation across multiple years. The All Years parent member does not include the No Year member.

Enhancements to Approvals

To allow greater flexibility and ease for administrators managing workflow, Approvals workflow now supports groups of users. Planning unit owners can be assigned as individual users or you can assign a group. Any user within the group can become the owner, but there can be only one owner at a time. Only the user appointed as owner can perform actions. Ownership can be taken away from the current owner by other group members. If there is not a designated owner, members of the group can perform actions on behalf of the group.

Runtime prompts now support Approvals security. This new feature allows the user to filter runtime prompt members based on access permissions and Approvals. Therefore, Approvals security can be determined and used for filtering members if set up properly.

Attach Multiple Documents

If the 'Enable Cell-Level Document' property is selected on the form by the administrator, planners can add, delete, and view EPM Workspace documents attached to the web form, or a single cell. A small red square in the cell's upper-right corner indicates that it contains cell-level documents. You can see the cell's intersecting members by hovering over the red square.

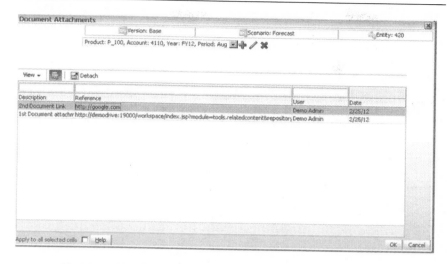

Multiple Comments

Multiple planners can add, view, edit and delete comments, and can subsequently view, edit, or delete comments in web form cells or cell ranges. A small red square in the cell's upper-right corner indicates that it contains cell-level documents. You can see the cell's intersecting members by hovering over the red square. Rich text formatting is now supported.

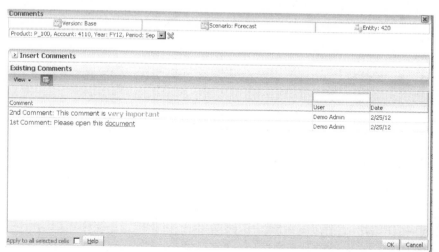

View Change History

Have you ever wanted to view a cell's history or changes? If the auditing for Data feature is turned on, planners can view the data history of any numeric, date, or text cell to which they have at least Read access.

To view a cell's data history, right-click in the cell and then selecting *Show Change History*:

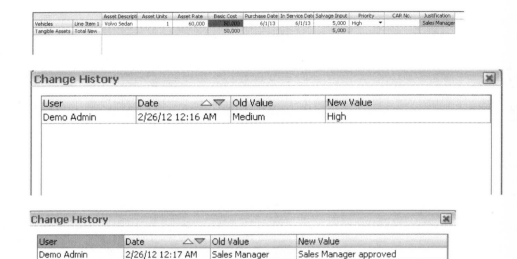

Predictive Planning

Planners can now use the new Predictive Planning functionality, located on the Planning menu, to forecast performance based on historical data. In order to be able to leverage this new feature, Administrators must design forms as described in the "Oracle Hyperion Planning Predictive Planning User's Guide".

Formatting, formatting, formatting

You can format text everywhere in Planning like instructions and comments. Planning also now supports formatting for data cells whose data type is Text.

Charts in Data Forms

In version 11.1.2.2, administrators can design composite forms that display the data in sections as charts.

Composite forms can be created where one or multiple forms can be designated as graphs. Both forms and ad-hoc grids can be added into a composite grid layout and either of them can be designated as graphs. Graphs are enabled for drill down to the lowest level of a dimension using the base form definition included in the composite.

Note: Graphs in Web-Forms are not displayed when the form is opened in Smart View.

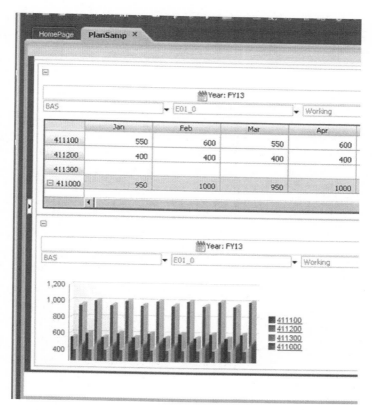

Planners can also drill down to the next level by clicking the underlined links or chart areas.

Configurable Message for Business Rules

When designing shortcut menus to launch business rules, designers can now add a customized configuration message within the rule's run time prompt (RTP). Through this, planners will now receive a message prior to running the business rule stating the result of launching the rule.

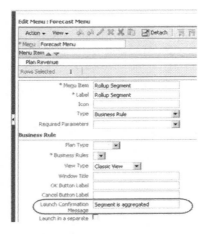

Smart Type Ahead for Smart Lists

Find it quicker. Smart type-ahead search is now enabled within the Smart List values. Type in a letter or string and the list will automatically filter based on the type-ahead you enter.

Global Currency Precision Setting

Have you ever wished that there was a Global Currency Precision Setting across all forms? There is now.

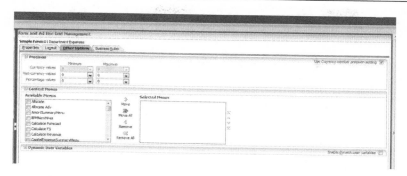

Grid Diagnostics Tool

The new Grid Diagnostics tool allows administrators to monitor the time it takes to open forms and ad hoc grids. It enables administrators to select on which forms and grids to run the diagnostics and to identify forms with poor performance.

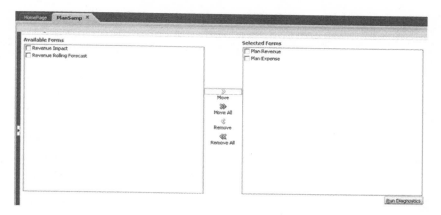

Substitution Variables Managed in Planning

Administrators can now manage substitution variables for all Planning applications. Admins can also designate the substitution variable's plan type, name, and value. Existing substitution variables can be edited or deleted as well.

CalcManager Enhancements

Calculation Manager will be the only Rules designer for Hyperion Planning going forward. Hyperion Business Rules will no longer be available from Release 11.1.2.2. There is an Upgrade Wizard to convert Hyperion Business Rules into Oracle Hyperion Calculation Manager business rules.

The key new functionality in this release is the 'Interactive debugging mode'. Interactive debugging provides following features to the end user:

- Ability to insert the break points
- Ability to Remove/Disable the break points
- Ability to add a condition to the break point
- Ability to view the members of the intersection
- Display a "Before" value and an "After" value of the execution of all the intersection(s) for member(s) in a statement.
- Display all execution variable values (present in the statement) before and after statement execution.

WHAT'S NEW IN 11.1.2.3?

ASO Plan Types Supported

Essbase allows two database types: aggregate storage databases (ASO) and block storage databases (BSO). ASO databases are designed to handle more dimensions and members, smaller batch windows for loads and aggregations of sparse data, and smaller database footprints. In versions prior to 11.1.2.3, only BSO plan types (databases) were supported.

Hyperion Planning now supports aggregate storage option (ASO) plan types in 11.1.2.3. ASO plan types can be created during application creation or the new Plan Type Editor provides an interface to build both ASO and BSO plan types. Users can use ASO plan types to provide write back to databases with larger number of dimensions and members.

Benefits of an ASO plan type include unified dimension maintenance and security for BSO and ASO planning and reporting. There is no longer a need to create a separate Essbase only cube in Essbase Administration Services. ASO plan types provide a higher level of granularity for requirements that dictate detailed planning. No aggregation is required for ASO databases so results at upper levels are available immediately. You can build composite forms that present data from both ASO and BSO plan types together.

ASO cubes maybe created during application creation or later in the process. Planning applications can still have 3 BSO plan types and now in 11.1.2.3, they can add ASO plan types. The number of ASO plan types allowed in an application equals the number of BSO cubes created plus one.

Create ASO Plan type

Planning administrators create ASO plan types during application creation or add a new plan types to existing Planning applications. You use the application creation wizard to create the Planning application in 11.1.2.3. The process is the same as 11.1.2.2 but with the new option of adding an ASO plan type.

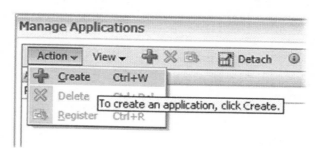

The Application Creation Wizard has a new option to add an ASO plan type. Note you must define the application name and the database name.

So what happens when you click the Create button? Planning creates the relational database tables in the underlying relational database and creates the underlying Essbase application(s); however, the Essbase databases have not yet been created. Planning will create one application which will contain all BSO databases and a separate application for ASO which will contain the ASO database.

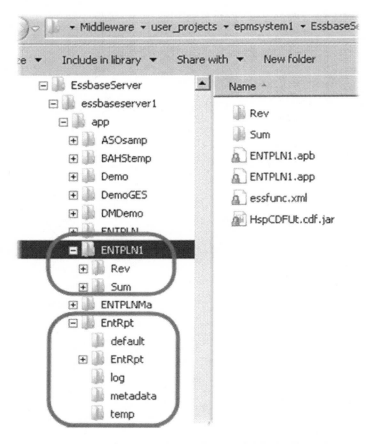

Add Dimensions and Members to an ASO Plan Type

Once the application and databases are created, plan types are selectable in the Dimension Editor so you can view all dimensions for all plan types or filter dimensions by plan type for both BSO and ASO:

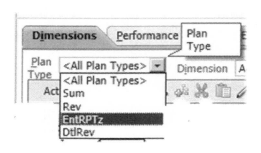

This filtering option is a great way to understand what dimensions, hierarchies and members will be built in each plan type.

Add dimensions and members to ASO plan types just as you have you in the past, choosing the *Valid For Plan Type* check box. Note a member can belong to both ASO and BSO plan types:

Dimensions

Edit Dimension Properties : FiscalYear

Dimension	FiscalYear
Description	
Alias Table	Default
Alias	
Valid for Plan Types	☑ Sum ☑ Rev ☐ DtlRev ☑ DtlRev
Two Pass Calculation	☐
Apply Security	☐
Data Storage	Never Share
Display Option	Member Name

You can associate dimensions and members for ASO plan types just as you do for BSO plan types.

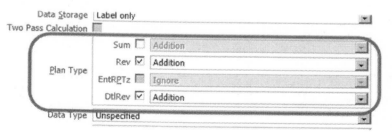

You can create dimensions that are only for an ASO plan type:

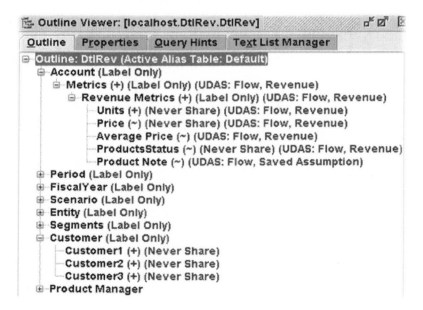

After you refresh to Essbase the ASO outline is updated with dimension and member information:

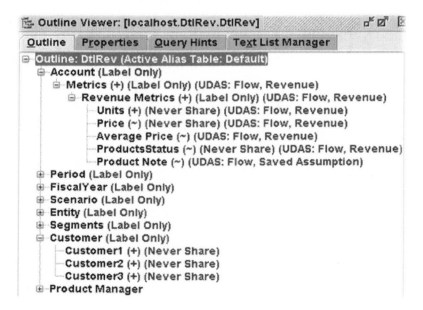

Input Data, Load Data, & Report

You load data to your ASO plan type just like the BSO plan type. The only requirement is that when loading to ASO plan types you must load to level zero members. You cannot load data to upper level members for ASO.

Once data is loaded or input, you can see the impact at in data forms or retrieve and analyze data via Smart View Planning connection or Financial Reporting documents that use the Planning ADM driver. ASO cubes require no further calculation steps.

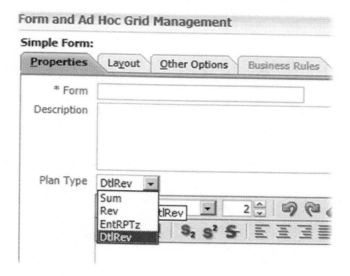

Considerations for ASO Plan Types

- ASO plan types are not supported using EPMA
- No business rule support for ASO databases
- No member formula support for ASO databases
- Planning does not generate XREFs on ASO databases
- Because Planning does not require all base dimensions on an ASO database, approvals may not apply to the ASO database if an approvals dimension is missing; If this is the case, normal security would apply
- Dynamic time series members are not supported for ASO plan types
- ^ Never consolidation tag is not supported for ASO plan types

- Must have ASO license
- Creating and refreshing security filters is not supported for ASO databases
  - This means you cannot retrieve data from ASO databases from a third party source (Smart View Essbase connection)
  - You can only retrieve data through Planning either directly or, for Financial Reporting, through the Planning ADM driver

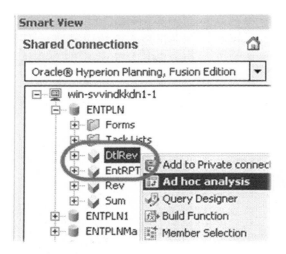

New Plan Type Editor

You can add or delete plan types to an existing Planning application via the Plan Type Editor. Select *Administration >> Manage >> Plan Types* to access the Plan Type Editor:

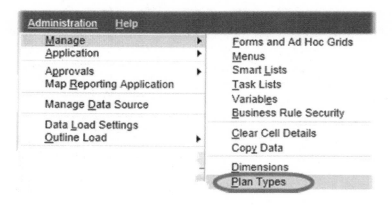

The Plan Type Editor displays:

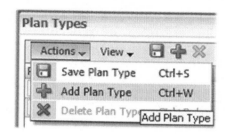

You can *Add* or *Delete* plan types from an application:

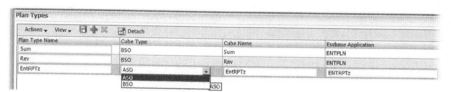

When adding a new plan type, you can choose *ASO* or *BSO*:

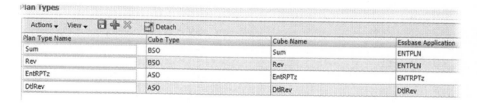

You may create up to 3 BSO plan types within a single application (just like before) and X ASO plan types where X equals the number of BSO plan types +1.

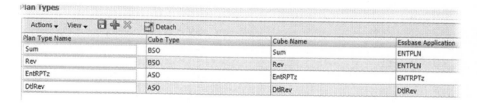

Flexible Custom Dimensions

You define and manage different dimension hierarchies by plan type.

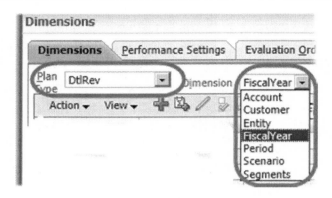

New Task List Types

Copy version and Job Console are now valid options to include in a task list.

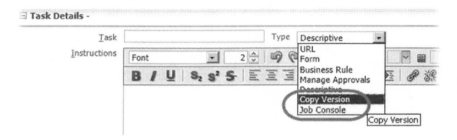

New Task List Dashboard and Report Page

Users can create new visualizations of Task List Status by status, type, user, date and then display task list status graphically. Users can filter relevant tasks from a graph:

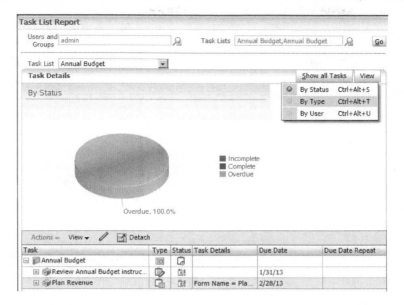

Users can export Excel or pdf reports displayed by column:

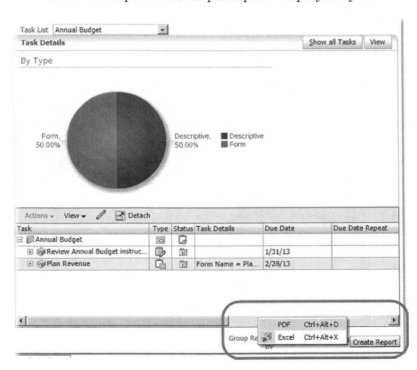

Update Dimensions and Members from Smart View

Hyperion Planning administrators can now use Smart View and Excel to maintain dimensions and members. Planning admins will download the Smart View for Office administrator client.

Once installed, admins can update dimensions, add and move members, and update member properties under the Dimensions folder in the Smart View Panel:

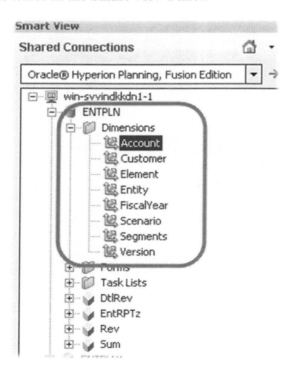

Right click on the desired dimension and choose *Edit Dimension:*

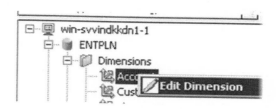

The Dimension editing option opens in Excel similar to an ad hoc query:

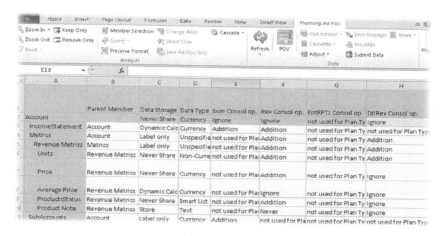

You can update member properties by selecting values from the drop down or in some cases, typing values:

DtlRev Consol op.	Two Pass Calculation	Smart Lists	Account Type	Var
Ignore	No	<None>		
not used for Plan Type	No	<None>	Revenue	Nor
Addition	No	<None>	Revenue	Nor
Addition	No	<None>	Revenue	Nor
Addition	No	<None>	Revenue	Nor
Ignore	No	<None>	Revenue	Nor
Ignore	No	<None>	Revenue	Nor
Ignore	No	Products St	Revenue	Nor
Ignore	No	<None>	Saved Assump	Nor
Ignore	No	<None>	Revenue ▾	r
not used for Plan Type	No	<None>	Type to search	r
			Expense	
			Revenue	
			Asset	
			Liability	
			Equity	
			Saved Assumption	

Right click to insert a new member using plain ol' Excel functionality. Type in the new member name in the blue section. Then enter the member properties. Click Submit Data to save changes to Planning.

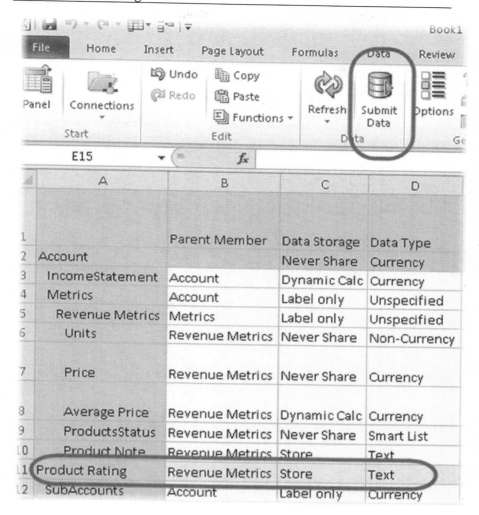

	A	B	C	D
1		Parent Member	Data Storage	Data Type
2	Account		Never Share	Currency
3	IncomeStatement	Account	Dynamic Calc	Currency
4	Metrics	Account	Label only	Unspecified
5	Revenue Metrics	Metrics	Label only	Unspecified
6	Units	Revenue Metrics	Never Share	Non-Currency
7	Price	Revenue Metrics	Never Share	Currency
8	Average Price	Revenue Metrics	Dynamic Calc	Currency
9	ProductsStatus	Revenue Metrics	Never Share	Smart List
10	Product Note	Revenue Metrics	Store	Text
11	Product Rating	Revenue Metrics	Store	Text
12	SubAccounts	Account	Label only	Currency

However you still need to Refresh the changes to Essbase. Right click on Dimensions in the Smart View panel and select *Refresh Database:*

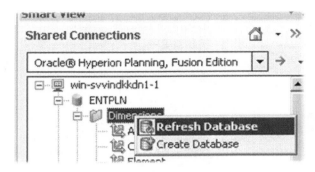

Choose the *Refresh* options:

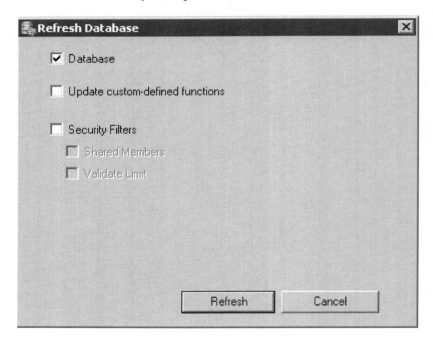

UI to Load Data and Metadata from the Web

Planning administrators can run the Outline Load Utility from the web (instead of command line on the Planning server). Planning admins can import and export data and metadata from Planning web client.

To use the interface, select *Administration >> Outline Load*, and then select *Import from File, Export Metadata to File, or Export Data to File*:

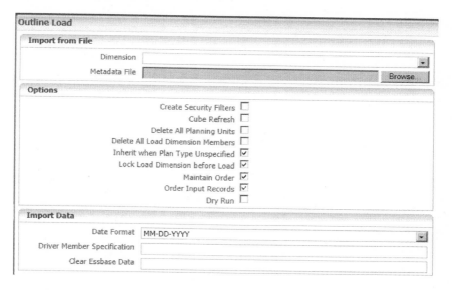

Import from File (import metadata and data) options include the import of Period, Year, Scenario, Version, Currency, Entity, user-defined dimensions, attributes, UDAs, exchange rates, Smart Lists, and planning unit hierarchies:

Export options include *Export Metadata to File* where you choose the desired dimension to export:

And *Export Data to File*:

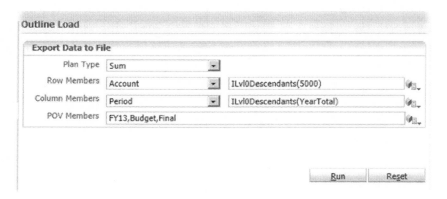

For *Export Data to File*, you will choose the plan type, row members, column members and POV members. A single dimension may exist in the Row and Column section. In the POV, all other dimensions must be referenced. Functions (e.g. @Chilren) are not supported for POV selection.

Click *Run* to process the import or export.

Here is a sample result of a metadata export:

	A	B	C	D	E	F	G	H	I	J	K	L	M	N
1	Account	Parent	Alias: Def	Alias: Lon	Valid For	Data Stor	Two Pass	Descriptio	Formula	UDA	Smart List	Data Type	Hierarchy	Account
2	IncomeSt	Account			false	dynamic c	false					currency	none	revenue
3	300000	IncomeSt	Net Incon		false	dynamic c	false					currency	none	revenue
4	310000	300000	Total Pret		false	dynamic c	false					currency	none	revenue
5	312000	310000	Other Exp		false	dynamic c	false					currency	none	revenue
6	311000	300000	Pretax Inc		false	dynamic c	false					currency	none	expense
7	400000	311000	Gross Pro		false	dynamic c	false					currency	none	revenue
8	410000	400000	Net Reve		false	store	false		"[OpenInputValueBlock]			currency	none	revenue
9														
10	IF (NOT ((Actual"")))													
11	IF (""ProductsStatus"" == [ProductsStatus.Active])													
12	""Units""*""Price"";													
13	ELSE													
14	#MISSING;													
15	ENDIF													
16														
17														
18	ENDIF													
19	[CloseInputValueBlock]													
20	, , ,													

Now that you can load metadata and data over the Planning web, do I still need Financial Data Quality Management? Yes! Use FDM when requirements dictate mapping processes, drill back to sources, and source integration.

Support for RDBMS in Outline Load Utility

The Outline Load Utility now supports relational databases as an import source and export target.

New Outline Load Utility commands to support this new feature are:

- /ER[:RDBConnectionPropertiesFileName]
- /ED CSV file to which to write exported data is written
- /EDD The row, column, and POV members being exported
- /ERA
- /REQ:exportQueryOrKey
- /REC:catalog
- /RED:driver
- /RER:url
- /REU:userName
- /REP:password

For Project Financial Planning, interface tables are available in 11.1.2.3 for use with this import/export feature.

Other New Command Line Parameters for Outline Load Utility

- /EDH: Exports a dimension header in Oracle Hyperion Planning internal HEADERBLOCK format in the output

.CSV file. This is used on import to dynamically create base and attribute dimensions before import.

- /ALS: Create alias tables on import if they do not exist (default). Use /-ALS to error out if the referenced alias tables do not exist.

- /C2A:(column1, alias1), (column2, alias2), ...: Creates aliases for columns for the /RIQ and /REQ commands. Use this parameter to avoid lengthy RDBMS character column and column alias restrictions.

- /DPU: Delete all planning units with the /R parameter otherwise error-out if members in planning units attempt to be deleted. Use /-DPU to prevent the delete operation from deleting members in planning units.

End User Preferences

Administrators apply Member name and display options by Application defaults, Application settings, Dimensions, Forms, and Member selections. Now in 11.1.2.3, end users can override alias displays for all areas of the application in Preferences. Users can choose one of the following in preferences:

- Default (determined by form, grid, or dimension settings)
- Member Name
- Alias
- Member name: Alias
- Alias: Member Name

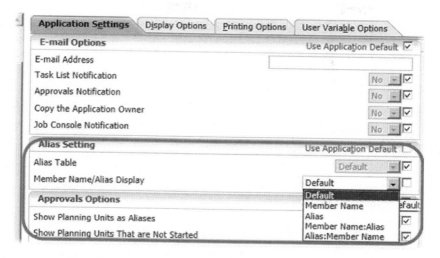

Grid Fetch Preferences

In data forms in the 11.1.2.2 user interface, by default, the data returned is only for the members that are visible on the screen. The benefit to this feature is that forms initially open much faster (because smaller data sets are returned). As you scroll through the data form and the members, additional data is retrieved and displayed (so there could be a "hesitation" in data form performance when scrolling as data is being retrieved).

In 11.1.2.3 you can control this behavior. You can accept the default behavior described above or administrators and end users can pre-set the grid rendering preference, defining the number of rows and columns returned in data forms.

What's New Smart View and Planning 11.1.2.3?

Hyperion Planning and Smart View 11.1.2.3 now supports *Submit* actions without requiring a *Refresh* first. As described above, administrators can update members and dimensions in Smart View. Composite forms with charts are supported in Smart View.

Hyperion Planning In the Cloud

Oracle is focusing more development efforts to lower the EPM adoption barrier and is beginning to offer mainstream EPM applications in the cloud. Hyperion Planning is the first supported EPM application in the cloud! The goal is to accelerate EPM adoption with the SaaS subscription model and lower IT resource requirements. Options include EPM cloud services stand-alone or with the Oracle ERP Cloud Service.

So what is delivered via the Planning & Budgeting Cloud Service (PBCS)?

- Fully Functional Hyperion Planning within EPM Workspace
- Financial Reports and Web Based Planning
- Data Integration Using Flat File loads from On Premise
- Smart View, Financial Reports Studio and Predictive Planning using a local client connecting into PBCS
- Lifecycle Migration

- Application migration from On Premise Planning to Cloud and vice-versa
- R11.1.2.2 Application migration from on-premise Planning to the Cloud

Deployment alternatives include:

Approach	Development System	Production Deployment
Pure On-premise	On-premise	On-premise
Pure Cloud	Cloud	Cloud
Hybrid	Cloud	On-premise

Dynamic Members on the Fly

The Hyperion Planning 11.1.2.3 modules (PFP, WFP, Capex, and PSB) support the ability for end users to add new member names on the fly in all dimensions except Period and Year.

How it works:

1. Administrator defines members to support dynamic members:
   - Property – *Enable for Dynamic Children*
   - *Number of Possible Dynamic Children* (what is the max number of members that users can create)
   - *Access Granted to Member Creator* – determines the access that users will have if they dynamically create members when launching rules (Inherit, None, Read, write)
2. Administrator refreshes to Essbase and placeholder members are created.

Child members that you load using either of the Outline Load Utilities or Lifecycle Management under parent members that are *Enabled for dynamic children* are added as dynamic child members if there are dynamic member placeholders in Essbase. Once the placeholders are full, any remaining children are added as normal members and cannot be used until the database is refreshed.

3. Members are available for use (no refresh needed).

The Catch! This feature is only available in initialized module applications such as Oracle Hyperion Workforce Planning,

Oracle Hyperion Public Sector Planning and Budgeting, Oracle Hyperion Capital Asset Planning, and Oracle Project Financial Planning.

Oracle Diagnostic Logging

Administrators can now configure logging parameters for Hyperion Planning and view log files via Oracle Diagnostic Logging. Different levels of debug logging may be set like INCIDENT_ERROR:1 (SEVERE.intValue()+100), ERROR:1 (SEVERE), WARNING:1 (WARNING), NOTIFICATION:1 (INFO), NOTIFICATION:16 (CONFIG), TRACE:1 (FINE), TRACE:16 (FINER), TRACE:32 (FINEST).

New parameters related to Calc Manager are also available in 11.1.2.3.

- BUSINESS_RULE_LAUNCH_LOG_ENABLED: Enables logging when Calc Manager business rules are run and checks whether the next two properties are set to true; default setting is true
- BUSINESS_RULE_LAUNCH_LOG_RTP_VALUES: If set to true, runtime prompt values are logged; default setting is false
- BUSINESS_RULE_LAUNCH_LOG_CALC_SCRIPT : If set to true, the calculation script sent to Essbase is logged; default setting is false

What New in PFP?

New features for Oracle Project Financial Planning (PFP) include a new business rule to calculate imported projects. PFP now supports Earned Value Management and Revenue planning for Capital projects (once the asset is in service). End users also have greater "what if" capabilities to set targets and shift start and end project dates, shifting the data to follow the new date and see the financial impact.

What's New in Capex and WFP?

Oracle Hyperion Workforce Planning and Oracle Hyperion Capital Asset Planning have undergone a major face lift. The updated application design leverages design best practices, functionality and features implemented in PFP.

If you currently use Capex or WFP, to use the new module design, you must initialize in a new application and migrate your data to the new application design (along with any custom artifacts or changes that have been applied).

Calculation Manager Enhancements

Version 11.1.2.3 contains many exciting new features to Planning administrators and end users:

- Searching for and replacing strings globally throughout Calculation Manager
- Filter objects by text string
- Suppress System Key Words while editing in Script mode
- Analyze business rule script for optimization

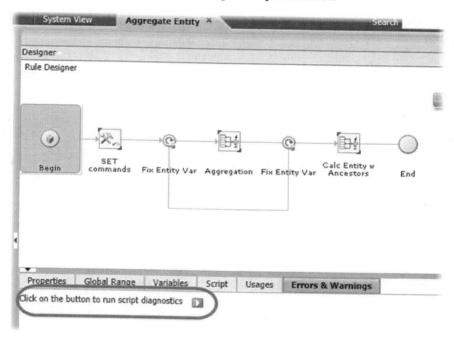

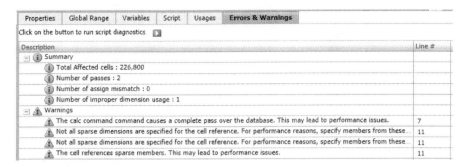

- Copy variables across different scopes
- Select variable within member block component
- Compare scripts of business rules

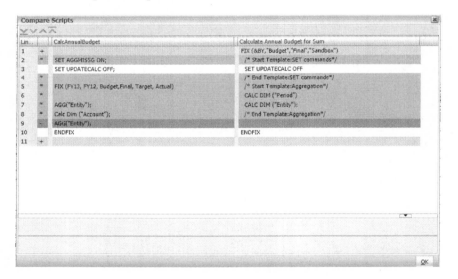

- Open a rule in rule set by double clicking
- Select Variables to display in variable selector
- Reset selections in Filter Dialog
- Select Planning Smart Lists within Condition builder
- Print BR from deployment view
- Enter Missing values for RTP during Validation, Debugging & Analysis
- Create Variables using Dim Names
- Search in Variable Designer
- Enable Template Macro Calls in a Script
- Allocate Simple Exclude Template

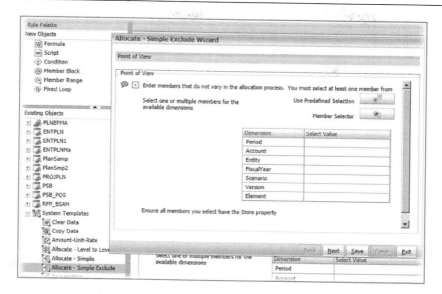

- Currency Conversion Template

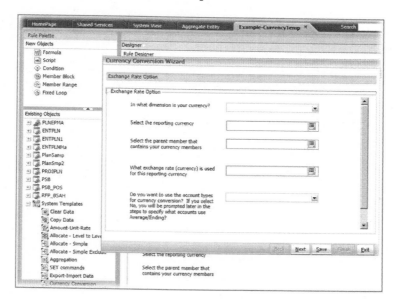

- Create and Delete Members Dynamically for WFP, Capex, PSB, PFP

LCM Enhancements

LCM enhancements include:

- Cross version LCM support
- Supported import from 11.1.1.4 to 11.1.2.3 (11.1.1.4 not available as of release date; watch for the supported patch levels!)
- Move app artifacts from one environment to another by downloading from the File System Node (saved as zip file)
- For faster deployment, you can import application metadata on an incremental basis
- Essbase Studio supported; Other new artifacts supported
- Artifact Change Report available over the web or in command line

Browse		Artifact Change Report					
Artifact Change Report:Details						1 of 1	
Application Group	Application	Artifact Name	Artifact Type	Modified User	Modified Date	Artifact Path	
Planning	ENTPLN	Customer	Dimension	admin	05/15/2013 19:57	/Plan Type/DtlRe...	
		Budget Travel by...	Data Form	admin	05/15/2013 21:52	/Plan Type/Travel...	
		Version	Version Dimension	admin	05/15/2013 20:58	/Global Artifacts/...	
		Scenario	Scenario Dimensi...	admin	05/15/2013 20:58	/Global Artifacts/...	
		Period	Period Dimension	admin	05/15/2013 20:57	/Global Artifacts/...	
		Entity	Entity Dimension	admin	05/15/2013 21:07	/Global Artifacts/...	
		Budget Travel by...	Data Form	admin	05/15/2013 21:36	/Plan Type/Travel...	
		Units Trend	Data Form	admin	05/15/2013 12:59	/Plan Type/Rev/D...	
		FiscalYear	Year Dimension	admin	05/15/2013 20:57	/Global Artifacts/...	
		SubAccount	Dimension	admin	05/15/2013 21:05	/Plan Type/Travel...	
		Account	Account Dimension	admin	05/15/2013 20:49	/Global Artifacts/...	
		Chart	Composite Form	admin	05/15/2013 12:55	/Global Artifacts/...	
		Segments	Dimension	admin	05/15/2013 19:57	/Global Artifacts/...	
		Chart2	Composite Form	admin	05/15/2013 13:06	/Global Artifacts/...	
		Plan Revenue	Data Form	admin	05/15/2013 11:41	/Plan Type/Rev/D...	
		ASO Form	Data Form	admin	05/15/2013 11:36	/Plan Type/DtlRe...	
Planning	ENTPLN1	Entity	Entity Dimension	admin	05/15/2013 08:46	/Global Artifacts/...	
		Scenario	Scenario Dimensi...	admin	05/15/2013 08:46	/Global Artifacts/...	
		Fill	Spread Pattern	admin	05/15/2013 08:46	/Global Artifacts/...	
		Period	Period Dimension	admin	05/15/2013 08:46	/Global Artifacts/...	
		Year	Year Dimension	admin	05/15/2013 08:46	/Global Artifacts/...	
		Version	Version Dimension	admin	05/15/2013 08:46	/Global Artifacts/...	
		EvenlySplit	Spread Pattern	admin	05/15/2013 08:46	/Global Artifacts/...	
		Account	Account Dimension	admin	05/15/2013 08:46	/Global Artifacts/...	

- EPM CLONE utility

EXALYTICS

Exalytics is the future of in-memory, virtually real-time analytics. Exalytics contains optimized versions of Essbase, OBIEE, and TimesTen all running in-memory on a really powerful server. If your users want a faster response time, we'll show how Exalytics continues to make Oracle Essbase & OBIEE a factor to be reckoned with going forward.

The Exa Family

Let's take a *Quick Detour* and review The Exa Family which includes Exadata, Exalogic, and Exalytics.

Exadata is the appliance for data warehousing / OTLP which delivers extreme performance via a pre-integrated, optimized Oracle DB platform. It includes an Enterprise data store and offloads data_intensive processing to storage by row filtering based on "where" predicate. The high speed IO System with smart caching and has at least ten times the efficient storage has at least ten times faster query processing. Ideally used for a consolidation platform.

Exalogic is the appliance for applications and has a high performance platform for Java, Oracle and Enterprise Applications. It is optimized to run applications, rapidly deploys new applications, scale vertically and horizontally, efficiently allocates resources, pre-engineered high availability and uses InfiniBand.

Exalytics is the appliance for OBIEE and/or Essbase and Planning.

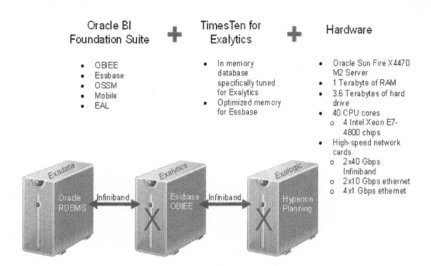

Figure 1 Exa- Family Appliance servers and the Exalytics application Suite.

1. Exalytics is a server with really powerful hardware:

Oracle has engineered this server to be the future of in-memory, virtually real-time analytics. Exalytics contains optimized versions of Essbase, OBIEE, and TimesTen all running in-memory on a really powerful server.

- Oracle Sun Fire X4470 M2 Server
- 1 Terabyte of RAM
- 40 CPU cores made up from 4 Intel Xeon E7-4800 chips
- High-speed network cards includes 2x40 Gbps Infiniband, 2x10 Gbps Ethernet and 4x1 Gbps Ethernet

2. Exalytics is tuned for analytics

Exalytics includes applications that contain in-memory data via TimesTen for OBIEE or memory optimized Essbase, running in-memory on a really powerful server. These applications have some features explicitly designed for Exalytics and are not available in standalone versions.

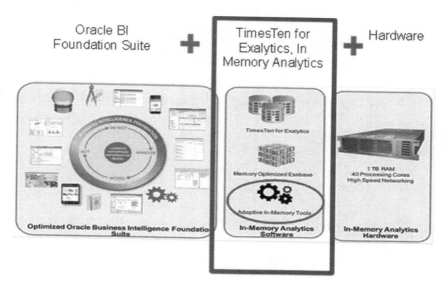

Figure 2 Exalytics Application Suite and Server Memory/Hardware

The memory optimized Essbase application delivered for installation is tuned with Exalytics which can achieve performance improvements and for BSO you will get faster parallel load, faster parallel export, faster calcs, faster cube restructuring, faster MDX, and more concurrent users. How? Better cache coherency, improved index navigation and locking, indexes and data blocks in memory, and better workload distribution across threads.

Essbase is now massively parallel with smaller CPU Utilization, improved thread/cache management. Essbase data is *not* brought into TimesTen (in memory) because Essbase already has data pre-aggregated in a superfast kernel so there is no need. You leverage Essbase's "natural" functionality with the super memory provided by the Exalytics machine.

3. Software included

Applications do not come preinstalled and must be installed and configured after delivery of the appliance. The Exalytics "stripe" of these products, OBIEE and Essbase, are included in the pricing. The Exalytics media pack will be downloaded and installed. The version stripe has coordinated patch set for Exalytics and cannot be upgraded individually. They are certified to work together.

There are numerous flags and settings that need to be enabled to take advantage of Exalytics features like the Essbase.cfg setting `OracleHardwareAcceleration TRUE`.

4. A pretty good price – All pricing is public

http://www.oracle.com/us/corporate/pricing/exadata-pricelist-070598.pdf

You will likely need more than one. It supports both Essbase and BI on the same server but in real life you may want to put them on separate machines depending on how much data, number of users, processes, etc. and beta testers tested Essbase only on the Exalytics server or OBIEE only on the Exalytics server. It is advisable to have your Test and Production instances match. You will need more if you cluster for high availability or need to scale for more users and applications.

5. Available Now!! Oracle announced the availability February 2012

So what benefits and value can companies expect? Benefits include happy users, speed of thought visualization, automatic movement of data driven by the end user experience and existing BI models, reduction in consulting needs because it eliminates the need for tuning DB experts, and repurposed FTE's to value added analysis roles.

Appendix D:
ODI and EPM

By Richard Magee, interRel Consulting

Introduction to ODI and EPM

Oracle Data Integrator (ODI) is a data integration tool that moves data across multiple systems. It has officially replaced Hyperion Application Link (HAL) as the tool to load Planning, Essbase and HFM metadata and data. You may sometimes hear it referred to as Sunopsis; this would be because like many of Oracle's products it was obtained through an acquisition.

All processes within ODI are based on metadata within the source and target systems. A really important and exciting feature of ODI is that actual data is not stored in ODI, only the metadata, mappings, connection parameters and translations required to move the data from one system to the other.

ODI is used to perform dimension and data integration with EPM applications. Examples would include loading dimensions to Planning, HFM and Essbase from a flat file or a relational database or loading data to these applications or exporting Essbase outlines.

Thankfully when ODI became the official tool to replace HAL they included knowledge modules (we will discuss this term later) that provide the following functionality:

	Planning	Essbase	HFM
Metadata discovery & model creation	✓	✓	✓
Load data	✓	✓	✓
Load Metadata	✓	✓	✓
Extract data	✗	✓	✓
Extract metadata	✗	✓	✓
Other	Refresh to Essbase	Calc, post and pre MaxL scripts	Consolidate

X indicates functionality that is not supported in the current release.

The following diagram is an example of a sequential data integration process that can be accomplished with ODI. The dimensions Accounts and Entities are loaded to Planning, HFM and Essbase. The Customer dimension is loaded to Essbase only. The last step is to load Forecast, Actual and Sales data. Once the data is loaded a MaxL script can be executed to allocate and aggregate data.

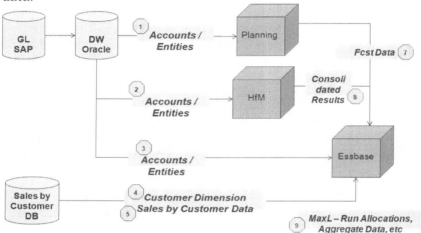

The ODI architecture has several applications that work together to provide a seamless data flow across technology independent platforms.

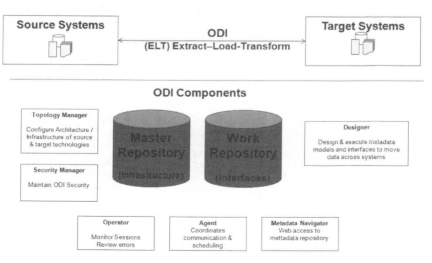

ODI uses two types of repositories: a Master repository and Work repository which are relational databases that store ODI configuration (similar to the BI Repository for EPM).

One of the first challenges of understanding ODI is learning all of the new terminology. Oracle thankfully uses terms most information system technologists are familiar with, but it does sometimes use these words uniquely.

The **Master repository** stores information that is configured in Topology Manager and Security Manager and version information from Designer.

The **Work Repository** stores the mapping and interface information created with Designer. It also stores the Operator information. It is possible to have multiple work repositories but each environment can only include one master repository.

Topology Manager is the application used to configure connection information for source and target technologies. This would include parameters such as server name, user id and password, connection strings, driver references, etc.

Security Manager is the tool used to create users, profiles and roles. It is separate from Shared Services. You can assign access to objects, methods and servers. In layman's terms you can lock it down to each item or you can do it role-based (metadata admin, security admin, interface designer, etc)

Designer is the application used to design and execute metadata models and interfaces.

Agent(s) is a Java service that is placed on one or multiple servers as the listening mechanism for enabling communication between multiple technologies and ODI.

Operator is the application that contains status and log information about each job that is executed.

Metadata is data about data. For example suppose you have a field in a relational database that stores Customer, metadata would include things such as the field length (20) and data type (string). Metadata is not the actual value that is stored for Customer (John Doe).

Metadata Navigator is a web based tool that allows business or technical users to maintain metadata about the source or target systems and field. They can also trigger and monitor jobs from this interface.

Oracle Data Profiling and Quality is another tool available when you install ODI. This tool provides more advanced capabilities for data cleansing and data enrichment in the source and target systems. Data cleansing examples include removing duplicates and parsing fields. Data Enrichment examples include user driven rules.

ODI Deployment

It is possible to have different configurations of ODI. The design of Topology Manager is such that you can have one master repository that points at all servers within a company network, including development, test and production. The advantage of this configuration is that you set up the connection parameters for all systems that will be used only once. This provides you the ability to take data from production and load it to development and vice versus. However, typically you would see three or more work repositories: one for development, one for test and one for execution only in production.

Many IT managers cringe at the idea of a production application talking to a development application. Therefore, another common configuration is to have one master repository for development, a separate one for test and a final one for production, all linking to their own work repository. This follows a more traditional and conservative approach which keeps objects completely isolated.

Dev	Test	Prod
• Master Repository • Work Repository (s)	• Master Repository • Work Repository (s)	• Master Repository • Work Repository (s) (**Execution Only**)

Topology Manager – A little more in-depth

To access Topology Manager, first start ODI Studio. Then from the menu bar select *View>> Topology Manager*. Again, think of Topology Manager as the ODI infrastructure layer that supports all of the other components. Many users want to skip this part all together and move onto Designer but it is essential to understand the topology layer.

Let's dive into some more terminology that is important in Topology Manager. There are multiple objects within Topology Manager.

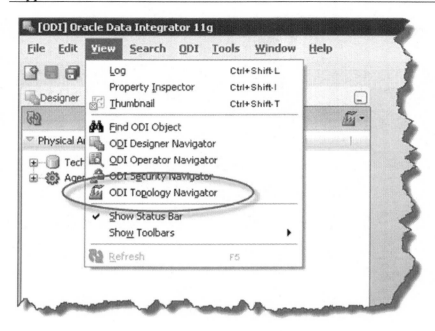

The **physical architecture** includes the connection and driver information for each data storage system that will ultimately be the source or target of the interfaces.

Within the physical architecture, the gold database level is a technology. ODI comes out of the box with drivers and predefined configuration options for these technologies.

The blue database level is a data server. A data server is considered any technology that can store data. That could include a file folder, a relational database or an Essbase server, etc.

The next layer down is referred to as the physical schema layer. A physical schema is considered an instance of the data server. For example within an Essbase data server, each application is considered its own physical schema. In Planning, the Planning server is the data server and each Planning application is a physical schema.

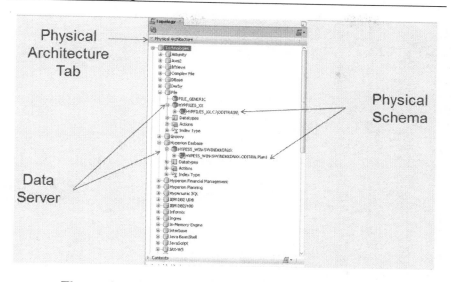

The required information to configure and use a data server is the computer name, user and password information. Please note: references to computer names should be fully qualified or ensure the host file on the ODI server where the agent is located refers to the computer name specified in this definition.

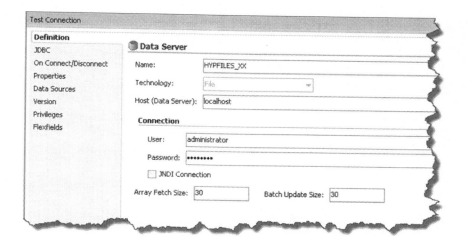

The connection string and driver reference is also specified on the JDBC tab.

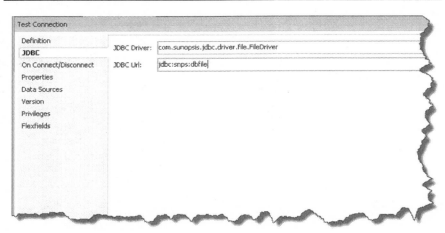

Once the physical architecture has been defined the next object to consider is the Logical Architecture. The Logical Architecture is the functional view of the physical architecture. This is what is referenced at design time. For example you may want to pull customers from the sales and marketing relational database to build the customer dimension in Essbase. Physically the S&M database has been split into three instances of a structurally identical database. (Structurally identical means they have the same tables, field names, field lengths, logic, etc.) There may be three instances because of performance reasons or storage reasons. When designing the interface in ODI, to pull the customer data, all three sources look the same from a metadata point of view. You only need to create this interface once by using the Logical architecture reference. At execution time you select which of the three physical databases to pull from.

The set up of the Logical Architecture looks similar to the Physical Architecture without all of the connection and driver parameters. In the Logical Architecture, a logical schema is set up for each physical schema in the Physical architecture.

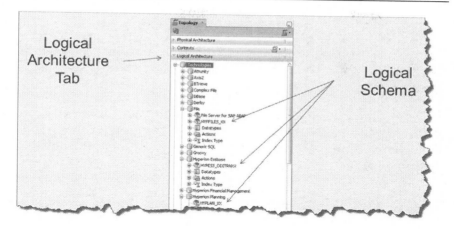

So the next question is, how does ODI know which physical architecture is relevant to each logical architecture? This is through an object called the Context.

In the Customer example we discussed earlier, you would have:

Physically:
Customer database 1
Customer database 2
Customer database 3
Logically:
Customer database
Context:
Customer db on db1
Customer db on db2
Customer db on db3

Another example of this concept is using the dev, test, prod model:

Physically:
Sample Basic – Dev
Sample Basic – Test
Sample Basic – Prod
Logically:
Sample Basic
Context:
Sample Basic on Dev
Sample Basic on Test

Sample Basic on Prod

When you design the interface you simply select Sample Basic. When you execute the interface you select the Context "Sample Basic on Prod" which tells ODI which environment to update.

Agents are another important concept to discuss related to Topology Manager. Both a physical and a logical agent are used to facilitate the communication between ODI and other servers. Similar to the architecture layers, the physical agent specifies the machine name. You can also set up options to perform load balancing and span sessions across multiple servers. One very important concept related to Agents to mention is that there are two types, a listener agent and a scheduler agent. The listener agent can be used in environments where jobs will be executed manually in designer. If the user is going to schedule jobs, they must configure the scheduler agent. Both types of agents should be run as a service in the background.

Languages are the final concept to discuss. Within ODI Topology, each technology uses a language to receive and give commands. For example, when writing queries to pull data from a Relational Source, you use SQL. Languages within ODI can be modified and updated for all technologies specified.

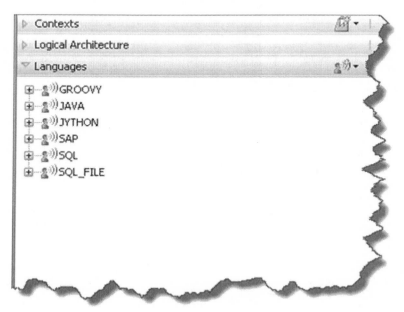

Design Time with Designer

Designer is the application that is used to define the interface, mappings and models. To access Designer from the Start menu select *Oracle >> Oracle Data Integrator >>Designer*.

Every object within Designer is contained within a Model or a Project. Models are the metadata for your source and target systems. Projects are the integrations that move data from your source and target systems. Within a project you can have:

- Interfaces
- Packages
- Procedures
- Variables
- Knowledge Modules

As a reminder, the Designer module stores this information in a work repository and it references the topology and the security information defined in the master repository.

Knowledge Modules

Knowledge Modules (KMs) are components with built-in knowledge (functions and logic) that connect technologies to ODI. KMs are similar to HAL Adapters but with many more connection options. KMs connect to the technology, extract data from it, transform the data, check it, integrate it, etc.

There are different types of Knowledge Modules:

- LKM (Loading Knowledge Modules) are used to extract data from the source database tables and other systems (files, middleware, mainframe, etc.).
- IKM (Integration Knowledge Modules) are used to integrate (load) data to the target system.
- CKM (Check Knowledge Modules) are used to check that constraints on the sources and targets are not violated.
- RKM (Reverse Knowledge Modules) are used to perform a customized reverse-engineering of data models for a specific technology.
- JKM (Journalizing Knowledge Modules) are used to create a journal of data modifications (insert, update and delete) of the source databases to keep track of the changes.
- SKM (Service Knowledge Modules) are used to generate the code required for creating dataservices.

To utilize a Knowledge Module within ODI, select the *Projects* tab. Right-click on the Knowledge Modules item (contained within the individual project) and select *Import*. Typically the available knowledge modules are stored within the OraHome1 directory under the impexp folder.

You can find a complete list of KMs at http://www.oracle.com/technology/products/oracle-data-integrator/10.1.3/htdocs/documentation/oracledi_km_reference.pdf.

Models

Models contain the metadata for source and target systems. RKM's are used to extract the metadata information from a source or target system. The below picture is a reverse engineered model for a Hyperion Planning application.

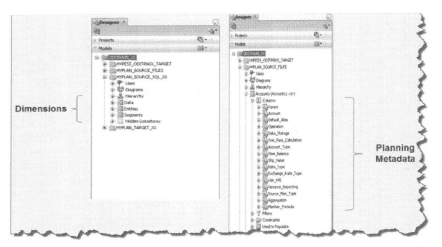

In the picture you notice that it translates the multidimensional format of planning into a more table friendly format. Each dimension has a set of columns that can be updated with an ODI interface. For each column, parameters such as field type and length are set during the reverse process.

Once a model has been configured for both the source and target system, an interface can be created. An interface is the object which loads one target data store with data from one or more sources, based on business rules implemented as mappings.

Projects

Within a project there are multiple objects that are created and grouped within Folders. Folders include Packages, Interfaces, Procedures, Variables, Sequences, User Functions and Knowledge Modules.

The interface is typically the first item to configure. All objects can typically be created or edited by right-click on the object name and using the appropriate selection from the menu. Initially, the source and target models are placed into their respective window frames in the interface designer. The expression editor is used to map the source and target columns. Columns with identical names are automatically mapped for ease of use.

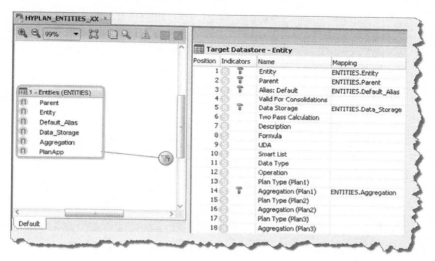

More options are available in the panel below, select the target column. From here you can access the expression editor, indicate whether the logic should be applied on the source or target, select whether the system should perform an insert or an update.

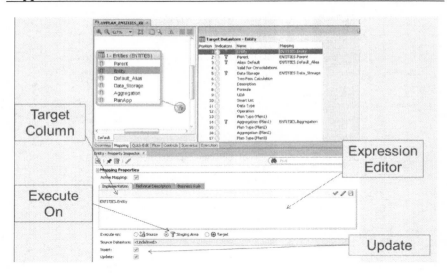

Filters can be applied to the source system by dragging the field into the gray area. A yellow funnel will appear indicating a filter has been applied. An example of a filter would be to extract all entities that have a PlanApp equal to ODITRNXX from the source system.

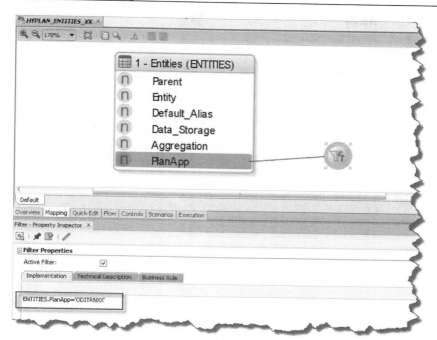

The illustration above only includes one source, but ODI provides the ability to join multiple sources and map them to a single target. This is useful in situations where some information is stored in the data warehouse and a user provides you another set of information in a file. As you can see below, advance joins can be applied.

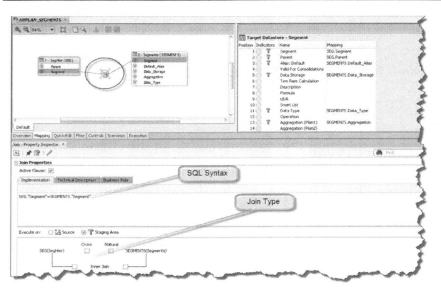

The Expression Editor can be opened in a separate window and provides more functionality. You can drag and drop columns, include variables, update the sql manually (ie. Append prefix to the column) and check syntax. The syntax follows the language of the source or target. However, it does allows you to apply sql to non sql sources that have been joined with a sql source.

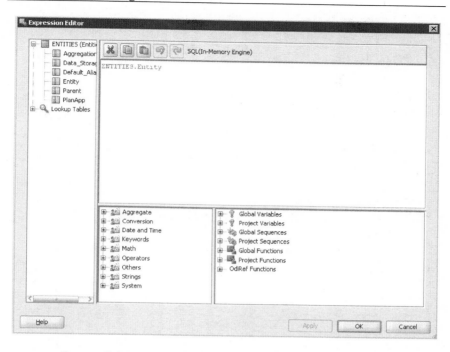

Once all mappings and translations are complete, it is time to move onto the Flow tab. The Flow tab depicts a graphical view of what is occurring in the interface. By clicking on each object, you are provided a list of options.

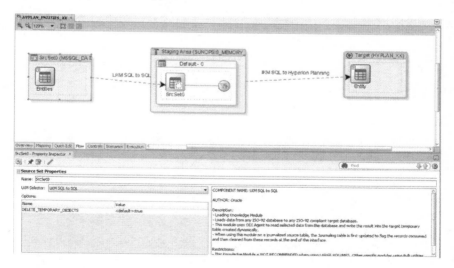

If you want to see the entire interface "at-a-glance" check out the Quick-Edit tab.

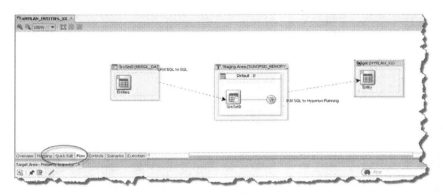

After clicking on Quick-Edit, you can see all of the moving parts in one place.

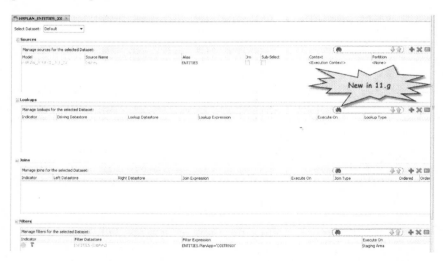

Each Knowledge Module comes with a predefined set of options. For example, the Planning IKM includes an option that specifies "sort the data in parent child format before loading". Behind the scenes this includes the SQL necessary to process the sorting. As you can see from the above picture, the flow tab illustrates the source, knowledge module used to take data from one place to the next.

If you pay close attention to the picture above you will see a staging area in the middle of the flow diagram. ODI has a default temporary staging area that ships with the product. It is referred to as the Sunopsis_Memory_Engine. You have the option to use a staging area or bypass the staging area and send data straight to the target. However, in most cases you will need to pump the data to a temporary location for the translations and mappings to occur properly. With the EPM Suite of products you must use the staging area. However, it is not recommended to use the Sunopsis Memory Engine when you have large volumes of data going through the interface. At this point you would want to create a separate staging area that you can allocate space to and manage database settings for optimal performance.

Once the flow options have been set, you can execute the job directly from this window.

You will always be prompted with a message that says session started. Then the place to go and look is the Operator.

The Operator

The Operator logs information about jobs in a hierarchical format of Sessions, Steps and Tasks. It is grouped and can be filtered by Physical Agent, Keywords, Date, Sessions, Status and User.

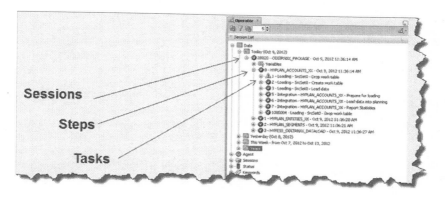

A plethora of information is kept about each session. You can find who submitted, what context was used, what code was run, if it was successful, etc. You can even restart and stop jobs from the Operator.

Error Logs

In the interface on the flow tab, error trapping and log files can be specified. This should be used to trap records and error messages that have not flown through to the target system.

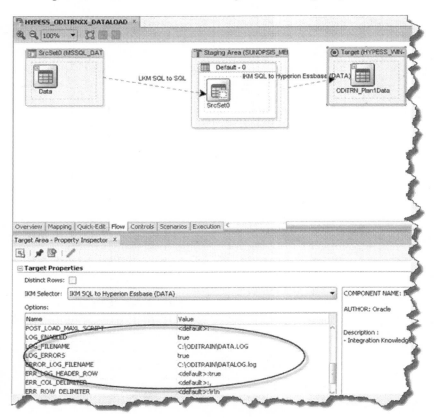

Another location to look for error or processing information is on the execution tab within the Operator. Typically in the message box, if there is a system error, it will be captured here. The Description tab will tell you more information about the series of steps and functions that are called during the execution.

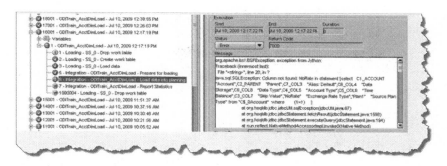

We should forewarn you that reading errors, trapping errors and understanding the messages from ODI can be the most challenging obstacle to overcome when learning the product. The more familiar you are with the source and target technologies, the easier it becomes to translate the technical "gobbly gook" to something meaningful.

Automation

The ODI objects Packages, Scenarios and Variables all come into play when it is time to automate or string multiple steps (interfaces) together. A package can include multiple interfaces, OS commands, Procedures, and variables. Variables can be used to pass in a parameter (month, file name, etc.) Once a package has been created a Scenario is generated and can be scheduled. Reminder: the Agent must be running as a scheduler agent!

There is also a batch utility that can be used to run an ODI Scenario. Use StartScen.bat in the \\..\OraHome_1\oracledi\bin directory. This would be useful if your organization has another scheduler that is used and supported in-house. It is also useful if you have a series of IT personnel that feel more powerful using the "black screen".

Shortlist of Steps

To summarize, let's recap the list of steps to create a source to target data integration with ODI.
1. Define and configure Topology.
   a. Physical Architecture
   b. Logical Architecture
   c. Map through a Context
2. Before you start building an interface you:
   a. Import Knowledge Modules into the project
   b. Create your Metadata Models

Then in the interface,

3. Define your source and target
4. Define the mapping and translations (business rules)
5. Define the flow requirements
6. Execute

To automate execution, you will need to create and work with packages, procedures, variables, and sequencing.

Real Life Tips

As always we like to pass along some time saving tips to our readers.

*   Watch out for the supported releases!
*   Design before you build!
*   Whiteboard the Topology before configuring in ODI
*   Standardize naming conventions for topology components
*   Incorporate as many error logs and error trapping processes as possible.
*   Consider using a staging area instead of the Sunopsis Memory Engine. This will allow performance optimization and error resolution.
*   If the source is a relational database, perform as many translations in a view as possible.
*   Instead of loading Essbase Data with ODI KM, write a MaxL script to load data to Essbase and add it as an OS Command step in the ODI package.
*   Plan extra development time; the learning curve is steep as ODI is more complex than Hyperion Application Link (HAL).

This concludes our brief overview of ODI and EPM applications.

Appendix E:
Planning & Crystal Ball

By Troy Seguin, interRel Consulting

One of the new features in the next release of Planning will be its interaction with Crystal Ball. Crystal Ball is a leading tool used to model risk in business.

MODELING RISK

Nothing is better than experience. If a person has 20 or 30 years of experience he will probably have a very good idea what will happen in the next year given the current environment. However, there aren't very many people with this level of experience and they probably won't be working in the Budgeting and Planning department of your company. So what do you do if you don't have decades and decades of experience and you are tasked to come up with an accurate prediction of the next year's budget? That's where tools like Crystal Ball and Hyperion Planning Predictive Analytics can help.

Risk vs. Uncertainty

Throughout business, as well as the rest of our lives, we must make decisions in the presence of uncertainty. But what exactly is uncertainty? Many people get the definition of risk and uncertainty confused. Let's look at the differences using an example. Let's assume that you are given a standard pack of playing cards. You know that there are 13 hearts, 13 clubs, 13 spades, and 13 diamonds. You are asked to draw one card. If you draw a diamond, you will win $1. What is the likelihood that you will draw a diamond? Since there are 52 cards in a deck and 13 diamonds, you have a chance of 13/52 or 25% to win a dollar. This is an example of probabilities and risk. You know that you are taking a risk to win $1 and that you have a 25% chance to win.

Now in the next scenario, assume you are given a stack of cards. You have no idea what type of cards. They could be playing cards, flash cards, or even tarot cards for all you know. You are still asked to draw a card and are told that you will win $1 if you draw a diamond. However, you don't even have the information to calculate a percentage of success. This is an example of uncertainty.

Reducing Uncertainty

Understanding the uncertainties that exist allows us to make better decisions. Let's illustrate this using a wolverine juggling business. Let's assume that the wolverine juggling business has really taken off and you are now looking to expand into other sports. The 2 main sports that you would like to start are badger wrestling and porcupine riding. Initial investments would cost $1 million for either venture. Also, your analysis says that they would both provide an average profit of $2 million. However, there are a lot of common skills with badger wrestling (obviously) and the range of values for profit is [$0, $3 million]. You don't know as much about porcupine riding so the profit falls in the range [$-1 million, $6 million]. Even though you have a chance to make more money porcupine riding, there is a great deal more uncertainty in the porcupine riding venture. Thus, the more predictable choice would be to start a badger wrestling business.

CRYSTAL BALL

You can take Predictive Analytics even further with Crystal Ball. Crystal Ball makes calculating risk and determining your uncertainties a lot easier. Crystal Ball works just like any other Excel add-in. There is a drop down menu to run different predictive modeling calculations. It's also very easy to upgrade existing Excel models to Crystal Ball applications. Crystal Ball uses three main components to build predictive models: Optimizer, Predictor, and Simulations.

Optimizer

Most Excel based models have a number of variables that you can change that affect the outcome of the model. In many budget models, a number of controllable factors will have an effect on the end result of the model. For example, investments in marketing will affect Sales figures. Usually, there are a large number of variables whose values you can change. Ideally, the people making the models would be able to find the perfect mix of values for these variables that will maximize profit. This is easier said than done. Usually, the only tool that modelers have is to manually change each variable and check the end result. This gets boring and tedious really fast. Optimizer automatically runs through all of the possible combinations of values of these variables and picks the combination that will optimize the end result.

Predictor

Predictor uses Time Series Analysis to predict variables that you cannot control. Examples of this would be inflation or oil prices. Predictor will look at historical data for these variables and make predictions based on patterns that emerge from the data. There are a number of sophisticated algorithms that Crystal Ball uses to do this and it will automatically choose the algorithm that is the best fit with the data. However, you do have the ability to choose which algorithm to use. This option works really well if you have a lot of clean historical data.

Simulations

The Simulations feature is Crystal Ball's version of Monte Carlo Analysis. Monte Carlo Analysis is a term that I have heard used a lot. However, most of the people that I've heard use the term don't seem to have a clear understanding of it. Since this is a book on Planning, you have heard the term "What If" analysis. Monte Carl analysis is What If analysis on steroids.

Let's review the concept of What If analysis. Usually you have a budget model set up with a few variables that represent numbers that you don't have a lot control over. So a lot of times people will say things like "What if I sell 5000 units this month instead of 3000?" or "What if I sell 500 units?" How will this affect profits? To do this in a model is simple enough. You just change you units sold variable from 3000 to 5000, run the model, and look at the profit. You then change you units sold variable to 500, run the model, and look at the profit again. This gives you a little information but it can be a slow tedious process.

Monte Carlo analysis takes this concept a step further. Keeping the same example, you would say "I know my units sold will be somewhere between 500 and 5000 units." Crystal ball will then run a number of simulations randomly picking numbers in that range and recorded the resulting profit. You specify the number of simulations. Most people run around 10000 simulations. Once the simulations run, you then have a report that graphs the different profit values and the percentage they occurred. This allows you to start asking questions like "Based on these simulations, what chance do I have of making any kind of profit?"

CRYSTAL BALL IN ACTION

The following group of screens shots shows an example of when Crystal Ball would be useful in a Sales Revenue model. In this case, sales managers were given sales goals by upper management.

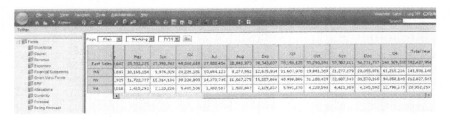

Penny added sales to her job responsibilities in addition to IT. The CFO just gave her the sales goals for the following year. The total amount is $382 million. This seems kind of high to her.

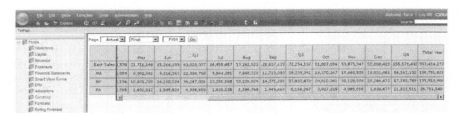

She looks at the Actual sales for FY09 and sees that they total $353 million. "What!!??" she says to herself. "How am I supposed to increase my sales by almost $30 million next year?" Her first reaction is to go to the CFO and yell and scream that this is a ridiculously high goal. But this approach might be extremely uncomfortable and often counterproductive. She remembers that she recently installed a tool called Crystal Ball and decides to change tactics.

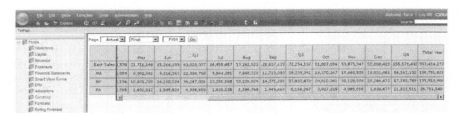

She clicks on the *Open in Smart View* icon to export the web form in Excel.

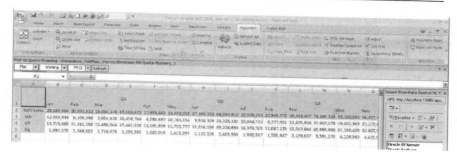

In Smart View, she wants to do 2 things. First, she would like to predict what her sales will be in the next year using Predictor. Secondly, she wants use Simulations to show the likelihood of achieving a goal of $382 million.

Using Smart View, she retrieves 3 years of monthly historical data from the Planning database.

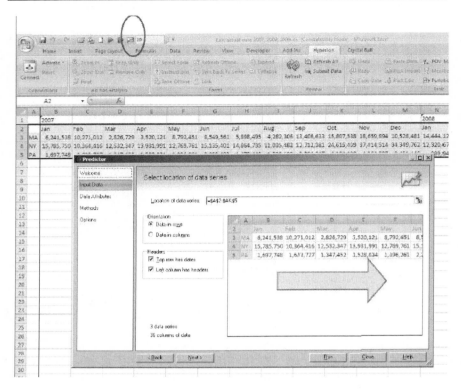

She then clicks on the *Predictor* icon to open up the Predictor wizard. The first screen is used to select the cells that contain the historical data.

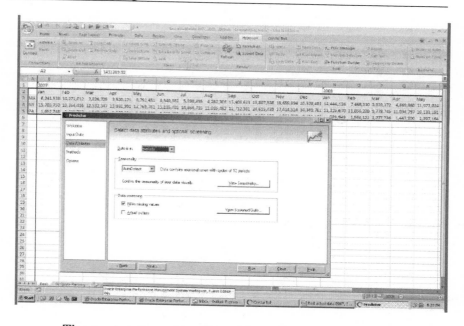

The next screen describes the periods and any seasonality that might occur in the data. Note that you have the option to let Crystal Ball automatically detect seasonality.

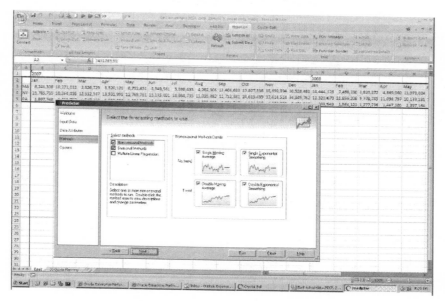

The next screen shows the forecasting methods that are available to you. Again, Crystal Ball automatically detects the best one but it also allows you to choose one yourself.

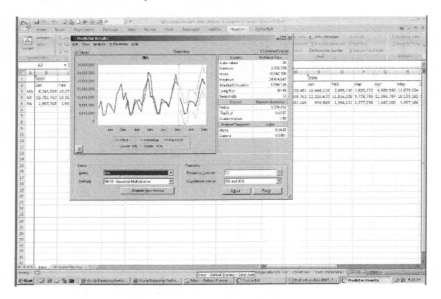

The next screen graphs the forecasted data for you. On the graph itself, the vertical black line represents the present. The past data is to the left of the line and the predicted data is to the right. The green line to the left of the vertical black line is the graph of the historical data. The blue line to the left of the vertical black line is the trend line created by the forecasting logic. The blue line to the right of the vertical black line is the forecasted values based on the forecasting logic. The dotted red lines to the right of the vertical black line represent the possible range of values of the forecasted data.

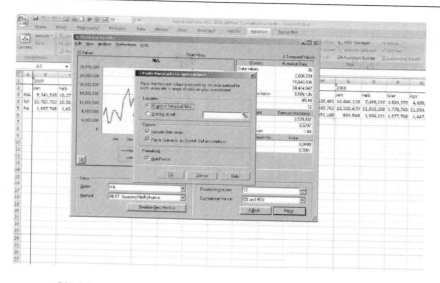

Clicking on the *Paste* button brings up the Paste Forecast to Spreadsheet dialog box. You can specify how you would like the predicted numbers onto the spreadsheet.

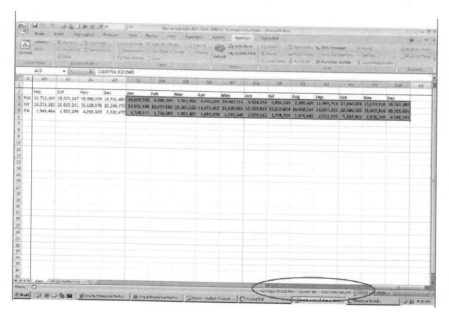

The cells holding the forecast values are highlighted in green. The sum of the cells is $366 million. This represents the more achievable goal for Penny to make.

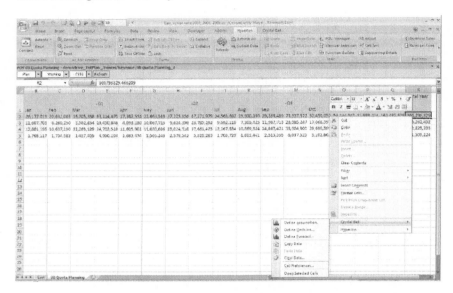

To determine the chances of making the $382 million goal, right-click on the cell representing total sales for the year. Select *Crystal Ball>>Define Forecast.*

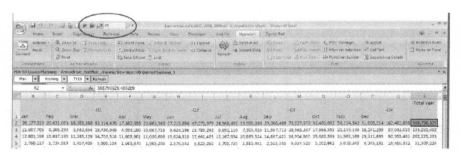

The cell will turn blue. A text box with the number 10 displays. This tells Crystal Ball to run 10 simulations. Change that to "10000". Click on the green *Play* button.

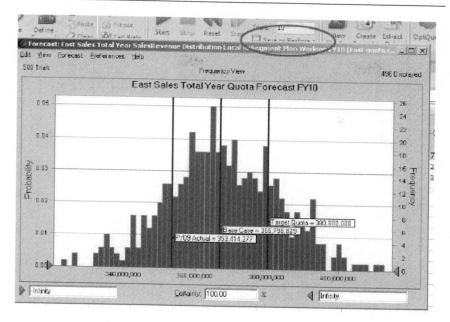

After 10000 trials, you will see a report like this. This shows all of the sales outcomes that occurred during the 10000 trials. Penny wants to see what her chances are of making her quota of $382 million.

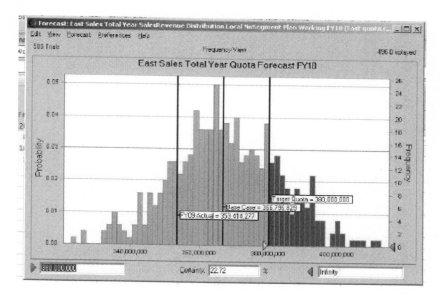

In the box at the lower left side of the report, she types in 380,000,000. This is telling Crystal ball to show the percentage of trials where the outcome of annual sales was between $380 million and infinity (i.e. where the sales was greater than $380 million). The percentage is in the center box labeled certainty. This shows that Penny roughly has a 22.72% chance of achieving the sales goal given to her by management.

Now, based on this analysis, Penny has a much more reasoned, logical argument for her boss to lower her sales goal. She can give a goal that she thinks will be success ($366 million). She can also present her chance of achieving her sales goal in the current environment. She can now go to the CFO and ask for more support to help her achieve her goal (e.g. more marketing dollars or more sales personnel).

PREDICTIVE PLANNING

In Hyperion Planning 11.1.2.2, Oracle delivers Predictive Planning with Hyperion Planning. This new feature provides statistical forecasting built into Planning and is accessible to all Planning users.

Predictive Planning uses Crystal Ball's Predictor to analyze historical data and projects trends and patterns into the future. Users can review forecasted values, override the values if needed, and then submit the data back to Planning in different scenarios and versions. Predictive Planning can automatically forecast best and worst case scenarios in addition to base case.

As we discussed earlier, Predictor uses Time Series Analysis to predict variables that you cannot control. Examples of this would be inflation or oil prices. Predictor will look at historical data for these variables and make predictions based on patterns that emerge from the data.

You can access Predictive Planning from the Planning Smart View ribbon:

To use Predictive Planning, you must first set up the Predictor. You will define the Predictor Scenarios, whether to use Bottom up or Top Down methods, and how much history needed to help create an accurate prediction. You will also have to create a data form with the specific design to include the base data needed for the analysis.

Let's get started in Predictive Planning!

Setting the Data Source

To set up Data Source (in the Set Up Predicator of Predictive Planning), click on the *Set Up Data Form* icon from the Predict Ribbon:

The Data Source window will pop-up:

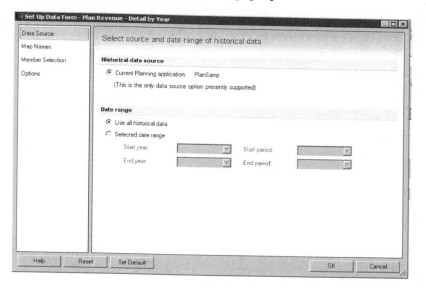

Notice that Predictive Planning can only use the current Planning application, in the present example *PlanSamp*.

To set up the Data Source date range, you have two different options: *Use all historical data* or define a specific time periods by selecting *Selected date range* (if you select this option, you will have to define a Start and End year as well as a Start and End period). While setting the Data Source, keep in mind that the more history you use, the more accurate the prediction will be. Also, it is highly recommended that the number of historical periods used should be at least twice the number of predicted periods, so much so that Predictive Planning will enforce this rule. If possible, try to select the *Use all historical data* option. The only times you would not use this is if you had so much data that it would greatly affect the performance of the form (this would most likely have to be decades of data). The other case would be if certain unlikely events happened in the past that will skew the data. In that case, you would want to disregard that data.

Setting Map Names

The *Map Names* tab of the Predicator wizard guides you to map data series to your Planning scenarios. This is where you can select your Historical data series Scenario and set two other options. You can set up the *Comparison Scenarios data series* to define which scenarios will be used to compare against the results calculated be Predictive Planning. These can be your Forecast or Budget or any other scenario you wish to use. *Prediction Scenarios data series* are similar to the comparisons scenarios; these scenarios can hold a base case, a best case and a worst case. These scenarios will be used as part of out of the box comparisons and analysis once the predicator has been run. The way the tool works is that it creates a range of possible values. It determines an upper bound of values, called the Best Case, a lower bound of values, called the Worst Case, and somewhere in the middle, called the Base Case. These three cases can be stored in members of the Version dimension. You tell Planning which members of the Version dimension to use in the Prediction Scenarios section.

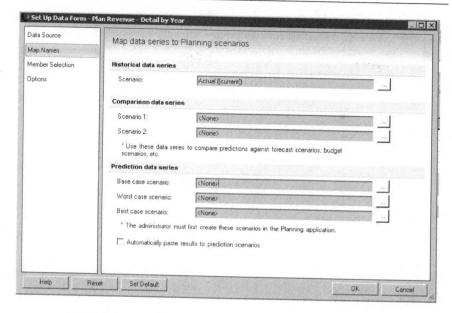

Member Selections

In the *Member Selection* section, you can select your type of prediction. *Bottom-up* will calculate predictions at the lowest level of the hierarchies on the web form. The predicted values can then be aggregated using the aggregation operators defined in the hierarchy

Top-down will calculate the predictions at higher levels of the hierarchies on the web form and distribute the values down along the dimension.

Full prediction predicts the values at all levels of the hierarchies on the web form.

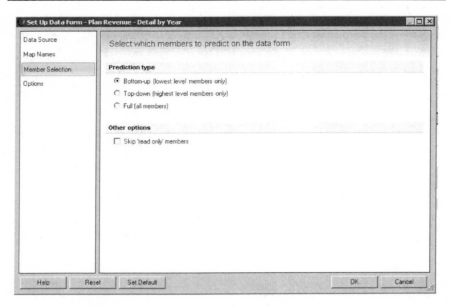

Options

In the *Data Attributes* section of the *Options* tab, you are able to define the seasonality of your data. Are there natural cycles in the data? If you don't know the answer to this question, you can let Predictor automatically detect seasonality by selecting the Automatic radio button. If you do know the seasonality, you can enter the number of time periods there are to a cycle of your data. If you data is not seasonal, you can enter 0 periods per cycle. If you have missing values in your history, you can have Predictor automatically fill them by checking the box next to *Fill in missing values*.

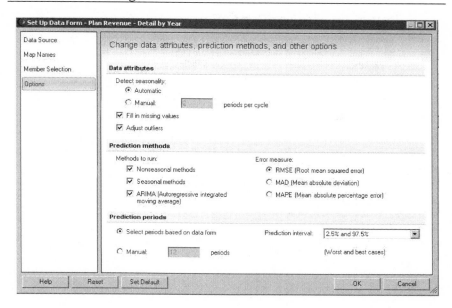

In statistics, outliers are numbers that vary widely from the pattern. Do you remember that kid in school that would always score a 100% on a test even if everyone else scored a 50%? Maybe you were that kid. Either way, that kid's score would be considered an outlier. You can have Predictor adjust the outliers if you are worried that they would skew your predictions.

The *Prediction methods* section allows you to choose the kind of prediction methods you want to run: *Nonseasonal, Seasonal,* or *ARIMA (Autoregressive integrated mobbing average),*

Warning! The following sections talk about some of the basic algorithms that are used in the background. It's here for informational purposes only. If you would like to learn more about it, you can pick up any basic introductory book on Time Series.

The Nonseasonal Methods include:

Single Moving Average – Good for volatile data with no trend or seasonality. Moving average of the last few time periods and projects the last one forward.

Double Moving Average – Does SMA twice. The second time to the projected data. It uses both sets to project forward. Good for data with a trend but no seasonality.

Single Exponential Smoothing – takes a weighted average with heavier weights given to later periods. (Exponentially decreasing going into the past) Good for volatile data with no trend or seasonality.

Double Exponential Smoothing – Does SES twice. The second time to the projected SES results. It uses both sets to project in the future. Good for data that has a trend but no seasonality.

There are also four Seasonal Methods that are run when Seasonal Methods is selected:

Seasonal Additive – Calculates a seasonal adjustment to give to exponentially smoothed forecasted values. Good for seasonal data with no trend.

Seasonal Multiplicative – Similar to additive but it multiplies the adjustment to the smoothed forecasted values. Good for data without a trend but whose seasonal changes increase over time.

Holt-Winters Additive – Uses the Holt Exponential smoothing algorithm but acts the same as Seasonal Additive.

Holt-Winters Multiplicative – Uses the Holt Exponential smoothing algorithm but acts the same as Seasonal Multiplicative.

ARIMA, Auto Regressive (AR) Integrated (I) Moving Average (MA) is a univariate process. Current values of a data series are correlated with past values in the same series to produce the AR component, also known as *p. Current values of a random* error term are correlated with past values to produce the MA component, *q. Mean and variance* values of current and past data are assumed to be stationary, unchanged over time. If necessary, an I component (symbolized by *d) is added to correct for a lack of stationarity through* differencing. AutoRegressive and Moving Average both look at past data and projects future data. They act differently with the way they handle White Noise. Sometimes it is necessary to incorporate an Integration component to transform the problem into one with equal probability distributions.

In the *Prediction Methods* section, you can also select the *Error Measure* to use. These Methods are used to reduce the deviations from the historical data that cannot be explained through seasonality or trending. There are 3 types of Error Measure:

RMSE (root mean squared error) is an absolute error measure that squares the deviations to keep the positive and negative deviations from cancelling out one another. This measure also tends to exaggerate large errors, which can help eliminate methods with large errors.

MAD (mean absolute deviation) is an absolute error measure that originally became very popular (in the days before hand-held calculators) because it did not require the calculation of squares or square roots. While it is still fairly reliable and widely used, it is most accurate for normally distributed data.

MAPE (mean absolute percentage error) is a relative error measure that uses absolute values. The absolute values keep the positive and negative errors from cancelling out each other. Because relative errors do not depend on the scale of the dependent variable, this measure enables you to compare forecast accuracy between differently scaled time-series data.

Select Data

Once the setup of data form is done, you can start selecting data. The data must be selected from a "proper" data form (with base data displaying) and the Predictor will automatically run along most granular time period.

Reading the Results

To read results, hit the *Predict* icon from the Planning Predict ribbon. The Predictive Planning Smart View windows will display offering three different tabs: Chart, Data and Statistics.

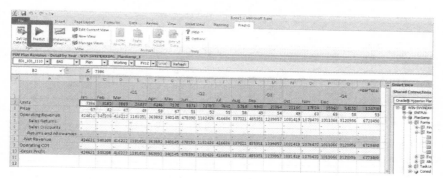

The *Chart* tab is showing a graphical representation of your Predictive Planning.

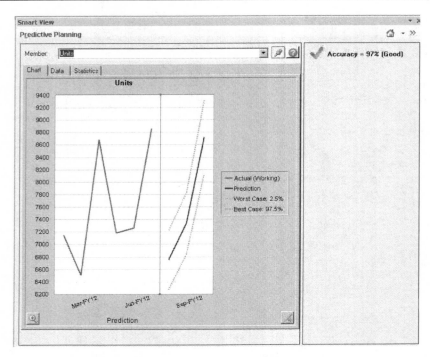

Four different graphical predictions will appear:

Prediction base case - Median prediction values calculated based on past historical data; median values mean that the actual values in the future are equally likely to fall above or below the base case values

Prediction worst case - A calculated lower confidence interval, by default the 2.5 percentile of the predicted range

Prediction best case - A calculated upper confidence interval, by default the 97.5 percentile of the predicted range

Prediction fit line - A line of the best fitting time-series forecasting method through the historical data

The *Data* tab is presenting the data in a table for the 4 following cases: Actual, Worst Case, Prediction and Best Case. The Prediction column is the same as the Base Case.

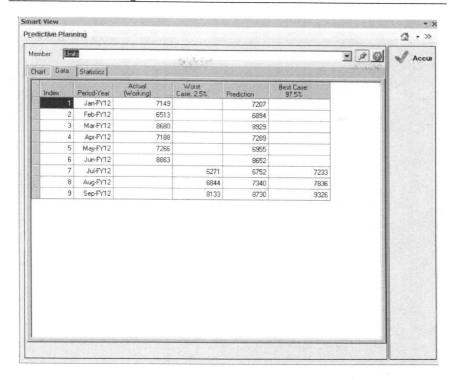

Index	Period-Year	Actual (Working)	Worst Case: 2.5%	Prediction	Best Case: 97.5%
1	Jan-FY12	7149		7207	
2	Feb-FY12	6513		6894	
3	Mar-FY12	8680		8929	
4	Apr-FY12	7188		7289	
5	May-FY12	7266		6955	
6	Jun-FY12	8863		8652	
7	Jul-FY12		6271	6752	7233
8	Aug-FY12		6844	7340	7836
9	Sep-FY12		8133	8730	9326

Finally, the Statistics tab displays several statistics on the prediction run:

Number of Data Values – Number of historical values used in the prediction. This should be a much larger number than what is in the example.

Minimum – The smallest value in the historical data set.

Mean – This is what most people think of when they say Average.

Maximum – The largest value in the historical data set.

Standard Deviation – The standard deviation the values have from the Mean of the historical data set.

Seasonality – The determination Predictor made about whether the data is seasonal or not.

Accuracy – The confidence level the Predictor has about its prediction.

RMSE – The value produced by the error method chosen in the previous tab.

Best Method – The algorithm that Predictor determined would be most accurate (ARIMA, Seasonal, or Non-Seasonal).

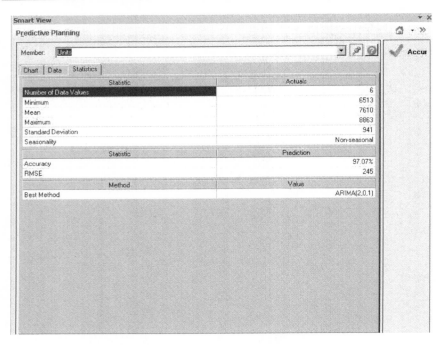

Once predictions are generated, they can be saved back into Planning as new versions.

Any questions?

We hope this introduction has shown you the exciting possibilities of improving the forecasting process with Predictive Planning and Crystal Ball.

Appendix H:
OTHER STUFF

Don't stop reading now; you've only got 2 more pages. This appendix has some helpful notes for consideration along with a "don't miss" finale.

NOTE ON THIS BOOK

We've tried to be as detailed as possible but if we described every single click or button, you'd be 100 years old before you were ready to use Planning (and at that point, Hyperion would probably not even be an independent company but rather bought by some totally awesome firm like Oracle and Hyperion's CEO would be replaced with a really great guy like Larry Ellison, who if he's looking for an heir apparent should contact me at eroske@interrel.com). So we don't mention the fairly obvious tasks and buttons. For example, if there is a Close button, we probably skipped defining what this button does. Cancel means Cancel (doesn't save anything that you just did). Nothing tricky there.

NOTE ON PLANNING VERSIONS

Our objective is to teach you how to use Oracle Hyperion Planning from an administrator perspective. While this book is based on version 11.1.2.2 with highlights of 11.1.2.3, most of the content in this book applies to version 11.2.1.

INDEX

Made in the USA
Lexington, KY
25 January 2017